P9-EDJ-992

Migration and Urban Development

Migration and Urban Development

A Reappraisal of British and American Long Cycles

BRINLEY THOMAS

METHUEN & CO LTD
11 New Fetter Lane London EC4

First published 1972
by Methuen & Co Ltd
11 New Fetter Lane London EC4
© 1972 Brinley Thomas
Printed in Great Britain by
Butler & Tanner Ltd
Frome and London

SBN 416 75130 X hardback
SBN 416 75140 7 paperback

This title is available in both hardbound and
paperback editions. The paperback edition is
sold subject to the condition that it shall not, by
way of trade or otherwise, be lent, re-sold, hired
out, or otherwise circulated without the
publisher's prior consent in any form of
binding or cover other than that in which it is
published and without a similar condition
including this condition being imposed on the
subsequent purchaser.

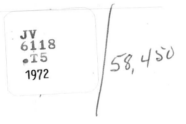

JV
6118
.T5
1972

58,450

Distributed in the USA by
HARPER & ROW PUBLISHERS, INC.
BARNES & NOBLE IMPORT DIVISION

To Simon Kuznets

CAMROSE LUTHERAN COLLEGE
LIBRARY

Contents

Contents

Preface

The challenging dilemmas facing modern cities have their most stubborn roots deep in past migrations, and this is especially true of America and Britain. Most of the population growth of conurbations such as Greater London, New York, Merseyside, Chicago and Philadelphia took place in the half century ending in 1913, the era of mass migrations; a study of this background is essential to an appreciation of the complex problems now besetting them. A strong impetus has been given to economic and demographic work in this area by public concern about population pressure, the environment, and the assimilation of non-white migrants; and international movements of educated manpower have become a major object of inquiry in many countries.

Drawing on the results of up-to-date research, this book is a reappraisal of my earlier work, *Migration and Economic Growth: a Study of Great Britain and the Atlantic Economy*. It takes a new look at the long cycles in migration and urban development in the Atlantic economy, with particular reference to the way in which the process of urbanization in Britain and America interacted as a result of international movements of population and capital. Special attention is paid to strategic factors in American growth arising from long cycles in immigration and urban development and in the internal migration of the black population. I have included an analysis of internal migration and the regional incidence of non-white immigrants in Britain. There is also a quantitative survey of the international circulation of professional manpower in the period 1950–70. A study of the causation of brain drain based on the concept of dynamic shortage is presented in Chapter 7. The diagnosis was first put forward in a lecture at the London School of Economics in March 1967 when I argued that the key explanatory variable was Federal expenditure on Research and Development in the United States. Chapter 7 shows that subsequent events confirmed this variable as an accurate predictor of the course of brain drain.

Some authors who have written on the Atlantic economy have attempted to show that there was no systematic relation between long swings in the United Kingdom and in the United States. These views are summarized in Chapter 1. Some American economists have argued that the periodic inflows of immigrants and capital to the United States were caused unilaterally by swings in American aggregate demand, whereas one or two economic historians interpret British building fluctuations as the result of purely fortuitous domestic factors. These critics show a surprising tendency to view the economic growth and fluctuations of particular countries (usually their own) exclusively in terms of internal determinants. The new evidence presented in Chapter 2 refutes these interpretations and amply confirms the primacy of the demographic determinants of building cycles in the United Kingdom and the United States as well as the inverse relation between them. I have extended the analysis to comprise Canada, Argentina and Australia. In Chapter 4 the process of interaction in the pre-1913 Atlantic economy is reassessed in the light of the latest findings, and the conclusion that long cycles in America, Canada, Argentina and Australia were inverse to British cycles is reaffirmed. With the aid of a model of the international economy, the *modus operandi* is explained in terms of inverse demographic cycles (with migration as a key variable) and the monetary implications of the international gold standard. In carrying out this reappraisal, I have felt that its technique bears a close relation to that of the new economic history in the United States; the next step will be to construct an econometric model on the basis indicated in Chapter 4. As a postscript to that chapter I have included a comparative note on the international economy between 1946 and 1971, with the United States as leading lender presiding over a 'dollar standard' with fixed exchange rates.

I see no reason to change the conclusion reached in *Migration and Economic Growth* that the decade of the 1890s was the end of one epoch and the beginning of another (ibid., pp. 118–22). The Atlantic economy as we conceive it went through a structural change and did not survive after the 1920s. The slump in the international flow of capital in the 1890s was different from previous slumps in one important respect: America was now so large and rich that she would not need to borrow much more from London. Very soon she was to become the world's leading creditor nation. New forces gave a special character to the last great upswing in Britain's foreign investment from 1900 to 1913, as is shown in Chapter 3. The profound changes which were in the making at the end of the nineteenth century have been brilliantly analysed by Geoffrey Barraclough in *An Introduction to Contemporary History*. In the following passage, stressing demographic factors, he strikes a note well in tune with the theme of this book.

Hence, as the twentieth century proceeded, the advantages which had ensured European predominance – namely, the monopoly of machine production and the military strength conferred by industrialisation – receded and the underlying demographic factors reasserted their importance. It is no exaggeration to state that the demographic revolution of the half-century between 1890 and 1940 was the basic change marking the transition from one era of history to another. At the same time the period of European political hegemony was drawing to a close and the European balance of power, which for so long had governed the relations between states, was being superseded by the age of world politics. (p. 92)

The question remains whether the long cycle was a phenomenon peculiar to the Atlantic economy and ceased to exist when the underlying conditions changed. My thinking on the whole subject of long cycles has been profoundly influenced by the works of Simon Kuznets, which have been a rich and abiding source of enlightenment and inspiration. One of his most significant findings was that the inverse relation between swings in population-sensitive and other components of capital formation disappeared when trans-Atlantic mass migration came to an end. For long swings to be inverse it is sufficient to have conditions similar to those set out in Chapter 4, but, as Kuznets has stressed, the long swing itself is not a transitory phenomenon but a fundamental component of the long-term movement. (*Capital in the American Economy: Its Formation and Financing*, p. 54.)

Fortunate indeed is the author who can say without fear of contradiction that he made no mistakes in his earlier work. I cannot claim this. In Chapter VIII of *Migration and Economic Growth*, dealing with internal and international mobility, I thought I had demonstrated that the hypothesis of an inverse relation between internal and external migration applied to countries of immigration as well as those of emigration (see pp. 130–4 of that work). Critics have rightly pointed out that this is refuted by the experience of the United States where swings in internal migration corresponded to those in immigration. But perhaps I was lucky after all, for that error turned out to be a blessing in disguise. What happened was that I took the migration of black people from the South to the North of the United States as a proxy for internal migration in general, and I found that its fluctuations were inverse to those of immigration. I thought I had detected symmetry, but the key was really to be found in asymmetry. I had stumbled across a fact of far-reaching significance. There was a clear inverse correlation between the proportion of Negroes and the proportion of foreign white stock in the population of the various States (see ibid., pp. 133–4). The black worker was in keen competition not only with poor whites in the South but also with unskilled whites from Europe; his chance of getting a job in the North depended very much on whether immigration was booming or dwindling. Kuznets extended the analysis to other variables and discovered long swings in black mortality and fertility rates, the former corresponding to and the latter inverse to the swings in immigration. (See 'Long Swings in the Growth of Population and in Related Economic Variables', p. 31.) If by a miracle there had been racial tolerance, the black workers from the South could have played their full part, in common with immigrants from Europe, in meeting the labour requirements of the rapidly growing cities of the North after the Civil War. The significance of Negro internal migration and its bearing on the modern urban dilemma are explored in Chapter 5.

The peopling of America by the 'huddled masses' of the Old

World was a boon to the whites and a curse to the blacks. One would expect the black migrant to come into his own after the ending of free immigration in 1924, and this tendency has gathered considerable strength. Net out-migration of Negroes from the South, which was 454,000 in 1910–20 and 749,000 in 1920–30, rose to 1,597,000 in 1940–50, 1,457,000 in 1950–60 and 1,400,000 in 1960–70. Nearly half (46·8 per cent) of the 22,672,570 black people enumerated in America in 1970 lived outside the South, as compared with 23 per cent of 12,866,000 in 1940. However, the sombre fact is that the cities which the Negroes are at last entering in large numbers are being evacuated by the descendants of the immigrants who founded them; hence the agonizing problems of a shrinking tax base, seething ghettos, mounting welfare rolls, and fierce racial conflict. The social ladder which made the 'American dream' a reality for the European immigrant, whatever his ethnic group, appears to the Negro to be just a pipe-dream.

The migration scene in America and Britain is now over-shadowed by the sinister legacy of racial discrimination. Chapter 6 shows how the one big influx of migrants from the West Indies, India and Pakistan into England has tended to produce a segregation pattern in some urban areas. The ghost of the first Atlantic economy, whose mainstay was the horrible traffic in African slaves, is now haunting the Anglo-Saxon world; but the present generation cannot be held responsible for what their forbears did. We all live in glass houses, even though some are more stone-proof than others. If the present generation of young whites retain their idealism and practise non-discrimination when they become middle-aged heads of families and if the blacks meet them half-way, the future will be bright.

Acknowledgements

I am grateful to the Principal and Council of University College, Cardiff, for giving me leave to accept a visiting Professorship at Johns Hopkins University for a term in 1968 and at Brown University for a term in 1971. Thanks to the generosity of my hosts in these universities, I was able to pursue my research in a most congenial environment. I wish in particular to express my thanks to Carl Christ at Johns Hopkins and George Borts and Jerome Stein at Brown for the stimulating experience of working with them and their colleagues and for the interest they took in my work.

Chapter 2 was given as a paper to the Mathematical Social Science Board Conference on the New Economic History of Britain, 1840–1930, held at Eliot House, Harvard University, in September 1970; and Chapter 3 is a shortened version of a paper which I contributed to a conference on Capital Movements and Economic Development held by the International Economic Association in Washington in 1965. Early versions of Chapter 4, the heart of the book, were read as papers to seminars at the Economics and Sociology Departments at Brown University, to the Economic History Workshop at Chicago University, to a seminar organized by J. J. Spengler at Duke University, and to an economics colloquium at the University of Wales. The critical probing which took place on those various occasions was of immense value to me. It has been my good fortune to participate in several of the American conferences on the new economic history, and I profited considerably from lively discussions on long swings with Moses Abramovitz, Douglass North, Richard Easterlin and Jeffrey Williamson. On the demographic side I am greatly indebted to Dorothy Thomas, Hope Eldridge and their colleagues at the University of Pennsylvania Population Studies Center.

One obligation stands out; I dedicate this book to Simon Kuznets in appreciation of what his works and his friendly encouragement have meant to me. Several friends have been kind enough to comment in detail on early drafts of some chapters. I wish to record my deep appreciation of the help I received from Conrad Blyth, Henry Phelps Brown and John Parry Lewis, especially in setting out rigorously the ideas of Chapter 4. On some methodological problems arising in Appendix B I had the benefit of expert comment by Bernard Benjamin. I learnt a great deal about the statistics of professional manpower and brain drain from discussions with Mrs Joan Cox of the Department of Trade and Industry in London, Dr Milton Levine of the National Science Foundation in Washington, and John D. Alden, Executive Secretary of the Engineering Manpower Commission of the Engineers Joint Council, New York. Any errors that may have crept in are entirely my responsibility.

I am grateful to the following for permission to base diagrams and tables on existing material: to Sir Alec Cairncross and the Cambridge University Press for table 6.6; to Drs Karl and Alma Taeuber and the American Sociological Association for table 5.8; to J. H. Adler, the Macmillan Press Ltd, and the International Economic Association for figs. 4.2 and 4.5; to Herbert Feis and the Council on Foreign Relations, New York, for tables 3.3 and 3.4; to H. D. Mitchell and R. Ash, the editor, and the *British Medical Journal* for table 7.5; to Professor Reynolds Farley and the Markham Publishing Company for fig. 5.2; to the National Science Foundation for table 7.1; to Drs Karl and Alma Taeuber and the University of Chicago Press for table 5.9; to the New York Times Company for table 5.7; to Allen C. Kelley and the Kent State University Press for table 4.2; to Dr Dorothy S. Thomas and the American Philosophical Society for fig. 5.1; and to Professor Arthur Bloomfield and the International Finance Section, Princeton University, for fig. 4.3.

I thank the following for permission to reproduce sections of work of mine which they have published: Donald N. McCloskey

Acknowledgements

and Methuen and Co. Ltd (*Essays on a Mature Economy: Britain after 1840*, 1971, Chapter 2); J. H. Adler, the Macmillan Press Ltd, and the International Economic Association (*Capital Movements and Economic Development*, 1967, Chapter 1); the editor of *Erhvervshistorisk Årbog*, Aarhuus, Denmark (*The Changing Pattern of Anglo-Danish Trade, 1913–1963*, 1966, Chapter VI); the University of Wales Press (*The Welsh Economy: Studies in Expansion*, 1962, Chapter 1); and the editor of *Minerva* ('The International Circulation of Human Capital', Vol. V, Summer 1967, pp. 479–506).

I am particularly grateful to Mrs Margaret Evans, a former research assistant, for her expert handling of original data which she collected at the Public Record Office; much of the credit for the methodology of Appendix B and the charts in Chapter 2 belongs to her. I thank the social sciences section of the library of University College, Cardiff, for excellent service and my colleagues, Hamish Richards and Roy Thomas, for their help in checking and proof reading. I am much indebted to my secretary, Mrs Vida Turner, who not only saw each draft through to its final stage with superb accuracy but was also responsible for drawing some of the charts. Finally, it is a pleasure to record my gratitude to my publisher and printer, to John Naylor for his enthusiastic cooperation, to Mrs Gillian Wright for organizing the book with such admirable efficiency, and to Craig Dodd for the cover design.

February 1972   Brinley Thomas

1 American Models of the Long Cycle

The central issue in this book is the significance of the inverse
relation between British and American long cycles in capital
formation and the mechanism by which migration and capital
movements influenced the course of urban development in the
two countries in the era of mass migration.

THE GAP IN SCHUMPETER'S SYSTEM

As a preliminary step, it is instructive to look again at Schumpeter's account of the growth of Britain, the United States and
Germany in the nineteenth century and to ask what difference
it would have made to his system if he had not treated international movements of population as an 'external' or exogenous
factor, i.e. not inherent in the working of the economic organism
itself.[1] He admits in the introductory chapter of *Business Cycles*
that '. . . migrations in particular are so obviously conditioned by
business fluctuations that no description of the mechanism of
cycles can claim to be complete without including them, and including them – at least some of them – as internal factors'.[2] And
then he adds:

> However, as we shall not deal with this group of problems in
> this volume – although the writer is alive to the seriousness of
> this breach in our wall – it will be convenient to consider

---

[1] This theme is dealt with in my article, 'The Rhythm of Growth in the
Atlantic Economy', in Hegeland, ed., *Money, Growth, and Methodology
and Other Essays in Economics in Honor of Johan Åkerman*, pp. 39–48.
[2] Schumpeter, *Business Cycles*, Vol. I, p. 10.

migrations over the frontiers of the territories to which our statistics refer, provisionally, as *an external factor*, while migration within those territories, which it would be impossible so to consider, will be noticed but incidentally.[1]

This decision had a far more profound effect on his investigation than he seemed to realize.

The method was to build a set of hypotheses for a closed system and then to seek verification in the economic time-series of each country – England, United States and Germany – taken separately. It was argued that the rhythm postulated in the system could be observed simultaneously in the history of the three countries. Unfortunately, there was one irritating exception and it could not be brushed aside as peripheral. Schumpeter found that 'England's economic history from 1897 to 1913 cannot, owing to the comparative weakness of the evolution (in our sense) of her domestic industries, be written in terms of our model – the only case of this kind within the epoch covered by our material.'[2] One cannot help wondering why perfidious Albion failed to toe the line in this period. There is a significant clue in Volume II of *Business Cycles* where the reader is reminded that 'the cyclical aspects of international relations . . . cannot receive due attention within this book'.[3] Then comes this important admission:

Of all the limitations imposed by the plan and purpose of this book, this is the most serious one. *Not only do cycles in different countries systematically affect each other, so much so that the history of hardly any one of them can be written without reference to simultaneous cyclical phases in other countries*, but cycles really are, especially as regards the great innovations which produced the Kondratieffs, international phenomena. That is to say, such a process as the railroadization or the electrification of the world transcends the boundaries of individual countries in such a way as to be more truly described as one world-wide process than as the sum of distinct national ones. Capitalism itself is, both in the economic and the sociological sense, essentially one process, with the whole earth as its stage.[4]

[1] Schumpeter, my italics. [2] Ibid., Vol. I, p. 435.
[3] Ibid., Vol. II, p. 666. [4] Ibid., my italics.

This is a crucial point. If the phenomena under review were 'one world-wide process' and not 'the sum of distinct national ones', one would have thought that Schumpeter might at least have indicated that his mode of verification, based on the notion that the process *was* the sum of distinct national ones, was to be regarded as merely a first approximation. Instead of that, he went on to say that

> both reasons – interactions and supernational unity of funda-
> mental processes – explain why in our historical survey the
> cycles in our three countries were found to be so much in step.
> The fact that they were is not more obvious than the mechanism
> that produced it and also – in principle, at least – the manner
> in which these relations affected the working of pre-war
> central banks and of the pre-war gold standard.[1]

Schumpeter was bent on having it both ways.

What happens when the basic postulates are changed? First, let us regard international factor movements as endogenous and the countries belonging to the Atlantic community as an entity, the Atlantic economy. Secondly, instead of confining our attention to fluctuations with an average span of forty months, seven to ten years, and fifty years, let us concentrate on the long swing with an average span of twenty years. In other words, we conceive the evolution of capitalism (as Schumpeter said we ought to) as a process transcending national boundaries, and we drop his three-cycle scheme. This was the starting-point of my earlier work.[2] As soon as we regard the separate nations as regions comprising an aggregate, and we ask what are the conditions under which the rate of growth of income in this aggregate can be maximized over time, there is no reason to expect each of the parts to pass through identical and simultaneous phases according to a theory of a closed system. Secular growth entails internal shifts within the aggregate via international factor movements; the expansion of the whole may well express itself through disharmonious rates of growth in the parts. This is what happened in the Atlantic

[1] Ibid.
[2] See my *Migration and Economic Growth: a Study of Great Britain and the Atlantic Economy*, Chapters III and VII.

economy between the middle of the nineteenth century and the First World War. There was an inverse relation between the long swings in capital formation in the United Kingdom and in countries of new settlement overseas. There were four major outflows of population and capital from Europe – 1845–54, 1863–73, 1881–8 and 1903–13. The upward phase of the long swing in trans-Atlantic migration and foreign lending coincided with an upswing in capital construction in the United States and a downswing in capital construction in the United Kingdom; the downward phase of the long swing in trans-Atlantic migration and foreign lending coincided with a downswing in capital construction in the United States and an upswing in capital construction in the United Kingdom.

It seems to be a condition of this inverse investment cycle that (*a*) a substantial part of capital formation is sensitive to the rate of population growth, and (*b*) the rate of population growth is mainly determined by the net migration balance. In the country exporting population there is an interesting inverse relation between internal and external migration. When capital exports to the United States were in the upswing phase and British home construction was relatively declining, surplus labour from the rural sector in Britain tended to migrate to America rather than to urban areas at home. In the succeeding phase when the rate of capital formation in Britain rose rapidly, the workers released from agriculture moved into the flourishing industrial towns and emigration ebbed away. A wave of home construction drew the rural surplus into urban employment at home; a wave of foreign investment drew the rural surplus into urban employment abroad. International movements of labour and capital were thus a pivotal element in determining the time-shape of economic development in the sending and receiving countries. One may summarize the process as an inter-regional competition for factors of production within the Atlantic economy, with the Old World and the New World alternating in their intensive build-up of resources. This is the essential characteristic which distinguishes these long swings from short business cycles. Long swings are fluctuations in the rate at which the whole network of urban infrastructure is developed, whereas the short business cycles are fluctuations in investment in producer durables and inventories.

From this analysis it is clear that Schumpeter was not justified in claiming that 'interactions and supernational unity of fundamental processes' gave added support to his finding that the cycles in his three countries were in step. On the contrary, this particular approach leads to inverse long swings and to the conclusion that the United States economy had fluctuations of a greater amplitude than the United Kingdom because in the latter country movements in home investment were counterbalanced by opposite movements in foreign investment and this was not the case in the United States. The difference between American and British experience could be put as follows. In the United States a wave of prosperity (or depression) in building would usually be transmitted to the rest of the economy; in the United Kingdom (where the export sector and the home construction sector were more evenly balanced) a wave of prosperity (or depression) in building was partially offset by an opposite swing in the export sector.

ONE-SIDED INTERPRETATIONS

Some American economists tend to seek an explanation of American long swings almost exclusively in terms of forces operating within the United States itself. According to Abramovitz,

> . . . a long swing in the volume of additions, perhaps even in the rate of growth of additions, to the stock of capital, that is, in capital formation, is likely to involve a fluctuation in effective demand and thus to generate an alternation between states of relatively full and relatively slack employment. A long swing in unemployment rates in turn appears to have been among the chief causes of Kuznets cycles in the volume of additions to the labor force and, perhaps, in capital formation.[1]

This mechanism interprets swings in immigration to the United States as '. . . responses to the occurrences of protracted periods of abnormally high unemployment and to the recovery from such

[1] Abramovitz, 'The Nature and Significance of Kuznets Cycles', p. 230.

5

periods'.[1] No significance is attached to an interaction between the United States and other economies. Similarly, Easterlin's analysis of European migration to the United States concludes that '. . . on the whole the movements were dominated by conditions in this country'.[2] This stress on unilateral causation finds adherents in O'Leary and Arthur Lewis who assert that '. . . the U.S. governed its own fortunes in the nineteenth century and if any adjustment had to be made it was made on the other side of the Atlantic'.[3]

This line of thought, at first sight, is not without some degree of credibility when applied to an economy of the stature of America even in the second half of the nineteenth century, but economic self-determination is hardly reasonable in the case of Australia. Net capital inflow from Britain to the Australian colonies in the 1860s and 1880s was about half their gross domestic capital formation in each decade; gross residential construction accounted for one-third of gross capital formation; unassisted immigration was by far the most important single factor governing housing demand; high levels of pastoral investment were increasingly financed in the 1870s and 1880s by Scottish law firms and solicitors advising clients to buy Australian debentures; the ratio of British to Australian-held deposits in Australian banks rose from 10 per cent in 1873–4 to 37 per cent in 1891; and by 1889 nearly 40 per cent of the proceeds of Australian exports were mortgaged for investment income payable to Britain. And yet, despite these significant evidences of the close economic dependence of the colonies on Britain produced by Noel Butlin in his monumental work on the period 1861–1900,[4] this author argues that the decisive influences on events were in Australia. For example, he states that '. . . the basic determinants of the speed, stability and complexity of Australian growth were in local Australian conditions';[5] and that '. . . the rate of inflow of British capital and

---

[1] Ibid., p. 243.

[2] Easterlin, 'Influences in European Overseas Emigration before World War I', p. 348.

[3] O'Leary and Arthur Lewis, 'Secular Swings in Production and Trade', p. 126.

[4] Butlin, *Investment in Australian Economic Development, 1861–1900*.

[5] Ibid., p. 31.

merchandise imports and the allocation of funds and resources between different activities were determined in Australia'.[1]

Is it plausible to think that the nature and time-shape of the economic growth of Australia were domestically determined? Surely what is called for here is an examination of the process of interaction between a small developing country with a population (in 1861) of just over one million and the advanced factor-providing country with a population of 23 million. Butlin dismisses the explanation of Britain's capital outflow in terms of inverse long swings in home and foreign investment, although the evidence for it in this period is overwhelming. Nearly all the data for a statistical test of this explanation and of Butlin's hypothesis are in his book. We shall explore this question in Chapter 4.

A similar preoccupation with the dominance of domestic factors in the United Kingdom is to be seen in the work of H. J. Habakkuk and S. B. Saul.[2] Their contention is that the effect of migration on British building fluctuations, 1870–1913, was of minor significance compared with domestic or fortuitous factors. This is refuted by the quantitative evidence presented in the next chapter. The same applies to the view of O'Leary and Arthur Lewis. Intrigued by the inverse relation but sceptical of the influence of migration and capital flows, these authors confess that they '. . . cannot rule out the possibility that the alternation of the U.S. and U.K. building cycles was a sheer accident, springing perhaps from the different effects which the Napoleonic Wars may have had upon the progress of residential building in the two countries'.[3]

Those who interpret the growth and fluctuations of individual countries as domestically determined seem to forget a fundamental truth which Alfred Marshall expressed in a famous analogy relating to the question whether value is governed by utility or cost of production.

> We might as reasonably dispute whether it is the upper or the under blade of a pair of scissors which cuts a piece of paper. . . . It is true that when one blade is held still, and the cutting

[1] Ibid., p. 38. [2] See Chapter 2, pp. 20–2 and 41–3.
[3] O'Leary and Arthur Lewis, op. cit., p. 127.

is effected by moving the other, we may say with careless brevity that the cutting is done by the second, but the statement is not strictly accurate, and is to be excused only so long as it claims to be merely a popular and not a strictly scientific account of what happens.[1]

This gem of Marshallian wisdom is highly relevant in the present context.

LIMITATIONS OF AMERICA-CENTRED MODELS

It was Simon Kuznets who first drew attention to the significance of the long swing as a feature of economic growth;[2] his work has inspired most of the analytical developments in this field. It is fitting that this type of fluctuation should now be known as the Kuznets cycle.

The mechanism of a self-perpetuating long swing in the United States up to the 1920s which Kuznets tentatively put forward was as follows.

> The long swings in additions to *per capita* flow of goods to consumers resulted, with some lag, in long swings first in the net migration balance and then in the natural increase, yielding swings in total population growth. The latter then induced, again with some lag, similar swings in population-sensitive capital formation, which caused inverted long swings in 'other' capital formation, and in changes in *per capita* flow of goods to consumers. The swings in the latter then started another long swing in the net migration balance, and so on.[3]

One of Kuznets' path-breaking contributions is the distinction between, on the one hand, population-sensitive capital formation – i.e. non-farm residential construction and capital expenditure by railroads – and, on the other hand, 'other' capital formation – i.e. construction other than non-farm residential or railroad

[1] Marshall, *Principles of Economics*, Book V, Chapter 3, p. 348.
[2] See Kuznets, *Secular Movements in Production and Prices*.
[3] Kuznets, 'Long Swings in the Growth of Population and in Related Economic Variables', p. 34.

(largely industrial plant, store and office building), producers' durable equipment other than railroad (i.e. largely industrial machinery), changes in inventories (largely in distributive channels), and changes in net claims against foreign countries.[1] He found an inverse relation between the swings in these two components of capital formation, and this was explained by the savings constraint on total capital formation having the result that '. . . acceleration (or deceleration) in the population-sensitive components left so much less (or so much more) room for the growth of other capital formation. This restraining influence of a limit on total capital formation appears to have been removed in the 1920s, and synchronism has prevailed since.'[2] The inverse relation between the two capital formation components is essential to the logic of Kuznets' model. However, the degree to which savings were a restraining influence depends to a considerable extent on an external factor – the inflow of funds from abroad, mainly Britain. The use which his formulation makes of the savings constraint is a tacit admission that the long cycle in America was partly determined by demand and supply conditions in the British capital market. The implications of this are not worked out.

Moreover, the explanation depends on a suspiciously long 'lag' between additions to the flow of goods to consumers and additions to population. The point to notice here is that Kuznets regards changes in the flow of goods to consumers *per capita* as an index of the varying strength of the 'pull' which the American economy exercised on net immigration: the empirical evidence shows an inverse relation between swings in immigration, additions to population and population-sensitive capital formation, on the one hand, and 'other' capital formation and the flow of goods to consumers *per capita* on the other. The argument then runs as follows.

The long swings in additions to flow of consumer goods *per capita* are inverted to those in additions to population before World War I – and quite prominent. *Yet they suggest one explanation of the swings in additions to population, if we allow for a*

[1] Ibid., p. 33.   [2] Kuznets, *Capital in the American Economy*, p. 333.

9

long lag that would, in a sense, turn negative into positive association . . .
Immigration, particularly in its timing, could be assumed to be responsive to the pull – that is, largely to conditions in this country rather than in the country of origin. This assumption of the responsiveness to the pull is clearly indicated by the fact that *net* additions were affected not only by gross inflow but also by emigration, which clearly reflected conditions in this country. It is indicated also by the fact that the long swings in emigration from various countries of origin were fairly similar. One could, then, argue that a sizeable reduction in additions to *per capita* flow of goods to consumers (with some lag), all other things being equal, would represent a discouragement to immigration, while a sizeable rise in additions to *per capita* flow of goods to consumers would represent an encouragement.[1]

Kuznets emphasizes that this '. . . is a tentative sketch designed to indicate lines of further exploration and does not claim even rough validity'.[2] The trouble is that to make it work he has to turn the inverse relation between immigration and flow of goods to consumers into a positive one and insert a long lag. This is asking too much. Since these are *long* swings with a span of about twenty years, the implied response interval stretches over so many years that it cannot be meaningful. And what justification can there be for singling out one particular case of inverse relation and calling it a long 'lag'? If it is right to do it in one case, why not in others too? One must reject this linking of swings in immigration to swings in flow of goods to consumers. Nevertheless, Kuznets' distinction between population-sensitive and other capital formation is crucial to an understanding of the international aspects of the long swing mechanism, as we shall see later.

A major contribution to the theory of long swings has been made by Abramovitz.[3] He regards them as 'the outcome of

[1] Kuznets, *Capital in the American Economy*, pp. 347–8. The italics for the sentence are mine.
[2] 'Long Swings in the Growth of Population and in Related Economic Variables', p. 34.
[3] Abramovitz, 'The Nature and Significance of Kuznets Cycles', pp. 225–48. See also his *Evidences of Long Swings in Aggregate Construction since the Civil War.*

interactions between the pace at which resources were developed, the generation of effective demand, and the intensity of resource use'.[1] The long swing in the inflow of labour from various countries depends on a 'common cause' in the United States, i.e. the long swing in unemployment. Abramovitz does recognize interactions via the foreign balance, international capital movements and the supply of money, but the whole emphasis is on the unilateral swing of demand in the United States. There is only one indirect mention of the inverse relation between American and British long swings when he says that '. . . the competing pressures for finance of British home investment and of demands in other areas of the world played their parts in determining whether the United States could continue to finance a large deficit'.[2] No attempt is made to quantify these competing pressures or to discuss their implications.

A comprehensive examination of the demographic aspects of Kuznets cycles is to be found in Easterlin's authoritative work.[3] Like Abramovitz, he regards immigration as depending on the swing of unemployment in the United States. He found that he could test this hypothesis adequately only in the period beginning in 1890 when estimates of unemployment began to be recorded. An analysis of reference cycle averages for the years 1890–1915, covering one long swing, gave a close correspondence between the rate of change of output and that of unemployment and between the average unemployment rate and the gross immigration rate, with the former leading. Extending the test back to 1870 in decennial periods, by using Lebergott's estimates of unemployment,[4] he obtained for 1870–1965 a correspondence between the first differences of the induced component of labour force growth, i.e. net migration plus participation rate change, and the first differences in the average unemployment rate.[5] From these findings, which are what one would expect, Easterlin concludes

---

[1] Abramovitz, 'The Nature and Significance of Kuznets Cycles', p. 246.
[2] Ibid.
[3] Easterlin, *Population, Labor Force, and Long Swings in Economic Growth*.
[4] See Lebergott, *Manpower in Economic Growth: the American Record since 1800*, pp. 403–20.
[5] Easterlin, op. cit., pp. 151–2.

that the swings in immigration were determined unilaterally in the receiving country; but this does not necessarily follow.

There is an important omission in Easterlin's analysis; at no point does he pay any attention to long swings in the inflow of capital. The mechanism of the long swing in the United States cannot be properly interpreted if this aspect is left out. The United Kingdom in the 1870s and 1880s carried much more weight in the international economy than the United States. In 1870 Britain accounted for 31·8 per cent of world manufacturing output as against 23·3 per cent in the United States and 13·2 per cent in Germany; in 1880–5 the proportions were 26·6 per cent, 28·6 per cent and 13·9 per cent respectively.[1] In 1880 Britain was responsible for 63·1 per cent of world exports of capital goods and 41·4 per cent of world exports of manufactured goods, as compared with 19·0 per cent and 19·3 per cent respectively in Germany and 5·7 per cent and 2·8 per cent respectively in the United States.[2]

Between 1869 and 1876 the net inflow of foreign capital into the United States was on the average 15·5 per cent of total net capital formation, and from 1882 to 1893 it was 10·3 per cent. In the period 1870–1914 Britain was the source of between 55 and 60 per cent of foreign investment in the American economy.[3] These are significant quantities. By ignoring them, Easterlin was bound to get a one-sided view of the long swing mechanism. As Williamson pointed out, '. . . with this knowledge, surely we must find that domestic investment opportunities for British capital had an important impact on the movement of foreign capital into the United States'.[4] This goes for the parallel movements of immigration as well.

At one crucial point Easterlin is assailed by doubt. He points out that '. . . several studies have indicated that economic activity in the European countries also shows long swings'. He then makes

[1] League of Nations, *Industrialisation and Foreign Trade*, p. 13.
[2] S. B. Saul, 'The Export Economy 1870–1914', in Saville, ed., 'Studies in the British Economy 1870–1914', pp. 12 and 16.
[3] See Jeffrey G. Williamson, *American Growth and the Balance of Payments, 1820–1913*, p. 145.
[4] Ibid.

this admission. 'If these were common in timing and *inversely* related to those in the United States, then the view attributing dominant importance to swings in American demand would be weakened.'[1] He discounts this possibility by saying that 'O'Leary and Lewis on the basis of series referring primarily to industrial output and exports in France, Germany, Great Britain and the United States lean towards the view that investment booms in the respective countries were fairly autonomous'.[2] This article by O'Leary and Lewis confirms the inverse relation between swings in capital formation in Britain and the United States. Having said that '. . . writers have sought to explain why investments in the U.S. and the U.K. should have fluctuated in opposite directions',[3] these authors go on to discuss possible reasons for this phenomenon. They suggest that the Kuznets cycles in these two countries and France and Germany were 'autonomous'; but this does not mean – and on their evidence could not mean – that there was no inverse relation between British and American swings.

Easterlin criticizes the thesis of Part III of *Migration and Economic Growth* and contends that '. . . Brinley Thomas, in his analysis, appears to suggest that swings in the British economy as *a whole* were inversely related to those in the United States (op. cit., pp. 108–13). His comparison of the movements in the United States and the United Kingdom national product series, however, shows little evidence of systematic inverse movements.'[4] Yet this is a question of fact. The statistics are plotted in fig. 1.1, and they display clear inverse swings in rates of change in real national income in the United States and the United Kingdom between 1869 and 1913. The evidence is also against R. C. O. Matthews' statement, quoted by Easterlin, that '. . . despite the elements of inversion referred to, fluctuations in *national income* in Great Britain have not generally stood in an inverse relation to those in the United States'.[5]

[1] Easterlin, 'Influences in European Overseas Emigration before World War I', p. 347. Italics in the original.   [2] Ibid.
[3] O'Leary and Lewis, loc. cit., p. 125.
[4] Easterlin, loc. cit., pp. 347–8, footnote 25. Italics in the original.
[5] Matthews, *The Trade Cycle*, p. 194. Italics in the original.

The theory of unilateral 'pull' has even been applied to United States growth in the 1850s where it is least plausible. Albert Fishlow maintains that '. . . pending further analysis, and more is needed, we should not be quick to overthrow the hypothesis advanced by Kuznets and others that the common response of

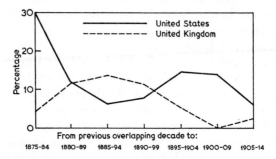

Figure 1.1 Rate of change in real national income *per capita* (from decade to overlapping decade) in the United States and the United Kingdom, 1869–1913.
Sources: United States – Kuznets, 'Long Swings in the Growth of Population and in Related Economic Variables', Table 15; United Kingdom – Mitchell and Deane, *Abstract of British Historical Statistics*, pp. 367–8.

many European countries suggests a single external cause, the state of the American economy . . . the railroad was an important determinant of that economy in the 1850s'.[1] In his attempt to justify this, he criticizes my analysis in Chapter VII of *Migration and Economic Growth* on the ground that the figures I used, based on *Poor's Manual of Railroads*, led me to locate the peak of railroad construction in 1856, whereas it is now established by Fishlow's more accurate estimates that the peak was in 1853–4.[2] However, this makes no difference to my argument. The fundamental point is that the peak in immigration from Europe came in 1851, two

[1] Fishlow, *American Railroads and the Transformation of the Ante-Bellum Economy*, p. 202. For an abridged version see Fishlow's paper, 'The Dynamics of Railroad Extension into the West' in Fogel and Engerman (eds.), *The Reinterpretation of American Economic History*, pp. 402–16.
[2] Fishlow, *American Railroads . . .*, p. 201.

or three years before the peak in railway building. Indeed Fishlow's own analysis confirms that settlement preceded railway building. He puts it very clearly in these words:

> If roads earned profits from the start, did not show an upward trend in net earnings, were built through areas of previous and abundant settlement and did not receive much government aid, virtually all would agree that construction ahead of demand had not taken place. *That these were the typical characteristics of railroad development in the West in the 1850s is exactly what we shall argue.*[1]

In the case of Iowa, '. . . the large increase in settlement occurred between 1850 and 1856, not later. Yet virtually no railway mileage was built before 1856, . . . and it is therefore clear that the principal wave of settlement had markedly preceded the rail network in that State.'[2] The same was true of Illinois and Wisconsin. Further confirmation comes from Robert W. Fogel who points out that '. . . the acceleration in urbanization that paralleled the rapid expansion of industry and commerce also preceded the railroads'.[3] An important element in the process of prior settlement was the arrival of nearly 3 million immigrants in the decade ending in 1854 (most of them expelled from Ireland by calamity and from Germany by agrarian crisis), an influx which was no less than one-sixth of the population of America in 1844. In the interaction process in that period the supply side had much more force than the demand side; this is also demonstrated by the results of lag analysis in *Migration and Economic Growth* (pp. 159–60).

On Easterlin's own admission, the existence of an inverse relation between European and American long cycles weakens the view that swings in American demand were dominant. However, the matter cannot rest there. The issue will not be settled by models of the long swing which ignore international interaction and which take no account of the transmission mechanism linking money with other economic variables. The long swing models referred to in this chapter are all deficient in

[1] Ibid., p. 171. My italics.   [2] Ibid., p. 175.
[3] Fogel, *Railroads and American Economic Growth*, p. 235.

this respect. From 1879, when the United States resumed specie payments at the pre-Civil War parity, to 1913 the leading countries of the Atlantic economy were on the gold standard. The financial dominance of London and the international repercussions of the Bank of England's policy were major factors. In each country there was an interaction between the 'real' economic magnitudes and the changes in the supply of money entailed by the discipline of the gold standard. In Chapter 4 we shall examine this interaction as part of an attempt to explain the alternation in phases of urban development in the United Kingdom, the leading lender, on the one hand, and the United States and other countries of new settlement, on the other.

Appendix A

A Note on Spectral Analysis of Long Swings

One or two statisticians, using the technique of spectral analysis, have tried to disprove the existence of long cycles. Such attempts have no bearing on the statistical verification presented in this book, since the basic series used here exhibit long cycles in the original data, e.g. for Britain – emigration, building, home investment, capital exports, and share prices, and for the United States – immigration, building, capital imports, incorporations, and railroad construction. The same is true for these variables in many other countries.

Spectral analysis is relevant only where smoothing techniques such as a moving average are used to bring out the cycle. Irma Adelman's conclusion was that '. . . it is likely that the long swings which have been observed in the U.S. economy since 1890 are due in part to the introduction of spurious long cycles by the smoothing process, and in part to the necessity for averaging over a statistically small number of random shocks'.[1] Apart from objections which might be raised against the methodology of this test, the result is unconvincing for two reasons. The series covered a period profoundly disturbed by two world wars, and the analysis left out two crucial variables, construction and population.

A more comprehensive test was made by Jon P. Harkness on 48 time series for Canada, the majority extending over about a hundred years.[2] He concluded that

> . . . we can accept the hypothesis that long swings exist both in rates of growth and in deviations from trend of economic magnitudes in Canada. This is particularly significant in the case of rates of change, which not only give the most favourable

[1] Adelman, 'Long Cycles – Fact or Artifact?', p. 459. See also Bird, Desai, Enzler and Taubman, 'Kuznets Cycles in Growth Rates: the Meaning', pp. 229–39.
[2] Harkness, 'A Spectral-Analytic Test of the Long-Swing Hypothesis in Canada'.

results but also represent the currently most popular version of the long-swing hypothesis. In the case of the deviation-from-trend version, acceptance is based on a preference for harmonic over log-linear trend elimination when using spectral analysis.[1]

The nature of Harkness's results is indicated by the following quotations.

In terms of a two-tail test, estimated spectra of the rate-of-change version are extremely favourable to the long-swing hypothesis. If we accept a frequency band centered on 9·6 years as being within the relevant range, then 45 of the 48 spectra estimated demonstrate quite sharp peaks in the long-cycle frequency bands. The estimates indicate an average period for the Kuznets cycle in all series of between 10 and 14 years, which conforms with the results obtained by Daly in Canada and Abramovitz in the United States, using less sophisticated techniques to test the rate-of-change version. . . . The over-all results of the harmonic-trend version are generally favourable to the hypothesis. Of the 48 spectra estimated 30 indicate relatively strong peaks within the long-cycle frequency domain. . . . The average cycle length indicated by the 30 definite series appears to be about 20 years. This conforms with results of other investigators who have dealt with deviations from trend using less sophisticated techniques.[2]

There is no reason to expect a different result if the methods used in this investigation were applied to the time series of other countries.

A rigorous analysis which cuts new ground is to be found in a paper by Charles M. Franks and William W. McCormick.[3] The technique is described as follows:

This model is designed to account systematically for a large set of possible interactions among the selected variables, both

[1] Ibid., pp. 435–6.
[2] Ibid., pp. 433 and 435.
[3] Franks and McCormick, 'A Self-Generating Model of Long Swings for the American Economy, 1860–1940'.

current and time-lagged, and to establish that subset of variables and their interactions that best describes the generation of Kuznets cycles. In mathematical terms the analysis involves the construction of a set of simultaneous linear difference equations which, when evaluated through a self-iterating process from some initial set of starting values, will generate series which closely reproduce the time series of variables from which the system was derived. The successful identification of such a system is a step towards discovering the types of endogenous relationships explaining long-term economic change. Thus, this study of long-swings concentrates on an estimated system of relations between variables, rather than on data series alone.[1]

The paper concludes that

. . . Adelman's suggestion that long swings may result from large exogenous shocks impinging upon the economic system is unnecessary in view of the self-generating model found in this study. Our results lend support to the hypothesis that long swings are endogenously explained without the need for any episodic shocks external to the basic long-swing process, whereas the explanation of business cycles may be far more contingent upon a series of erratic shocks to supply the necessary energy for continued fluctuations.[2]

[1] Ibid., p. 297. [2] Ibid., p. 342.

2 Demographic Determinants of British and American Building Cycles, 1870–1913

In the course of the debate on the working of the Atlantic economy, no critic has been able to refute the existence of an inverse relation between long swings in construction in Britain and the United States and in British home and foreign investment, at least in the period 1870–1913. There has indeed been ample confirmation.[1] Where disagreement enters is in the interpretation of the nature of the mechanism by which the economies of the two countries reacted on each other. Contributors to the discussion can be divided into two broad schools – those who accept the reciprocal character of British and American long swings as systematic rather than fortuitous, and those who argue that the operative forces were in the domestic sphere and not in any interacting process. The line taken by this second group is seen in the work of H. J. Habakkuk and S. B. Saul.[2] Habakkuk is a sceptic not only

[1] An outstanding work is Parry Lewis, *Building Cycles and Britain's Growth*. This thorough study confirms the inverse relation between home-construction cycles from the 1850s to 1913 in Chapter 7, pp. 164–85. See also Bloomfield, *Patterns of Fluctuation in International Investment before 1914*. Bloomfield points out that not only did British home and foreign investment move inversely over the long swing between 1870 and 1913 but they also tended to move inversely *in the short run*. 'The correlation coefficient of the first differences of net capital exports and gross domestic fixed-capital formation from 1860 to 1913 was −0·32, significant at the 5 per cent level. Compare this result with Cairncross' assertion (*Home and Foreign Investment 1870–1913*, pp. 187–8) that in the short run home and foreign investment generally moved together.' Ibid., p. 22.
[2] Habakkuk, 'Fluctuations in House-building in Britain and the United States in the Nineteenth Century', reprinted in A. R. Hall, ed., *The*

about systematic influences in the alternation of British and American long swings but even about the existence of a British building cycle, as the following quotation indicates.

> There has recently been some suggestion that in England after the 1860s the trade cycle was not an independent phenomenon but simply the result of lack of synchronization between the long swings in foreign and domestic investment. [Footnote: Matthews, *A Study in Trade-Cycle History*.] The view taken here is the reverse of this: it was the long swings which were the epiphenomena and the trade cycles the reality, in the sense that when the character of the individual cycles has been explained there is no residue which needs to be attributed to the behaviour of a long cycle. The appearance of alternation in British and American long swings is the result of the fact that British trade cycles no longer came to a violent end but the American ones often did.[1]

It is not easy to summarize Habakkuk's paper, but the essence of his thesis can be put as follows. Housebuilding in Britain before the 1860s did not exhibit long swings but fluctuated with the trade cycle. There were special reasons of domestic origin why the relation between building fluctuations and the trade cycle changed after the 1860s. For example, internal migration became more an affair of the middle classes and less connected with changing business conditions, and financial institutions became more stable so that building could be sustained after cyclical downturns. The increasing tendency for building booms to continue after cyclical downturns gave rise to regional long cycles which were not necessarily synchronized. The 1880s were an exception; even in that decade the volume of emigration was largely the result of domestic influences. 'The alternation of British and American housing activity in the eighties and nineties partly reflects the different rate at which electricity was applied to traction in the two countries. This was, in the present context,

---

Export of Capital from Britain 1870–1914. The references here are to the latter. Saul, 'House Building in England 1890–1914'.

[1] Habakkuk, op. cit., p. 120. The footnote reference must be an error: it should be 'Matthews, *The Trade Cycle*'.

almost certainly fortuitous.'[1] With the exception of the later 1880s, the effect of emigration and foreign investment on British building fluctuations was '. . . of minor importance compared with domestic factors'.[2] This is a challenging argument deserving attention, although it rests mainly on speculations which are not subjected to rigorous testing. The issue can be decided only by an appeal to the empirical evidence.

S. B. Saul, in his study of local authority records for a large number of English towns in the period 1890–1914, has thrown light on matters such as the relation of building activity to the proportion of empty properties and the effect of changes in the availability of short-term funds.[3] His general conclusion is as follows:

> Migration, external and internal, was certainly an important matter and money-market conditions often helped to determine the timing of the upswing of the cycle. But the evidence for a complex interaction of the British and American economies at least as far as investment in housing in Britain is concerned, is slender. The facts certainly seem to point to an industry whose fate was largely determined internally by the state of demand and by the nature of the operation of the trade itself.[4]

The two contributions referred to lay stress on so-called fortuitous domestic influences on the course of housebuilding in Britain: neither has paid enough attention to demographic factors. An adequate interpretation of building fluctuations must give a prominent place to the role of population change.

In order to carry out a rigorous test, I have re-examined the course of housebuilding in England and Wales in the period 1870–1913 on the basis of new data yielding a more comprehensive record of regional cycles. The analysis seeks to attain a more accurate measurement of the demographic determinants of building cycles, regionally as well as in the aggregate. These results are then related to corresponding data on the demographic

[1] Habakkuk, op. cit., p. 137.
[2] Ibid., p. 141.   [3] Saul, op. cit.
[4] Ibid., p. 136. For a critique of Saul's analysis see Parry Lewis, op. cit., pp. 203–5.

determinants of the building cycle in the United States in the same period.

STATISTICAL SOURCES AND METHODS

The sources used are the Inland Revenue ledgers deposited in the Public Record Office. Inhabited House Duty statistics, available for each county, provide a basis for regional building estimates for the years 1875–1913.[1] The ledgers also contain figures of profit income assessed under Schedule D. The characteristics of these sources and the method used are described in the Appendix to this chapter.

We have information about the number of dwelling houses assessed and not assessed to house duty as well as 'messuages and tenements' not used as dwelling houses. Sir Josiah Stamp pointed out that the income tax Schedule A figures '. . . undoubtedly represent most closely the real facts but in revaluation years far more closely than at other times'.[2] To test the reliability of these data we expressed the annual change in the number of premises in Britain shown by the House Duty statistics as an index (1900–1909 = 100) and compared it with Weber's estimates of house-building.[3] Fig. App.B.1 indicates clearly that the two series yield virtually the same long swing, and this justifies the use of the Record Office data for our purpose. It also reveals that the House Duty figures were affected by periodic revaluations and cannot be used for year-to-year changes. Both values and numbers were affected by revaluations. To overcome this difficulty we have averaged inter-revaluation years plus the revaluation year following them; this prevents any misleading impression that the series can be used for annual changes and at the same time provides an adequate indication of the time-shape.

The counties of England and Wales have been divided into two broad sectors, urban and rural. The urban counties form seven regions – the Midlands, counties surrounding London, North-

---

[1] The series for England and Wales, Scotland, and Britain are given in Mitchell and Deane, *Abstract of British Historical Statistics*, pp. 236–7.
[2] Stamp, *British Incomes and Property*, p. 31.
[3] Weber, 'A New Index of Residential Construction, 1838–1950'.

west of England, Yorkshire, Northern England, South Wales and Monmouthshire, and London. The rural regions comprise the southern agricultural counties, those near the Midlands, the South-west plus rural Wales. We shall deal mainly with the urban regions, defined as predominantly urban in that they contained the greater part of the population of England and Wales at the end of the nineteenth century.

The purpose of this analysis is to test the proposition that British building fluctuations in the period 1870–1913 are to be explained mainly by demographic variables and, in particular, by migration. Also, by relating this analysis to recent studies of population change and the building cycle in the United States since the middle of the nineteenth century, we can carry out a new test of the inverse relation between British and American building cycles and the process of interaction between the two economies.

To illuminate the connection between changes in building and changes in the house-seeking age group we have made estimates of the quinquennial change in the population aged 20–44 in each region, separating the effects of natural increase and migration. Figures on recorded deaths were obtained from the Registrar-General's annual reports and decennial supplements, and these were combined with census population figures in quinary age groups to estimate the quinquennial changes which would have occurred in the absence of migration.

The following demographic factors are relevant in explaining the volume of housebuilding in any region in a given period: (*a*) natural increase in the 20–44 age group, (*b*) internal migration, (*c*) external migration, (*d*) the headship rate (the ratio of heads of households to the total population in an age group). In this analysis we shall ignore changes in the headship rate: instead we shall refer to changes in the marriage rate. The age group 20–44 is taken as comprising the vast majority of the house-seeking section of the community. We shall concentrate on (*a*), (*b*) and (*c*), and examine the course of the demographic and building series quinquennially in each region and in the seven regions as a whole. Our method of obtaining regional estimates for both natural increase and migration is explained in Appendix B.

'Natural increase' in the 20–44 age group is an estimate of the

24

population change which would have occurred in this age group in the two quinquennia following each census, if there had been no migration in either of these periods. Changes in natural increase reflect movements in the excess of births over deaths in previous periods. A five-year boom in the birth rate is followed twenty years later by a bulge in the 20–25 age group and after thirty years by a bulge in the 30–35 group and after thirty-five years by a bulge in the 35–40 group. In any given quinquennium the natural increase is thus a composite of past influences. There is much to be explored under this heading, both nationally and regionally, but we cannot deal adequately here with echo effects.[1]

The other element to be taken into account is migration, internal and external, affecting the age group 20–44. The estimate is, of course, a balance of inward and outward movements. There is no means of distinguishing between 'immigrants' who come into a region from one of the other six regions and those who come from outside, i.e. from the rest of the United Kingdom or from abroad; and similarly with 'emigrants' from a region. Despite the limitations of the data, it is possible to make a reasonably firm estimate of the extent to which natural increase in the age group 20–44 in each region was augmented or reduced by migration. Parallel with our aggregate migration series for the seven regions, we have plotted from an independent source the quinquennial emigration of occupied persons from England and Wales to the United States.

Having estimated natural increase and the balance of migration in the age group 20–44 in each quinquennium for each region, we derive an estimate of the change in the population in the house-seeking age group.[2] This series is then compared with the course of building in each region and in the seven regions as a whole.

[1] Comprehensive studies of echo effects for the United States are to be found in Easterlin, *Population, Labor Force, and Long Swings in Economic Growth*, and Campbell, *Population Change and Building Cycles*.
[2] A similar analysis of the potential demand for houses from population aged 20–44 in Great Britain as a whole quinquennially from 1871–5 to 1906–10 was carried out by Feinstein in his unpublished Ph.D. dissertation, *Home and Foreign Investment 1870–1913*, pp. 291–6. The methods used here, as explained in Appendix B, are different from Feinstein's.

REGIONAL BUILDING CYCLES, 1870–1910

Figs. 2.1 *A–C* show the course of the building cycle in each of the urban regions of England and Wales from 1871 to 1910. This series gives the average annual number of houses built in each quinquennium (years between revaluations plus the revaluation year following them being averaged). For brevity I shall refer to the Inhabited House Duty figures as the IHD index. With it we plot for each quinquennium from 1870 to 1910 the average annual increase in the population aged 20–44; this registers the net effect of natural increase and migration which are also shown in the charts.

The picture emerging from these charts dispels the uncertainty as to whether regional fluctuations were synchronized or were the result of diverse local circumstances. With the exception of London and South Wales there was a high degree of conformity between regional building swings, although the amplitude varied. London was particularly affected by outward shifts of population to the home counties; in the early part of the period, however, there was considerable net in-migration. The reason why South Wales is an exception is that its economy was entirely in the export sector.[1]

It would be unreasonable to expect the peak of the building cycle to occur in the same year in every region: there is usually a cluster of individual peaks within a neighbourhood of three or four years. Our building series, beginning in 1875, reveals a high level of activity, though often declining in the late 1870s in every region except the counties surrounding London where the peak came in the early years of the 1880s. The downswing lasted until the early 1890s in all regions except London and South Wales. Building activity was rising during the 1890s in all regions, with a peak at the turn of the century everywhere except in South Wales and London.

It might be argued that the averaging technique which has been used to overcome the difficulty of the reassessment years

[1] See Thomas, 'Wales and the Atlantic Economy'.

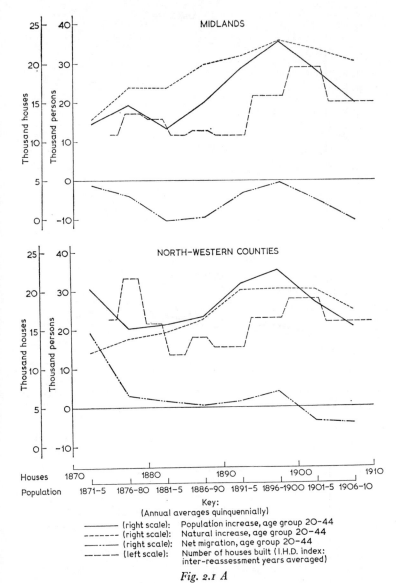

Fig. 2.1 A

Figure 2.1 Population change and regional building cycles, 1871–1910.
A Midlands and North-west. *B* Yorkshire, North, and South Wales and
Monmouthshire. *C* London and counties surrounding London.
Source: Appendix A.

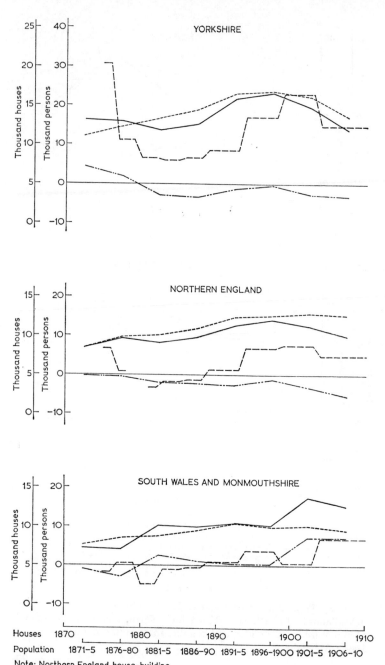

YORKSHIRE

NORTHERN ENGLAND

SOUTH WALES AND MONMOUTHSHIRE

Note: Northern England house-building
1879 and 1880 not charted – series distorted by boundary revisions

Fig. 2.1 B

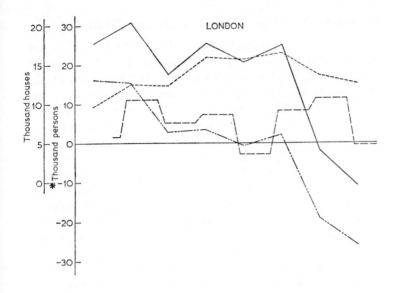

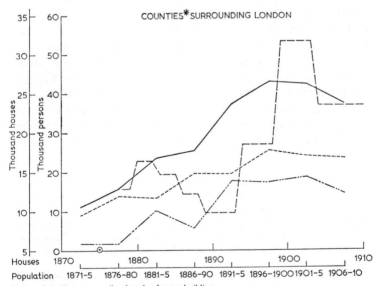

Notes: Counties surrounding London house-building
⊙ 1875: 5·1 thousand houses. 1876 and 1877 not charted —series distorted by
    boundary revisions
✱ London population age group 15-44

Fig. 2.1 C

tends to blur the peaks and troughs of the cycle. In order to test the reliability of the new regional indexes, I shall look at the North-west (Lancashire and Cheshire) in more detail and partially disaggregate the IHD index by plotting alongside it annual estimates of building in the Manchester conurbation and Liverpool, based on local authority data.[1] These are shown in fig. 2.2 together with the demographic series.

The peak of 1877–9 in our index coincides exactly with the peak in the number of houses erected by private enterprise in Liverpool. The peak in the Manchester conurbation index comes a year earlier, as one would expect since these figures relate to houses for which planning permission had been obtained. The steep descent from the top to a very low trough in 1883–5 shown by the IHD index corresponds exactly to what happened in the Manchester conurbation; in both series building then continues at a very low level until the upturn in 1892–4. The downswing in Liverpool is less steep and there is no early trough in 1883–5; the revival takes place at the same time as is indicated in the other two indexes.[2] There is a close resemblance between the final peak and the subsequent decline in the IHD series from 1899 to 1910 and the dominant Manchester component, again allowing for the fact that the latter registers building plans and not houses built. The high average level of activity in the region between 1899 and 1903 recorded by our index reflects a balance between the weakening boom in the Manchester conurbation and a continuation of buoyant conditions in Liverpool. A vigorous boom continued in Liverpool, with another high peak in 1906, whereas the level of activity in the conurbation was midway between the

[1] The figures for the towns in the Manchester conurbation are the number of houses on approved building plans. For Manchester itself there is a gap from 1871 to 1890 and values for these years were estimated from other sources. See Parry Lewis, op. cit., pp. 307–17. The Liverpool series are the number of houses erected by private enterprise. They were supplied to B. Weber by the Town Clerk of Liverpool. See ibid., pp. 335–6.
[2] The kink and sharp rise in the Liverpool index in 1895 is explained by the extension of the boundaries of the city in November of that year, adding 23,263 dwelling houses to the original stock of 106,962. See ibid., p. 335.

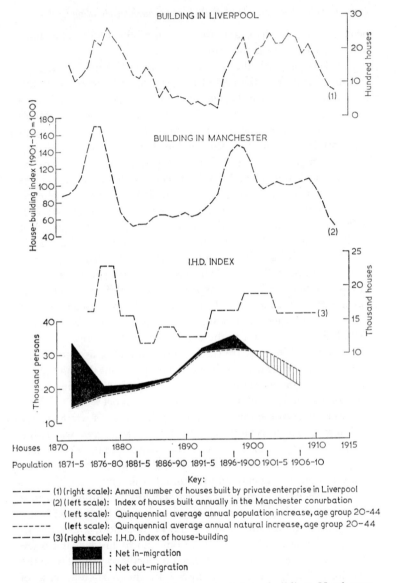

Figure 2.2 Migration, natural increase and housebuilding, North-west region, 1871–1913.
Sources: (1) Parry Lewis, *Building Cycles and Britain's Growth*, pp. 335–6; (2) ibid., p. 317; (3) Figure 2.1 *A*.

31

peak of the late 1870s and the trough of the 1880s. The sharp decline in 1909–13 is the same in both.

The IHD index is the nearest one can get to full coverage of regional building in the period 1875–1910. The comparison with local authority data in two large component parts of the North-west region has been reassuring; the close fit with Weber's national index is reproduced regionally. Even before we bring in the population variable, the evidence points strongly against the argument that regional building was shaped largely by diverse local influences. S. B. Saul came near to the main explanation in the following sentence of his: 'Liverpool followed the national index to the recovery after the Boer War, but then building continued at a high level until as late as 1909, just as it did in South Wales and in the cotton towns.'[1] It is essential to distinguish between the Home-Construction Sector and the Export Sector. Coal-exporting and cotton-exporting towns belong entirely to the export sector; building in such areas has a different time-shape from that of the home-construction sector (areas other than purely export areas). There is always some building going on in the export sector; the regional as well as the national indexes are composites of building activity in the two sectors. It is clear from the national index that the high phase of the long swing were the years when the ratio of building in the home-construction sector to building in the export sector was high and vice versa in the low phase. The purest case of export sector building is South Wales; the index for that region was rising in the 1890s and in the late 1900s, contrary to the national swing. The same phenomenon was at work in parts of other regions but it was seldom strong enough to dominate the regional composite.

Saul presents a number of charts showing building in various towns in Cheshire between 1890 and 1913, and finds an upswing in a number of dormitory towns and in Stockport, and a downswing in Crewe.[2] The more it becomes local history, the more variety we are going to see; but this is perfectly consistent with the presence of major ebbs and flows.[3] In the particular case of

[1] Saul, op. cit., p. 122.　　　　　　　　　　　[2] Ibid., p. 124.
[3] Analysis is concerned with phenomena which exhibit statistical uniformities. In the words of Sir John Hicks, '. . . every historical event has

32

Cheshire, the boom in building in the dormitory towns was part of a universal tendency in the economic growth of large cities – the overspill (internal migration from the point of view of the region). This is part of the migration variable which, as we shall see, is the major determinant of the ebb and flow of building.

A glance at fig. 2.2 shows for the North-west region the quinquennial course of natural increase and population change in the age group 20–44 from 1871–5 to 1906–10. The excess of population change over natural increase (the shaded area) indicates the volume of net in-migration, and the excess of natural increase over population change (the area with broken lines) indicates the volume of net out-migration. There is a close correspondence between the long swing in housebuilding and the curve of population change in the 20–44 age group, with the former lagging after the latter. The shape of the curve of population change is determined by the swing in the balance of migration.

The period begins with a very heavy net movement of migrants into the region in the years 1871–5, and this leads to a sharp rise in building activity which reaches a high peak in the years 1877–9. There was a marked contraction in in-migration in 1878–80, and it remained negligible through the 1880s and beginning of the 1890s. This was accompanied by a sharp downswing and long trough in building activity. Meanwhile, beginning in 1885–90 the curve of natural increase rose sharply until it reached a record level in the 1890s. The quinquennium 1896–1900 saw the powerful echo effect of the sharp increase in the birth rate twenty-five to thirty years before, and superimposed on this very high level of natural increase was a renewed rise in net migration into the region. There was also a considerable increase in the marriage rate in the 1890s. This time the lag relationship is

some aspect in which it is unique; but nearly always there are other aspects in which it is a member of a group, often of quite a large group. If it is one of the latter aspects in which we are interested, it will be the group, not the individual, on which we shall fix our attention; it will be the average, or norm, of the group which is what we shall be trying to explain. We shall be able to allow that the individual may diverge from the norm without being deterred from the recognition of a statistical uniformity.' (Hicks, *A Theory of Economic History*, p. 3.)

between the natural increase build-up which attained its maximum in 1891–1900 plus the migration increase with peak marriage
rate in 1896–1900 and the upswing in building which began about
1894–5 and went to a peak at the turn of the century and a few
years afterwards. After 1900 net migration was negative until the
end of the period and the level of natural increase was falling;
this induced with a lag a downswing in the volume of building.

Now that we have taken a preliminary look at the pattern in
the North-west region, with our IHD index partially disaggregated, we shall examine the evidence for the other regions.

DEMOGRAPHIC DETERMINANTS: REGIONAL
AND NATIONAL

The time-shape for the North-west is repeated in the North,
Yorkshire, the Midlands and the counties surrounding London.
The dominant influence of the course of migration is clearly
brought out in all regions. It is interesting to compare the picture
for London with that of the counties surrounding the capital. In
the Home Counties building has a long swing corresponding to
that of the rest of industrial England, with a very high peak in the
early 1900s: in London, however, there is only a mild swing. The
annual volume of building in the capital in 1902–6 was only
slightly above the level of 1877–81, and the troughs in 1892–6
and 1907–10 were relatively shallow. Net migration into London,
which was fairly high in the 1870s, fell to low levels in the 1880s
and 1890s, and became a large net outflow in the 1900s. The
gross outflows to the Home Counties were an important factor.

Some of these outflows went beyond the periphery of the
capital, as can be seen from fig. 2.3, which gives the course of
building in the predominantly rural areas of England and Wales.
In the agricultural Midlands there was a steady low level of activity with hardly any fluctuation; in the southern counties movements were more erratic and the South-west plus rural Wales
showed mild peaks in the late 1870s and early 1900s. Putting the
three together as a residual rural sector, we find a definite peak
in the early 1900s, as in the Home Counties, the Midlands, the
North-west and Yorkshire. This was chiefly the reflection of the

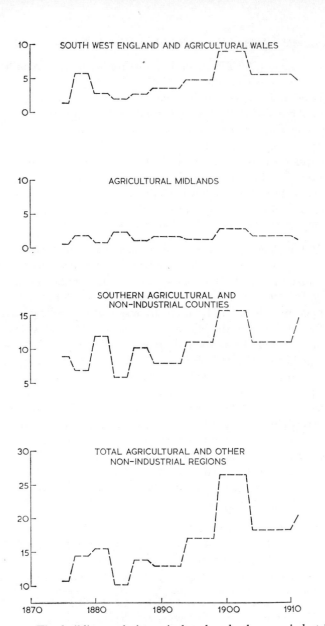

Figure 2.3 The building cycle in agricultural and other non-industrial regions, 1871–1910 (figures in thousands).
Source: Inland Revenue Inhabited House Duty records (see Appendix B).

35

demographic echo effect and the growth of residential and military towns in southern counties during the 1890s.

London displayed a unique pattern because it was a congested capital bursting at the seams. Behind the bare summary record of building and demographic change in fig. 2.1 *C* is a fascinating story of population mobility, transport innovations and the expansion of suburbs. To do justice to it would need several volumes of the calibre of the admirable study of Camberwell by H. J. Dyos.[1] The following summary of Camberwell's demographic history is in miniature a faithful reflection of the course of population change in London shown in the chart.

> Of the 75,000 persons by which the suburb had grown during its years of maximum development in the 1870s, about 52,000 represented the balance of migration into and out of the district, and 23,000 were the result of natural increase. But the stream of migrants which had been chiefly responsible for the growth of the suburb since the beginning of the century, and which was now in full flood, soon declined, and it had dried up all together by the end of the century. Of the increase of about 49,000 persons recorded between 1881 and 1891, only about 17,000 could be accounted for by net immigration, but in the last ten years of the century the increase of about 24,000 persons was wholly accounted for by natural increase, and would have been higher had not more people – over a thousand – left the suburb than came into it. By 1911, the balance of migration had detached a further 25,000 from Camberwell, and this attrition continued, despite the comparatively low average population density, in the post-war years.[2]

The natural increase component of the population curve rose everywhere to a peak in the late 1890s; this was the result of the high level of fertility a quarter of a century earlier (the number

[1] Dyos, *Victorian Suburb: A Study of the Growth of Camberwell*. See also Welton, *England's Recent Progress*, pp. 188–206; Bowley, 'Area and Population', and Ponsonby and Ruck, 'Travel and Mobility', both in *The New Survey of London Life and Labour*, Vol. I: *Forty Years of Change*; Cairncross, 'Internal Migration in Victorian England', in *Home and Foreign Investment 1870–1913*, pp. 65–83.

[2] Dyos, op. cit., p. 56.

of births per 1,000 women aged 15–44 in England and Wales rising from 150·7 in 1863 to 156·7 in 1876). In addition, the marriage rate was at a peak in 1896–1900, 16·1 per 1,000 as against 14·7 per 1,000 in 1886–90.

In all regions, except London and South Wales, population change in the age group 20–44 was at a maximum in the five-year period 1896–1900; there was a combination of a powerful echo effect on natural increase, a deep trough in emigration overseas, and heavy internal migration particularly into the Home Counties and the North-west. In each of these five regions the peak in housebuilding came at the turn of the century and there can be no doubt that there was a common demographic determinant. South Wales, which was out of step, had relatively low building activity in 1899–1904 and then came a vigorous boom (in the wake of high in-migration) in the years 1905–10, when every other region was experiencing a decline in house-building.

The building cycle and the demographic variables for the seven regions as a whole (largely England and Wales) are shown in fig. 2.4. There is a very close similarity between the movements in our IHD building index and those of the Parry Lewis weighted index. Population change in the age group 20–44 is the result of 'natural increase' and current migration. The charts show the quantitative significance of these two components. Fig. 2.4 indicates the part played by migration in determining the *shape* of the curve of population change in the urban regions of England and Wales taken together. The verdict of the analysis is that nationally and regionally the swing in housebuilding follows with a lag the swing in the population aged 20–44 as determined by migration. With regard to timing, the divergent fluctuations in London and South Wales did little to modify the major uniform swings in the other five regions which governed the aggregate. The inverse relation between internal and external migration is clearly shown. When internal migration was high, emigration was low; and it was in those years that building, with a lag, expanded; the opposite occurred when internal migration was low and emigration was high. The swings in housebuilding conform to the swings in the migration-dominated curve of population change. As Cairncross

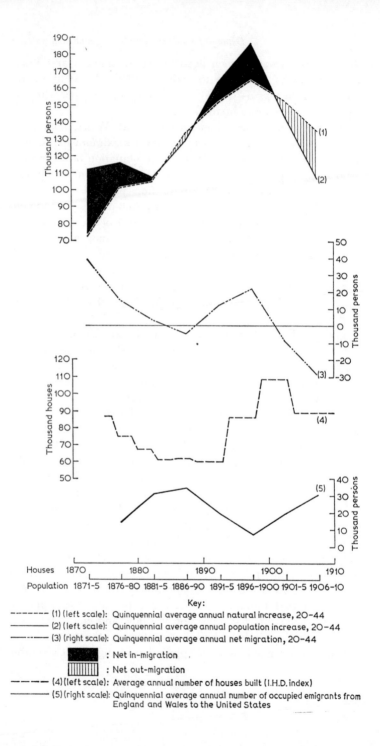

Key:

‒‒‒‒‒‒ (1) (left scale): Quinquennial average annual natural increase, 20–44

———— (2) (left scale): Quinquennial average annual population increase, 20–44

—·—·— (3) (right scale): Quinquennial average annual net migration, 20–44

    ■■■   : Net in-migration

    |||||| : Net out-migration

‒ ‒ ‒ ‒ (4) (left scale): Average annual number of houses built (I.H.D. index)

———— (5) (right scale): Quinquennial average annual number of occupied emigrants from England and Wales to the United States

observed in his well-known analysis of fluctuations in the Glasgow building industry, 1860–1914, '. . . the building cycle was little more than a migration cycle in disguise.'[1]

THE ALTERNATION OF BRITISH AND AMERICAN CYCLES

Much new work has been done on building fluctuations in the United States. To round off this reappraisal, I shall compare the British pattern with that of the United States in the period 1870–1910, drawing on the valuable researches of Burnham O. Campbell.[2] To take advantage of improvements in earlier building series, I shall use John R. Riggleman's index of the value of building permits as adjusted by Walter Isard and Clarence D. Long's index of the value of permits as adjusted by Miles L. Colean and Robinson Newcomb.[3]

Burnham Campbell has conducted a detailed examination of the influence of demographic variables, particularly immigration, on the residential building cycle in the United States. By isolating movements in the headship rate, i.e. the ratio of households to total population in an age group, he has reached illuminating conclusions about the causation of the post-1945 building cycle. In the present context we shall be concerned only with his results for the period ending in 1913. He defines 'required additions' as the population change in each age group during a given period multiplied by the headship rate for the age group at the beginning of the period. He has calculated for the United States the change

[1] Cairncross, op. cit., p. 25.
[2] Campbell, op. cit.
[3] For an account of the characteristics of these indexes see Abramovitz, *Evidences of Long Swings in Aggregate Construction since the Civil War*, pp. 206–20.

Figure 2.4 Population change and the building cycle in urban regions of England and Wales, 1871–1910.
Notes: (i) London's population includes 15–20 age group. (ii) Method of averaging housebuilding is based on reassessment years for areas outside London. Different reassessment years for metropolitan areas are ignored.
Sources: (1) to (4) Figure 2.1 (*A–C*); (5) Thomas, *Migration and Economic Growth*, Tables 81 and 84.

in population by age group in each quinquennium from 1850–5 on, and he then estimates the change in required additions by age group due to immigration in each quinquennium.[1] It is this latter series for the period 1870–5 to 1905–10 which I have reproduced in fig. 2.5.

Campbell concludes that

> ... from the Civil War to the 1890s the rate of change in required additions – and from the 1890s to the 1930s, the direction of change – was controlled by the long swing in immigration. . . . Not only was the long swing in required additions greatly influenced by immigration, but from the 1870s to the 1910s and again in the 1930s there was a close connection between the long swing in immigration and the long swing in household forma- tions and housing starts or residential capital formation. . . . The argument that fluctuations in immigration were the sources of those in residential building can be stated most strongly in terms of quinquennial data. From the 1870s to the 1930s residential building and required additions due to immigration varied together in all but three half-decades, and the lagged adjustment of residential construction to changes in housing demand could explain all three exceptions. In summary, from the Civil War to World War II the long swing in immigration was the dominant source of the long swing in required ad- ditions and so of the residential building cycle in the United States.[2]

In fig. 2.5 we plot the British data for the period 1871–1910 with the corresponding American quinquennial data on required additions in the age group 20–44 due to immigration, and three indexes of building activity. There is an impressive inverse relation between the quinquennial increase in population in the age group 20–44 in Britain and the quinquennial change in required additions due to immigration in the age group 20–44 in the United States. The building cycles are inverse and the time- shape of each is governed by the course of migration. If it were

[1] For details of the statistical treatment of immigration see Campbell, op. cit., Appendix C, pp. 189–94.   [2] Ibid., p. 110.

possible to produce quinquennial estimates of internal migration for the United States, this would complete the picture. Kuznets has shown, on the basis of decadal estimates, that changes in internal migration of natives born in the United States were synchronous with changes in additions to total population and that the volume of internal migration in any decade was probably at least equal to the total additions to population.[1]

Fig. 2.5 amply confirms the conclusions of *Migration and Economic Growth*. The crux of the problem is the mechanism of the migration cycle. Housebuilding is an important part of population-sensitive capital formation, and the fluctuations in the latter are crucial in the process of interaction between the British and American economies in the period under review.

The demographic factor is of course not the sole determinant of the building cycle; there are other factors on the demand and the supply side, e.g. income levels, the stickiness of rents, the rate of interest, the quality of houses, the rate of demolitions, and the organization of the building trades. Various elements can be combined to form a satisfactory explanation based on the cobweb theorem (see p. 98). What the empirical evidence demonstrates unequivocally is that migration is a major determinant.

Our analysis refutes the assertions of the writers quoted earlier, e.g. S. B. Saul's statement about British experience in the period 1890–1914, that it is '. . . hard to believe that migration of itself could account for more than a small part of the wide fluctuations in house construction'.[2] Habakkuk's speculations about possible lack of synchronization between regional fluctuations in Britain in the period 1870–1914 are also wide of the mark. Starting from the notion that the only real cycle is the trade cycle, he suggested that regional trade cycles were behaving in such a way as to produce a bogus long swing in aggregate building which became more moderate in its amplitude. The evidence contradicts any such notion. Statistical analysis confirms that there was a real building cycle determined mainly by migration. The degree of synchronization or lack of it between regional building cycles has

[1] Kuznets, *Capital in the American Economy*, pp. 325–7.
[2] Saul, op. cit., p. 131.

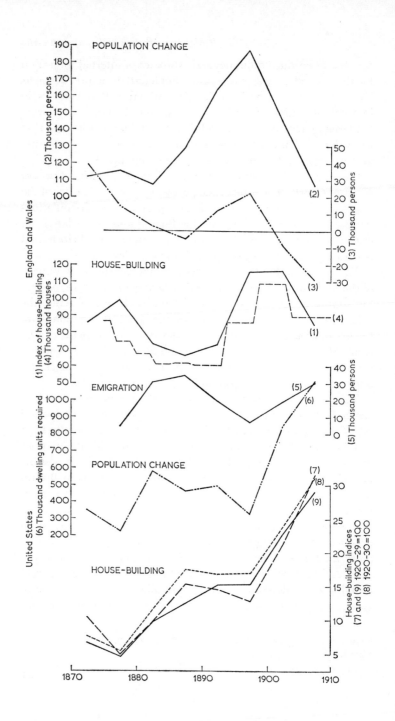

very little to do with the trade cycle.[1] Moreover, instead of moderating, the amplitude of the aggregate long swing increased, the high peak of the early 1900s reflecting the force of the demographic determinants in the late 1890s.

So far as the United States is concerned, Habakkuk says that '. . . an increase in immigration did not *initiate* a revival of building; the revival was started by changes in migration within the United States which preceded changes in immigration. . .'[2] There is no statistical support for this assertion; the figures for internal migration cannot be used for this purpose. What we do know about annual time series for immigration and building in the United States refutes the assertion. Lag analysis has demonstrated that throughout the period 1845–1913, except for the years 1869–79, immigration consistently preceded American building activity.[3]

According to Habakkuk, '. . . the problem posed by the hypothesis of the Atlantic economy is the balance between domestic – and in this context fortuitous – influences on the one hand, and foreign and systematic influences on the other',[4] and he comes down heavily on the side of the former. The empirical evidence presented in this chapter strongly confirms the proposition that migration, internal and external, played a major role in the housebuilding cycles in Britain and the United States in the period 1870–1913. To those who contemplate the tides of building activity and are impressed only by what seem to be accidental,

[1] The whole question of housebuilding and the trade cycle was thoroughly examined by B. Weber. He concluded that '. . . taking the period from 1842 to 1913 as a whole, neither an emphatic anti-cyclical movement in building nor the reverse can be established unequivocally'. See Parry Lewis, op. cit., p. 359.
[2] Habakkuk, op. cit., p. 121. Italics in the original.
[3] See *Migration and Economic Growth*, pp. 159–63.
[4] Habakkuk, op. cit., p. 133.

Figure 2.5 Population change and building cycles, England and Wales and the United States, 1871–1910.
Sources: (2), (3), (4) and (5), see Figure 2.4; (1) Parry Lewis, *Building Cycles and Britain's Growth*, p. 317, col. 7; (6) Campbell, *Population Change and Building Cycles*, p. 194; (7), (8) and (9) Abramovitz, *Evidences of Long Swings in Aggregate Construction since the Civil War*, pp. 147–9.

wayward or local influences, I commend the well-known lines of Arthur Hugh Clough:

> For while the tired waves, vainly breaking,
> Seem here no painful inch to gain,
> Far back, through creeks and inlets making,
> Comes silent, flooding in, the main.

Appendix B

Population Change and Regional Building Cycles in England and Wales, 1870–1910 : Sources and Methods

The sources used are Inland Revenue ledgers deposited at the Public Record Office, Ashridge, Hertfordshire.[1] They comprise revenue raised from the Inhabited House Duty and profits assessed under Schedule D. The data are available for each county.

INHABITED HOUSE DUTY STATISTICS

The Inhabited House Duty was introduced in 1851 and was levied on dwelling houses of £20 annual value and over. There is information about dwelling houses assessed and not assessed to duty as well as 'messuages and tenements' not used as dwelling houses. We took the series showing the total number of houses assessed and not assessed to duty from 1875 to 1910, and obtained a measure of housebuilding activity from the change in the numbers recorded.

It is important to be clear about the limitations of these data and how we have sought to overcome them. The first difficulty is the effect of the periodic reassessments of properties. In England and Wales, with the exception of London, reassessment took place in 1876, 1879, 1882, 1885, 1888, 1893, 1898, 1903 and 1910; the revaluation years for London were 1876, 1881, 1886, 1891, 1896, 1901, 1906 and 1911. Josiah Stamp, in his authoritative work, stated that '. . . the income tax, Schedule A, figures undoubtedly represent most closely the real facts, but in re-

[1] Thanks are due to the authorities at the Public Record Office at Ashridge for their courtesy and cooperation in granting facilities for this research. The work was carried out by Mrs Margaret Evans and Mr Kenneth Richards when they were Research Assistants in the Department of Economics at University College, Cardiff. I wish to pay tribute to the substantial contribution which they made in collecting and analysing these data. I am particularly indebted to Mrs Evans for preparing the material for this Appendix and for drawing the charts.

45

valuation years far more closely than at other times'.[1] In years
between revaluations the series tend to be below the true figures.
'The reason is that while effect is given in practice to all *bona fide
reductions* in rent wherever they occur, no effect is, or can be,
given to *increases* in rent, and the totals are only maintained by new
properties and structural alterations. There is a continuous drag
downwards, and the "slack" is not taken up until the next revaluation year.'[2] In some areas the figures for revaluation years
showed a decline rather than an upward revision; this was likely
to happen where a large number of houses were becoming empty
or where there was a general fall in rents and the revaluation
provided an opportunity for a general revision of assessments.
The numbers of houses as well as the values were affected by the
reassessments. Another awkward fact about these data is pointed
out by B. R. Mitchell and Phyllis Deane, namely, that '. . . the
figures are of net quantities, offsetting much demolition against
new building, and it seems probable that demolition was nothing
like constant from year to year'.[3]

For the above reasons the Inhabited House Duty figures are
not an accurate guide to *year-to-year* changes in housebuilding,
but this does not necessarily rule them out as an indication of the
time-shape of housebuilding. Their reliability for this purpose can
be tested by comparing them with Weber's building index. From
the House Duty records we have taken the annual change in the
number of premises in Great Britain[4] and produced an index
for the years 1875–1910 (1900–9 = 100). This is shown together
with Weber's index of residential construction in fig. App.B.1.

The chart brings out clearly the effect of the periodic revaluations and the impossibility of using the series for *annual*
changes. On the other hand, it also demonstrates that the long
swing in building revealed by the Inhabited House Duty statistics
follows closely that of the Weber index. It was therefore decided
to overcome the reassessment difficulty by averaging the years
between revaluations plus the revaluation year following them.

[1] Stamp, *British Incomes and Property*, p. 31.

[2] Ibid. Italics in the original.

[3] Mitchell and Deane, *Abstract of British Historical Statistics*, p. 233.

[4] This series is given in ibid., pp. 236–7.

The year is the financial year ending on 4 April; thus, for example, the difference between the number of houses in existence at 4 April 1876 and 4 April 1875 is taken as an estimate of house-building in 1875.

The counties of England and Wales are divided into two sectors, roughly urban and rural. The urban sector has seven regions – Midlands, counties surrounding London, North-west England, Yorkshire, Northern England, South Wales and Monmouthshire,

Figure App.B.1 Two indexes of housebuilding in Great Britain, 1875–1910.
Source: Mitchell and Deane, *Abstract of British Historical Statistics*, pp. 236–9.

and London. The three rural regions are the Southern agricultural counties, Midlands agricultural counties, and the South-west plus rural Wales.

In compiling these regional estimates we had to consider the effects of the frequent changes in income tax districts. Since our classification splits the country into large sections, most of the district revisions fell within (and not between) regions and can therefore be ignored. Where major revisions distort our series we have noted these in the tables as boundary revisions and left breaks in our charts for the years affected.

For the years 1893 and 1894 two volumes were missing from the

Ashridge ledgers. Counties are entered alphabetically, and the missing ledgers contained those beginning S–W (including Wales) for 1893 and B–R for 1894. It was therefore necessary to produce estimates. In most regions we had records for one or more counties and we applied the percentage change for available counties in the region to the missing counties. Where figures for all the counties in a region were missing we used the percentage change in ledger section totals as a guide. The sections were alphabetical and we took the most appropriate ledger section in two cases; section 4 containing Lancashire, Leicester and Lincoln was used for the North–west; section 9 containing Wiltshire, Worcester and Yorkshire was used for Yorkshire. A third method seemed preferable for Wales. In view of the slow rate of increase in numbers of houses for rural Wales, we assumed there was no change here between 1892 and 1893, and allocated the whole increase for Wales to the urban section – South Wales and Monmouthshire. The counties composing the regions are as follows.

MIDLANDS

Derby
Leicester
Northampton
Nottingham
Staffordshire
Warwick
Worcester

NORTHERN ENGLAND

Cumberland
Durham
Northumberland
Westmorland

LONDON

SOUTHERN AGRICULTURAL

Bedfordshire

Berkshire
Buckinghamshire
Cambridge
Gloucestershire
Hereford
Norfolk
Oxford
Suffolk
Sussex
Wiltshire
Hampshire

COUNTIES SURROUNDING LONDON

Essex
Hertford
Kent (extra-metropolitan)
Middlesex (extra-metropolitan)
Surrey (extra-metropolitan)

NORTH-WESTERN COUNTIES	MIDLAND AGRICULTURAL
Lancashire	Huntingdon
Cheshire	Lincolnshire
	Rutland
YORKSHIRE	Shropshire
Yorkshire	SOUTH-WESTERN ENGLAND AND RURAL WALES
SOUTH WALES AND MONMOUTHSHIRE	Cornwall
	Devon
Brecon	Dorset
Cardigan	Somerset
Carmarthen	Anglesey
Glamorgan	Caernarvon
Monmouth	Denbigh
Pembroke	Flint
Radnor	Merioneth
	Montgomery

A grouping of this kind is bound to be arbitrary and parts of regions classified as urban are rural; but the seven regions are urban in the sense that they contained the greater part of the population of England and Wales in the last quarter of the nineteenth century. A great advantage of the Inhabited House Duty data is that they give even coverage of all parts of the country, so that a comprehensive picture of regional cycles can be obtained.

PROFITS ASSESSED TO SCHEDULE D

The Inland Revenue ledgers contain a great deal of information on profit income assessed to Schedule D. They show gross and net profits, with allowances for wear and tear and life assurances, and a table is given of profits arising from foreign and colonial securities and possessions. Stamp approved the use of Schedule D profits as a guide to trade prosperity. 'This test is generally regarded as one of the most reliable and it has been made by many writers. There is no doubt a close correspondence between the assessments and trade. . . .'[1] Breaks affect the gross assessment

[1] Stamp, op. cit., p. 257.

series in 1876 and 1894, i.e. the financial years ending 5 April 1877 and 5 April 1895, and Stamp presents six alternative methods of allowing for these. We have applied a form of the second method (using abatements) described in his Appendix I,[1] and the series are linked accordingly.

There is one more break in 1874. From 1866 to 1874 the profit figures described as gross were actually net of life assurance allowances,[2] and to make them comparable with later series some adjustment for this should be made. Also, from 1866 to 1873 we have not deducted profits arising from foreign securities and possessions. If we take the North-western counties, for example, we find that in 1874 the allowances for life assurance amounted to £57·9 thousand and the profits from foreign securities were very small, certainly never more than £100 thousand, and were probably in the region of £50 thousand annually. Therefore the two adjustments required would seem to be almost entirely offsetting.

The records contain two sets of figures separating 'Trades, Manufactures, Professions and Employments' from 'Public Companies, Societies etc.' Since there would have been transfers over time from one group to the other with the extension of limited liability, we have taken the two groups together, and have used gross profit figures to avoid breaks caused by statutory changes in allowances and abatements. From this total profit income we have deducted (except in 1866–73) profits earned from foreign securities and possessions. We should also have deducted profits on railways outside the United Kingdom which are listed separately, in order to get a more accurate figure for domestic profits. However, they were negligible in relation to total profit income, so that they were ignored, except for London where they were deducted.

Before 1874 abatements were not included in profit income but given separately, so that they had to be added to the figures for profits to make them comparable with subsequent years. With regard to London, before 1875 separate figures are not given for the Metropolitan and extra-Metropolitan parts of the counties

[1] Ibid., pp. 473–90.
[2] Ibid., p. 207.

of Kent, Middlesex and Surrey. Therefore an assumption is made that the proportionate distribution of profits between the two areas was the same before 1875 as in the years immediately following. For each of the years 1875–8, 94 per cent of the profits were assessed in the metropolis and so this figure forms the basis for our metropolitan estimates of profit income in 1867–74.

Some of the ledgers are missing in the years 1892 (i.e. the year ended 4 April 1893) and 1893. An estimate has had to be made for profit income (as well as building) for those years. Summary totals in ten sections are available and the percentage change in profits recorded in the relevant year in these section totals is applied to the particular county which forms part of the section. Space does not allow an analysis of these data on profits, but the figures have been used as part of the method of handling the demographic data, as explained below.

DEMOGRAPHIC DATA

We have concentrated on population change as reflected in the 20–44 age group and have made quinquennial estimates for each region, separating the effect of natural increase and migration. Data on recorded deaths for each region were collected from the Registrar-General's Annual Reports and Decennial Supplements, and these were used with census population figures in quinary age groups to estimate the quinquennial changes which would have occurred in the absence of migration.

The method was as follows. We took the population in quinary age groups at each census date, and allocated recorded deaths for the next five years to these groups, thus obtaining an estimate of the survivors from each group (now five years older) at a mid-census point. In the allocation we assumed that the deaths, say, of persons aged 15–19 during the five years could be allocated on a 50 : 50 basis between the persons aged 10–14 at the census date (moving up into the 15–19 group) and those aged 15–19 at the census date (moving up into the 20–4 group). From these estimated mid-census survivors we then deducted deaths for the following five years in a similar way to produce an estimate of survivors from the previous census population at the subsequent census date. The difference between actual census population and estimated survivors from the previous census indicates the decade's migratory flow.

Where population is flowing into an area, some of the persons dying would be migrants, and to adjust for this we assumed that migrant deaths bear the same proportion to total deaths in their age groups as these migrants' life years in the decade bear to total life years of all persons in the area within the relevant ages for the same decade. That is, we applied the following equation:

$$x = d \, \frac{C(m - x)}{10(i + x) + C(m - x)}$$

where

    x is migrants' deaths
    d is total deaths in relevant age groups
    C is life-year coefficient for migrants
    m is migratory flow before adjusting for migrant deaths
    is our estimate of survivors from the previous census population at the subsequent census date (i.e. natural increase component of population) before adjusting for migrant deaths. (The life-year coefficient for i is, of course, 10).

The figure for x thus obtained was deducted from m and added to i, producing final estimates of migration and natural increase which take account of migrant deaths.

Our 'natural increase' in population aged 20–44 is the change in the number of persons within these age groups shown by the survivor estimates five and ten years later. It should be noted that the increase is based in *both* quinquennia on the population of the preceding census. For the second quinquennium it would have been preferable to calculate from a mid-census population. In order to obtain a mid-census population in quinary age groups, however, we must be able to allocate migration quinquennially for each group of persons as they move up through two succeeding age groups. As we cannot do this with the information available, the base for the second quinquennium has been left as the population of the census taken five years earlier. The definition of natural increase in this context must therefore be carefully noted. The natural increase figures are estimates of the population changes which would have occurred in the two quinquennia following each census if there had been no migration in either of these periods. At each census date the population base is changed, but between census reports it remains the same.

Although it was not possible to split the migration figures quinquennially within each age group, we have used the domestic profit income series as the criterion for allocating the total migration. We have already noted that there is a close correspondence between assessments and trade, and it seems reasonable to assume that migration into an area is likely to occur mainly during times of rising local business activity and that this local activity will also influence the amount of any outflow, with perhaps, in each case, a short lag before the effects are transmitted.

We have taken the years of rising profit income assessed as the probable years of migratory inflow, and the Inland Revenue's use of a preceding year basis of assessment has the effect of introducing a short lag. The next step was to compare the number of probable years of inflow in each interdecadal quinquennium, and split the decade's migration in the proportions indicated by this comparison. For example, if migration probably occurred in five years of the first quinquennium of a decade and in one year of the second, the decade's migration would be split between the quinquennia in the proportions of 5 : 1.

Since we wish to compare the demographic features with the other long swing series, it would have been more satisfactory to use some independent indication of migration. Where population is flowing out of an area we have brought in external factors by looking at the Board of Trade figures for external migration, and taking an average of the proportions indicated by internal and overseas criteria. Where net decennial flows were very small, we have not attempted any division of numbers, but merely divided the migrants equally between the two periods. A low decennial total could be misleading where a flow in one direction during one quinquennium is offset by a flow in the opposite direction during the next.

We compare our decadal migration figures with those obtained from the census reports, having first adjusted our totals to take account of any boundary changes which occurred. The best way of doing this was to compare, say, the 1901 population of a region given the 1891 area with the 1901 population given the 1901 area, the difference being actually due to a change in boundary. Assuming that 35 per cent of the total population is contained in the age groups 20–44, we reduce or increase migration figures by an amount corresponding to 35 per cent of the numbers spuriously gained or lost by a change in boundary.

A special note needs to be added about London. As already mentioned, our method produced estimates of natural increase based, in each interdecadal quinquennium, on the population at the preceding census date. This did not allow for the effects of migration during the first quinquennium on the natural increase in the second quinquennium. In certain circumstances this could give misleading results, as in London where the heavy inward movement of young women (under 20) made the method inappropriate. Since we could find no way of arriving at a reasonably accurate mid-census population, we took the age group 15–44 for the analysis of London. This avoids the distorting effect which a swollen age group can have on the results shown by our usual method.

TABLE APP.B.1

Natural increase and migration, population aged 20–44
Seven urban areas of England and Wales, 1870–1910

	1871–5	1876–80	1881–5	1886–90	1891–5	1896–1900	1901–5	1906–10
Natural Increase				*Thousands*				
North-western England	70·3	88·7	96·1	113·2	150·5	156·6	152·4	123·0
Northern England	35·1	48·1	50·5	59·9	74·6	77·1	79·7	76·4
Midlands	78·1	117·5	117·0	147·2	158·8	179·2	166·6	151·0
London (ages 15–44)	46·4	75·3	73·7	109·7	106·3	115·0	86·5	77·1
Counties surrounding London	46·1	69·4	66·9	98·0	97·2	128·2	119·9	116·6
South Wales and Mon.	26·4	35·2	37·5	44·5	53·1	49·2	50·8	45·0
Yorkshire	60·3	71·1	82·0	94·6	115·9	118·8	111·2	86·3
	362·7	505·3	523·7	667·1	756·4	824·1	767·1	675·4
Migration								
North-western England	+ 96·6	+ 14·5	+ 9·5	+ 2·1	+ 8·0	+ 20·0	− 18·9	− 20·8
Northern England	− 0·3	− 0·9	− 10·0	− 11·2	− 11·8	− 6·4	− 16·9	− 27·6
Midlands	− 7·0	− 20·5	− 51·4	− 47·5	− 16·9	− 1·9	− 27·0	− 51·9
London (ages 15–44)	+ 80·7	+ 78·3	+ 15·0	+ 17·7	− 2·9	+ 10·8	− 96·0	− 130·1
Counties surrounding London	+ 9·7	+ 9·2	+ 50·9	+ 28·8	+ 88·7	+ 86·6	+ 92·4	+ 71·6
South Wales and Mon.	− 5·0	− 14·6	+ 13·1	+ 4·8	+ 1·4	+ 1·4	+ 36·6	+ 35·7
Yorkshire	+ 20·9	+ 8·5	− 14·2	− 18·2	− 6·3	− 1·6	− 13·1	− 17·8
	195·6	74·5	12·9	− 23·5	60·2	108·9	− 42·9	− 140·9

TABLE APP.B.I contd.

Natural increase and migration, population aged 20–44
Seven urban areas of England and Wales, 1870–1910

	1871–5	1876–80	1881–5	1886–90	1891–5	1896–1900	1901–5	1906–10
Natural Increase and Migration								
North-western England	+166·9	+103·2	+105·6	+115·3	+158·5	+176·6	+133·5	+102·2
Northern England	+ 34·8	+ 47·2	+ 40·5	+ 48·7	+ 62·8	+ 70·7	+ 62·8	+ 48·8
Midlands	+ 71·1	+ 97·0	+ 65·6	+ 99·7	+141·9	+177·3	+139·6	+ 99·1
London (ages 15–44)	+127·1	+153·6	+ 88·7	+127·4	+103·4	+125·8	− 9·5	− 53·0
Counties surrounding London	+ 55·8	+ 78·6	+117·8	+126·8	+185·9	+214·8	+212·3	+188·2
South Wales and Mon.	+ 21·4	+ 20·6	+ 50·6	+ 49·3	+ 54·5	+ 50·6	+ 87·4	+ 80·7
Yorkshire	+ 81·2	+ 79·6	+ 67·8	+ 76·4	+109·6	+117·2	+ 98·1	+ 68·5
	553·3	579·8	536·6	643·6	816·6	933·0	724·2	534·5

Source: Population Census and Registrar-General's Decennial Supplements.

TABLE APP.B.2

Inhabited House Duty statistics: total number of houses assessed and not assessed to duty in England and Wales, by region, 1875–1912

Year ended 5 April	North-western counties	Northern England	Midlands	London	Counties surrounding London	South Wales & Mon.	Yorkshire
1875	766·4	266·3	677·9	479·1	370·4	113·1	567·4
76	788·5	276·3	690·9	485·4	375·5	117·9	584·0
77	798·9	282·8	699·7	490·9	381·5	121·0	607·8
78	824·7	289·4	720·6	501·1	385·1	125·9	616·0
79	849·5	293·5	734·8	513·6	394·2	128·1	630·7
1880	868·1	302·6	740·4	520·7	410·8	132·3	639·2
81	888·5	315·2	753·1	535·9	424·2	134·3	652·3
82	905·1	316·8	762·1	543·4	438·2	137·4	660·8
83	915·1	322·1	778·7	556·6	459·9	139·0	684·2
84	931·8	326·7	790·6	569·2	475·8	141·8	674·6
1885	945·8	330·9	800·1	572·8	489·5	145·1	681·8
86	950·1	334·5	811·1	579·9	504·0	150·1	688·1
87	966·4	339·4	821·7	581·5	515·7	154·5	696·4
88	979·1	343·3	834·8	591·3	526·4	158·2	706·3
89	992·2	347·3	844·9	600·8	540·4	162·1	713·7
1890	1010·5	351·9	855·5	613·3	550·2	165·8	725·5
91	1025·2	356·6	866·6	621·7	559·8	170·0	736·8
92	1038·8	363·1	878·6	625·0	569·9	175·0	748·8
93	1053·1			630·4			
94				636·7			760·5

TABLE APP.B.2 contd.

Inhabited House Duty statistics: total number of houses assessed and not assessed to duty in England and Wales, by region, 1875–1912

Year ended 5 April	North-western counties	Northern England	Midlands	London	Counties surrounding London	South Wales & Mon.	Yorkshire
1895	1066·0	380·4	912·0	635·8	600·8	192·4	771·5
96	1083·5	388·2	927·7	641·7	616·7	199·5	783·6
97	1104·9	396·8	946·9	643·4	635·4	206·0	798·5
98	1124·1	403·9	962·5	652·1	650·7	210·7	809·6
99	1137·8	417·7	977·9	669·0	682·6	217·4	828·1
1900	1170·5	428·5	1004·2	673·0	713·9	221·9	845·6
01	1193·3	438·5	1024·2	681·9	745·0	225·4	865·0
02	1211·3	450·2	1044·1	689·4	776·0	229·0	881·2
03	1224·4	459·7	1060·4	700·3	803·5	234·5	892·4
04	1232·3	461·5	1074·8	711·3	840·5	239·2	910·4
1905	1251·5	471·2	1093·4	725·9	868·4	245·0	925·9
06	1271·2	480·0	1119·0	738·4	900·7	254·9	941·8
07	1289·0	489·3	1134·7	742·8	923·0	259·9	955·6
08	1291·4	495·8	1143·2	744·4	935·9	265·9	957·9
09	1322·0	505·2	1164·2	751·4	964·4	275·3	974·3
1910	1338·8	516·1	1179·8	755·9	984·2	283·9	992·1
11	1343·6	513·5	1180·1	759·0	1003·8	289·8	996·4
12	1359·2	524·2	1194·9	766·8	1022·5	299·4	1009·2

Source: Inland Revenue ledgers.

3 The Role of International Capital Movements

A clear pattern may be seen in the population and capital flows of the period 1860–1913; each of the three upsurges in emigration from Europe – 1863–72, 1879–90, and 1898–1907 – was accompanied by a boom in British capital exports. That international migration synchronized almost exactly with international investment is evident from Table 3.1

The destinations of the 24 million European emigrants in the

TABLE 3.1

Peaks and troughs in British foreign lending and European overseas emigration, 1860–1913

United Kingdom net income available for foreign investment*		European emigration to overseas countries†	
Trough Year	Peak Year	Trough Year	Peak Year
1862	1872	1861	1872
1877	1890	1877	1891
1898	1908	1898	1907

Sources: * Imlah, 'The Balance of Payments and the Export of Capital of the United Kingdom, 1816–1913', pp. 234–9.
† Sundbärg's figures in *Emigrationsutredningen*, Bilaga IV, *Utvandringsstatistik*, pp. 102–3.

CAMROSE LUTHERAN COLLEGE
LIBRARY

years 1891–1914 were roughly as follows: 54 per cent to the United States, 25 per cent to Latin America, and 17 per cent to the British Empire. By 1913 aggregate British foreign investment amounted to £3763 million distributed geographically as follows: 47 per cent in the British Empire, 20 per cent in the United States, 20 per cent in Latin America, and 6 per cent in Europe. We shall now examine in detail the scale and significance of these capital movements.

THE WORLD INVESTMENT PICTURE IN 1913

The great era of accumulation and international lending which ended in 1913[1] had created a world sharply divided into creditor and debtor nations, as shown in Table 3.2.

TABLE 3.2

Main creditor and debtor countries, 1913

	Gross Credits			Gross Debts	
	$000 mn.	%		$000 mn.	%
United Kingdom	18·0	40·9	Europe	12·0	27·3
France	9·0	20·4	Latin America	8·5	19·3
Germany	5·8	13·2	United States	6·8	15·5
Belgium, Netherlands			Canada	3·7	8·4
& Switzerland	5·5	12·5			
			Asia	6·0	13·6
United States	3·5	8·0	Africa	4·7	10·7
Other countries	2·2	5·0	Oceania	2·3	5·2
	44·0	100·0		44·0	100·0

Source: United Nations, *International Capital Movements in the Inter-War Period.*

Britain's gross creditor position in 1913 amounted to $18 billion, or 41 per cent of the world total of $44 billion. This mirrored the prominent part played by British long-term lending

[1] The analysis is restricted to long-term capital.

in the nineteenth century. At first glance it is remarkable that the five continental creditor nations, France, Germany, Belgium, the Netherlands and Switzerland, had between them built up a creditor position of $20·3 billion, over $2 billion larger than that of Britain; even France by herself seemed to be half as important as Britain. This simple comparison, however, is misleading. There were significant differences between continental and British outflows of capital, in terms of quality, motivation and consequences. Private enterprise subject to mild British Government regulation was the mainspring in England, whereas in France and Germany foreign investment was an instrument for the attainment of national objectives.

French long-term foreign lending increased threefold between 1880 and 1914 when the aggregate reached 45 billion francs, a quarter of which was in Russia, a fifth in French colonies and Latin America and only 2 per cent in North America.[1] The political designs of the French Government resulted in the equivalent of £500 million being invested in Russian bonds, and the Russian Government was spending half the proceeds on armaments. Similar ill-fated loans were made to Turkey, Austria-Hungary, the Balkan States and Latin America. The yield was lower than that on domestic securities, and the borrowing countries did not increase their demand for French exports. Nearly all the loans were ultimately repudiated. It is estimated that French investors lost no less than two-thirds of the capital placed in foreign bonds, an amount equal to six times the German indemnity of 1870.

Germany experienced rapid economic expansion in the period 1871-1913. The domestic rate of interest was higher than in Britain and France, and the Government was determined that foreign investment should be subordinated to the needs of the German economy. The priorities to be observed were described by a contemporary writer as follows:

(a) The issue of foreign securities in the domestic market, like the establishment of branches of domestic enterprise and

[1] Feis, *Europe: the World's Banker, 1870–1914*, p. 51.

participations abroad, is permissible only after the domestic demand for capital has been fully satisfied, since the first duty of the banks is to use the available funds of the nation for increasing the national productive and purchasing power and for strengthening the home market.

(*b*) International commercial dealings as well as international flotations ought to be but the means for attaining national ends and must be placed in the service of national labor.

(*c*) Even when the two foregoing conditions have been fulfilled, the greatest care will have to be used in selecting the securities to be floated.[1]

In interpreting the national interest the German banks had an important influence on the volume of foreign investment, and there is evidence that, particularly up to 1900, they were to a large extent engaged in 'borrowing short' in London and Paris and 'lending long' in foreign countries. Germany's foreign lending was much greater than the surplus in her trade and services account. On the eve of World War I a little over half of the total of $5·8 billion of foreign investment was in Europe, partly inspired by the desire to increase the military effectiveness of her allies. The flow of capital to her colonies was very small; nearly a third of her total foreign assets was in North and South America.[2]

We may thus conclude that the State-controlled lending activities of France and Germany in the forty years before World War I, although considerable in scale, had only a small effect on the growth of the international economy. The dominant influence was the flow of long-term capital from Great Britain.

The distribution of Britain's overseas investments in publicly issued securities, by country and by category, is shown in Tables 3.3 and 3.4.

[1] Riesser, *The German Great Banks and their Concentration*, p. 384, quoted in Feis, op. cit., p. 162.
[2] For an excellent summary of the influence of government policy on foreign lending in France and Germany up to 1914, see Feis, op. cit., pp. 118–88.

TABLE 3.3

British overseas investments in publicly-issued securities,*
December 1913, by country

	£ Mn.	%
Canada and Newfoundland	514·9	13·7
Australia and New Zealand	416·4	11·1
South Africa	370·2	9·8
West Africa	37·3	1·0
India and Ceylon	378·8	10·0
Straits Settlements	27·3	0·7
British North Borneo	5·8	0·2
Hong Kong	3·1	0·1
Other British colonies	26·2	0·7
British Empire	1,780·0	47·3
United States	754·6	20·0
Argentina	319·6	8·5
Brazil	148·0	3·9
Mexico	99·0	2·6
Chile	61·0	1·6
Uruguay	36·1	1·0
Peru	34·2	0·9
Cuba	33·2	0·9
Other Latin American States	25·5	0·7
Latin America	756·6	20·1
Russia	110·0	2·9
Spain	19·0	0·5
Italy	12·5	0·3
Portugal	8·1	0·2
France	8·0	0·2
Germany	6·4	0·2
Austria	8·0	0·2
Denmark	11·0	0·3
Balkan States	17·0	0·5
Rest of Europe	18·6	0·5
Europe	218·6	5·8
Egypt	44·9	1·2
Turkey	24·0	0·6
China	43·9	1·2
Japan	62·8	1·7
Other countries	77·9	2·1
All foreign countries	1,983·3	52·7
Grand total	3,763·3	100·0

* Investments in shipping are excluded.
Source: Feis, op. cit., p. 23.

TABLE 3.4

British overseas investments in publicly-issued securities,*
December 1913, by category

	£ Mn.	%
Dominion and colonial governments	675·5	17·9
Foreign governments	297·0	7·9
Overseas municipalities	152·5	4·1
Government and municipal	1,125·0	29·9
Dominion and colonial railways	306·4	8·1
Indian railways	140·8	3·7
United States railways	616·6	16·4
Other foreign railways	467·2	12·4
Railways	1,531·0	40·6
Electric light and power	27·3	0·7
Gas and waterworks	29·2	0·8
Canals and docks	7·1	0·2
Tramways	77·8	2·1
Telegraphs and telephones	43·7	1·2
Other public utilities	185·1	5·0
Coal, iron and steel	35·2	0·9
Breweries	18·0	0·5
Other commercial and industrial	155·3	4·1
Commerce and industry	208·5	5·5
Mines	272·8	7·2
Nitrates	11·7	0·3
Oil	40·6	1·1
Rubber	41·0	1·1
Tea and coffee	22·4	0·6
Raw materials	388·5	10·3
Banks	72·9	1·9
Financial, land, and investment	244·2	6·5
Banks and finance	317·1	8·4
Miscellaneous	8·1	0·3
Total	3,763·3	100·0

* Investments in shipping are excluded.
Source: Feis, op. cit., p. 27.

In the early phase Britain lent a great deal to governments; it is estimated that of the £1,150 million of foreign assets in 1880 nearly a half (£500 million) was in foreign government loans and guarantees, and about a fifth (£240 million) in railways in Europe, the United States and South America. British entrepreneurs like Thomas Brassey had been responsible for a large-scale direct investment in railway-building on the continent of Europe. In 1913 the aggregate of investments in publicly-issued securities amounting to £3,763·3 million was distributed geographically as follows: 47 per cent in the British Empire, 20 per cent in the United States, 20 per cent in Latin America and 6 per cent in Europe. The large part played by investment in railways is clearly brought out in Table 3.4; it amounted to no less than £1,531 million, or 40 per cent of the total. Government and municipal securities at £1,125 million accounted for 30 per cent. Of the £1,780 million invested in Empire countries, 47 per cent comprised holdings of government and municipal bonds, and 25 per cent were in railway securities. The net income from foreign investments had grown from £58 million in 1875 to £200 million in 1913.

The great era of British foreign lending had been unique. At the end of the period her capital exports were at the rate of 9 per cent of her national income. It had been largely portfolio rather than direct investment, and mainly in securities yielding a fixed return; the plantation type of investment associated with colonies did not occupy a prominent place. Most of the capital went to developing countries of new settlement, particularly the overseas descendants of Western Europe – the United States, Canada, Australia and New Zealand – which are now in the world's top income bracket. Much of their urban development and infrastructure was financed by the savings of the British private investor. The leading creditor country had a high propensity to import; and the growth of the Atlantic economy was marked by alternating phases in which Britain was putting her money back into world circulation either through a wave of lending or an upsurge of imports. Under this regime it was possible for the effects of differential productivity increases to be transmitted internationally without serious disequilibrium.

STATISTICAL FINDINGS ON INVERSE CYCLES

Some of the important statistical findings relating to the mechanism of inverse cycles, mainly over the period 1870–1913, may be briefly noted.

United States

(*a*) Population-sensitive capital formation (non-farm residential construction and durable capital expenditure by railroads) display long swings coincident with (or lagging slightly behind) those in population additions, immigration and internal migration.[1]

(*b*) Between 1817 and 1917 there were five long swings in net capital inflow and merchandise imports, with an average span of about eighteen years. Deflated imports tend to lag behind domestic activity, and the rate of capital inflow tends to be synchronous with domestic activity at troughs and to lead by about a year at peaks.[2]

(*c*) From 1870 to 1914 between 55 and 60 per cent of the net foreign investment in the United States was contributed by Britain.[3]

(*d*) The gross volume of population-sensitive capital formation was over 40 per cent of total capital formation in the 1870s, and even in the first decade of the twentieth century it was still 25 per cent of the total.[4]

(*e*) Long swings in population-sensitive capital formation were inverse to those in other capital formation (i.e. net changes in inventories, foreign claims and producer durable equipment). This inverse relation ceases and becomes a positive association from the 1920s.[5]

[1] See Kuznets, *Capital in the American Economy*, Chapter 7.
[2] Williamson, *American Growth and the Balance of Payments 1820–1913*, pp. 75 and 96.
[3] Ibid., p. 145.
[4] Kuznets, *Capital in the American Economy*, Chapter 7.
[5] Ibid.

United Kingdom[1]

(*a*) From 1870 to 1913 there were long swings in additions to population inverse to those in the United States.

(*b*) The long swings in British domestic capital formation were inverse to those of population-sensitive capital formation in the United States.

(*c*) Long swings in British capital exports and in British and European overseas migration were coincident with the long swings in population-sensitive capital formation in the United States.

(*d*) Long swings in British imports at constant prices were positively related to swings in British domestic capital formation and in American 'other capital formation', and negatively related to swings in American population-sensitive capital formation.

(*e*) Swings in British internal migration were inverse to those in the United States.

CAPITAL MOVEMENTS AND THE TERMS OF TRADE

One of the problems to be examined is whether there was a causal relationship between fluctuations in the terms of trade and those of capital movement. Cairncross, in his analysis of British experience between 1870 and 1913, concluded that '. . . it was upon the terms of trade that the distribution of investment between home and foreign, as well as the course of real wages, ultimately depended'.[2] On this reasoning, when the terms of trade moved against Britain in favour of the countries supplying her with imports, British capital was attracted to these countries; the downswing in capital exports would be brought about by a movement of the terms of trade against the overseas countries. In seeking to verify this thesis, Cairncross was troubled by the fact that the great upswing in foreign investment in the 1880s was accompanied by a movement of the terms of trade *in favour* of Britain, and he had to go to considerable pains to explain this away.[3] Since the same phenomenon is to be observed during part

[1] See Thomas, *Migration and Economic Growth*, Chapters VII and XI, and 'Long Swings in Internal Migration and Capital Formation'.
[2] Cairncross, *Home and Foreign Investment, 1870–1913*, p. 208.
[3] Ibid., pp. 192–5.

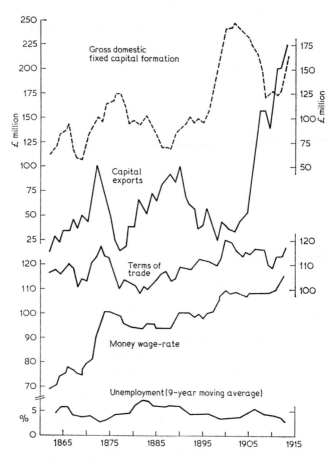

Figure 3.1 United Kingdom capital exports and the terms of trade, 1862–1913.

Sources: Gross domestic fixed capital formation in current prices – Feinstein, 'Income and Investment in the United Kingdom, 1856–1914', p. 374; capital exports – Imlah, *Economic Elements in the Pax Britannica*, pp. 72–4; net barter terms of trade (export price index divided by import price index) – ibid., pp. 96–8; money wage-rate (1890–99 = 100) – Phelps-Brown and Hopkins, 'The Course of Wage-rates in Five Countries', p. 276; unemployment: nine-year moving average of the percentages of trade unionists recorded as unemployed – Mitchell and Deane, *Abstract of British Historical Statistics*, pp. 64–5.

of the other two upswings in foreign investment, 1863–72 and 1902–13, it is necessary to examine these phases more closely. There may be an alternative explanation which better fits the facts.

There are serious objections to using the net barter terms of trade as an indicator of the distribution of gain between trading countries. What is significant is not so much the ratio between the average price of exports and the average price of imports as the quantities – factor movements, volumes of exports and imports, and rates of productivity – lying behind the ratio. A glance at fig. 3.1 shows that the three major upsurges in foreign investment between 1862 and 1913 shared one common feature; in the second half of the boom, when capital exports were at their heaviest and moving towards the peak, the terms of trade were moving sharply in favour of Britain, i.e. 1868–72, 1883–90, 1910–13. Further examination brings out other common elements shown in the data in Table 3.5.

In each upswing we note an initial phase during which the terms of trade move against Britain and there is a moderate revival in capital exports; then the terms of trade turn in favour of Britain and it is in this second phase that the rate of capital outflow is greatest. It is significant that the absorption of capital by overseas countries was at its height during years when the terms of trade were moving against them. Those who believe that the terms of trade played a decisive causal role will find it hard to explain this phenomenon. Perhaps an explanation can be found if we look behind the ratio. Given the inverse relation between home and foreign investment, the beginning of an upswing in foreign lending and exports is accompanied by a fall in the level of activity in domestic capital formation. Thus, during the first phase of a lending-export boom there is a high elasticity of supply of factors for the export sector due to the downturn in the construction sector. Unused labour and existing equipment are being re-absorbed in the export sector; this entails a rise in productivity, and money wages and export prices are kept down. As the boom gathers momentum a turning-point is reached; marginal costs rise sharply under the influence of bottlenecks at the higher level of employment in the export sector, while demand is running high in overseas construction activity; productivity has now ceased

TABLE 3.5

United Kingdom
Terms of trade, money wages, and unemployment during upswings in capital exports, 1863–1913

	(1) Net Capital exports (£ Mn.)	(2) Terms of trade (1880 = 100) Export price / Import price	(3) Money wage-rate (1890–99 = 100)	(4) Unemploy- ment %
1st Upswing				
1863–5 (annual av.)	28·1	106·3	73	3·6
1868	36·5	100·3	75	7·9
1869–72 (,, ,,)	65·0	106·9	80	4·1
1872	98·0	113·0	89	0·9
2nd Upswing				
1878–80 (annual av.)	29·3	101·0	94	7·9
1883	48·8	98·5	94	2·6
1884–90 (,, ,,)	81·8	104·1	95	6·3
1890	98·5	109·1	100	2·1
3rd Upswing				
1902–4 (annual av.)	43·3	112·8	106	4·9
1910	167·3	107·9	107	4·7
1911–13 (,, ,,)	206·1	113·7	111	2·8
1913	224·3	116·2	115	2·1

Sources: (1) Imlah, *Economic Elements in the Pax Britannica*, pp. 72–5; (2), (3) and (4), see fig. 3.1.

to rise and may be falling, hence a steep rise in export prices relatively to import prices. Although the statistics at our disposal are inadequate for the measurement of productivity, the figures in Table 3.5 are a rough guide. In the 1863–72 upswing the first phase saw the terms of trade move against Britain (from 106·3 to 100·3), money wages rose only slightly, and unemployment was heavy. Then in the second phase, 1868–72, the terms of trade moved sharply in Britain's favour (from 100·3 to 113·0), wages rose by nearly 20 per cent, and unemployment fell to 0·9 per cent. A similar pattern is seen in the 1878–90 and 1902–13 upswings in capital exports. Between 1880 and 1887 British export prices fell by 30 per cent while money wages remained constant; this is a strong suggestion of rising productivity in the export sector which did not lead to higher money wages. Then between 1887 and 1890 export prices rose by about 18 per cent and money wages went up by 8 per cent; we may infer that in those years productivity declined. On this reading of the interaction between the terms of trade and the inverse swing in home and foreign investment, one is led to regard movements in the net barter terms of trade as a consequence of the fundamental forces at work, rather than a causal factor determining the distribution of the flow of capital between home and foreign investment.

This is consistent with our argument about the inverse relation between long swings in domestic capital formation in the lending and borrowing countries. In each country, the capacity of the export sector in the upswing phase is a function of the rate of home construction in that country in the previous phase. The export performance of the underdeveloped country in a given period is based upon the amount invested by the creditor country in its construction sector in the previous period; and the ability of the industrialized country to expand its own construction in a given period is promoted by the increased flow of food and raw materials from the underdeveloped country. Given these intertemporal relationships, there was a fundamental long-run community of interest between lender and borrower; but after the turn of the century the situation had altered in important respects.

THE EDWARDIAN CLIMAX

As the financial centre of the world, London had acquired an unrivalled expertise. *The Economist* proudly declared in 1909 that '. . . we enjoy at present an undisputed right to place our money where we will, for Government makes no attempt to twist the stream into a given channel, and every borrower – native, colonial and foreign – has an equal opportunity of satisfying his needs in London.'[1] The great upswing in Britain's foreign lending in the years 1903–13, following the boom in home construction in the 1890s, was a continuation of the rhythm which had marked the country's growth over most of the nineteenth century. But this time there was a subtle difference. After the turn of the century there were ominous signs, though not yet perceived amid the pomp and glitter of the Edwardian age, that foreign investment was proving to be too much of a good thing.

Between 1907 and 1913 the outflow of British capital averaged £176 million a year compared with average gross domestic fixed capital formation of £132 million a year. This was the climax of the age described by Keynes in 1919 as the 'economic Eldorado' in which the inhabitant of London

> . . . could secure forthwith, if he wished it, cheap and comfortable means of transit to any country or climate without passport or other formality, could despatch his servant to the neighbouring office of a bank for such supply of the precious metals as might seem convenient, and could then proceed abroad to foreign quarters, without knowledge of their religion, language or customs, bearing coined wealth upon his person, and would consider himself greatly aggrieved and much surprised at the least interference. But, most important of all, he regarded this state of affairs as normal, certain, and permanent, except in the direction of further improvement, and any deviation from it as aberrant, scandalous, and avoidable.[2]

Some statesmen were dimly aware that there was a serpent in this paradise; Balfour and Joseph Chamberlain thought they recognized it in the shape of insular free trade.[3] But there was no one who asked whether Britain, by investing so much abroad, was paying too high a price in terms of domestic productivity and employment.

The period 1897–1913 saw a wave of fundamental innovations

[1] *The Economist*, Commercial History and Review of 1908, 20 February 1909.

[2] Keynes, *The Economic Consequences of the Peace*, pp. 9–10.

[3] See Balfour, *Economic Notes on Insular Free Trade*.

in electricity, chemistry and the automobile industries. Countries such as the United States, Germany and Sweden took full advantage of this technological revolution; their domestic investment and the physical productivity of their industries rose rapidly between 1900 and 1913. One cannot escape the conclusion that the technical efficiency of the British economy lagged behind in this period. It would be wrong to try to demonstrate this by analysing the preponderance of foreign issues on the London market. At the turn of the century the typical domestic entrepreneur was still a private company or a family business which had hardly any access to the new issue market. Cairncross has estimated that in 1907 the aggregate capital of manufacturing industry was about £1,000 million and net industrial investment about £50 million. If two-thirds of the latter came from profits, and only one-tenth from new issues, the remaining quarter must have come from other sources of borrowed capital.[1] The fact remains that adequate facilities for industries to avail themselves of the benefits of technical innovation were lacking. The domestic rate of interest rose from 2·76 in 1900 to 3·39 in 1913. There was a pronounced shift to profit and, unlike the 1880s, real wages were falling; and there was bitter industrial warfare. The pursuit of private investment profits overseas had become inconsistent with the long-run social productivity of the British economy in a changed environment. The technical performance of British industry and the welfare of the wage-earners would have been improved if foreign lending had been on a smaller scale, with the domestic rate of interest reduced to the level consistent with full employment of home resources.

[1] Cairncross, 'The English Capital Market before 1913', p. 145.

4 The Atlantic Economy: The Process of Interaction

A significant part of migration, whether international or internal, was a cyclical transfusion from agriculture to the burgeoning urban areas, facilitated by the rise in agricultural productivity. In the words of Schumpeter, 'the story of the way in which civilized humanity got and fought cheap bread is the story of American railroads and American machinery.'[1] The role of agriculture in the economic involvement between America and Europe must not be underestimated. Output per man-hour in the production of wheat and oats in the United States went up fourfold between the early 1840s and the early 1900s.[2] Even as late as the 1880s farming in the United States accounted for over half the labour force, and foodstuffs and crude materials comprised as much as 80 per cent of total exports, the major market being the United Kingdom. There was a high industrial input (drawing heavily on the metal industries) into agriculture and new settlement. Leontief has estimated that a dollar's worth of agricultural output requires far more iron and steel output and machinery production than does an equivalent dollar volume of output generated by textiles or miscellaneous manufacturing or even by the iron and steel industry itself.[3] A significant proportion of agricultural investment was devoted to land-clearing which

[1] Schumpeter, *Business Cycles: A Theoretical, Historical and Statistical Account of the Capitalist Process*, Vol. I, p. 319.
[2] See Parker and Klein, 'Productivity Growth in Grain Production in the United States, 1840–60 and 1900–10', in *Output, Employment and Productivity in the United States after 1800*.
[3] Leontief, 'Factor Proportions and the Structure of American Trade', Appendix III.

entailed substantial demands for breaking ploughs, axes, scythes and hoes.[1]

The evolution of American agriculture reflected closely the process of interaction between the New World and the Old. In the words of Robert E. Lipsey,

> . . . since agricultural exports played so large a role, the development of American trade during this period must be studied against the background of shifting and interacting supply and demand conditions for agricultural production in the United States and her chief market – Europe. These supply and demand changes were interrelated; long term shifts in supply conditions encouraged and yet depended on the changes in demand. . . . The Eastern seaboard of the United States played the same role vis-a-vis the West that Europe played in relation to the United States as its population shifted from rural to urban areas and from agriculture into manufacturing.[2]

> For some commodities, foreign trade . . . quickly provided an extensive market which could only have been created much more slowly by the growth of the American economy itself. In this respect American development depended on the willingness of the older industrial nations, particularly the U.K., to permit their domestic resources to be shifted out of agriculture by the influx of cheaper products from the developing areas.[3]

Any interpretation of the interaction between the British and American economies in the pre-1913 period must also account for the fact that all the overseas developing countries, e.g. United States, Canada, Argentina and Australia, had their investment upswings and downswings at the same time. Those who have attempted a one-sided explanation of the long swing in terms of variations in American aggregate demand see supporting evidence in the fact that there were *simultaneous* swings in migration from a number of European countries to the United States:[4] they never

[1] Lebergott, 'Labor Force and Employment 1800–1960', in *Output, Employment and Productivity in the United States after 1800*, pp. 126–31.
[2] Lipsey, *Price and Quantity Trends in the Foreign Trade of the United States*, p. 45.   [3] Ibid., p. 52.   [4] See Chapter 1, p. 10.

posed the question why there were *simultaneous* immigration and investment swings in a number of countries of new settlement. This latter phenomenon, which can hardly be explained by swings in United States demand, is an important part of the problem of the causation of the inverse cycles.

The answer is to be sought in two basic features of the period. First, the opening up of new sources of food and raw materials required flows of population and capital funds to be invested in infrastructure overseas, and there was necessarily a long lag between the input phase and the output phase. As Schumpeter said, this was essentially one vast process transcending national boundaries, with the whole earth as its stage. Secondly, the countries were linked together by the gold standard dominated by London, the financial centre of the world. When an infrastructure boom overseas became intense, there was a serious problem of undereffected transfer; and strong action by the Bank of England to protect its reserve had powerful repercussions on the supply of money in all overseas borrowing countries.

Space does not allow an analysis of British fluctuations in investment and trade in relation to those of European countries. That the primary causal forces were within the Atlantic economy is attested by the following comparison between Germany and Britain based on the matrix of world trade in 1887.[1] Germany was responsible for 11·7 per cent of world exports, about nine-tenths going to Europe, including the United Kingdom, and under one-tenth to the United States; she took 11·5 per cent of world exports, only 8 per cent of which came from the United States and 88 per cent from Europe, including the United Kingdom. The United Kingdom was responsible for 16·5 per cent of world exports, two-thirds going overseas and one-third to Europe; she took 25 per cent of world exports, of which 54 per cent came from overseas (22 per cent from the United States) and 46 per cent from Europe. Since one-fifth of German exports went to the United Kingdom, the German export sector was geared to home construction swings in Britain and not those in the United

[1] See O'Leary and Arthur Lewis, 'Secular Swings in Production and Trade', p. 129.

States, and this would make the German construction cycle coincide with that of America.

THE MONETARY FACTOR

In *Migration and Economic Growth* I argued that an explanation of inverse long swings would be found in 'the "real" type of theory' then being developed.[1] Monetary influences were not ignored, but they did not form an important part of the mechanism of interaction.[2] In this re-examination it is necessary to take into account recent developments in monetary economics and particularly the new empirical work on the supply of money in the period under review. Thanks to the monumental work of Milton Friedman and Anna Schwartz, our knowledge of the evolution of the money stock of the United States has been immensely enriched,[3] and there is also Phillip Cagan's illuminating book, *Determinants and Effects of Changes in the Stock of Money 1875–1960*.

There is plenty of room for improvement in British historical monetary statistics.[4] Take, for example, the sources on the rate of growth of bank deposits in Britain over the period 1878–1914. Confident conclusions were based by several writers (e.g. Pigou, Schumpeter, Tinbergen, and Rostow) on a series which give *The Economist*'s totals for *reporting* banks only, but they are very misleading, particularly in the earlier decades.[5] René P. Higonnet, who unearthed comprehensive estimates from the relevant issues of *The Economist* for the years 1877–1914, revealed the fragile

[1] Chapter XI, p. 189.
[2] See Chapter XI, pp. 181–3, and 'Migration and International Investment' in Thomas, ed., *The Economics of International Migration*, pp. 3–11, reprinted in Hall, ed., *The Export of Capital from Britain 1870–1914*, pp. 45–54.
[3] Friedman and Schwartz, *A Monetary History of the United States, 1867–1960*.
[4] Fortunately, Sheppard's authoritative work, *The Growth and Role of U.K. Financial Institutions 1880–1962*, has now appeared. It was not available in time for me to use any of his data in this book.
[5] These are the figures in Layton and Crowther, *An Introduction to the Study of Prices*, Appendix C, Table III, p. 253.

character of arguments founded on the incomplete estimates. 'Econometric research, monetary theory and business cycle theory have been seriously led astray; for it makes little sense to compare the deposits of, say, 60 per cent of the banks with those of 90 per cent of the banks at another time, without any adjustment.'[1] An influential article by J. T. Phinney, using these defective data, purported to show that between 1875 and 1913 there was '. . . a relatively constant rate of growth of bank reserves and bank currency, quite unaffected by variations in gold production or by trends in prices'.[2] The corrected estimates show that this is not true: there were clear fluctuations in the growth of bank money.[3] Rostow, relying on Phinney, reached spurious conclusions about the monetary interpretation of the fall in the price level from 1873 to 1896.[4] And so did Schumpeter.[5] In a penetrating critique of Rostow's views, D. H. Robertson concluded with the comment: 'Respectfully, I do not believe the last has been heard of the view that gold had something more than other kinds of dirt to do with the behaviour of money prices in the gold-using nineteenth century.'[6]

Friedman and Schwartz, in their summary of the course of the money supply in the United States in the years 1867–1913, recognize the existence of long swings; but they are reluctant to regard them as cyclical in character. They prefer to interpret the period 1873–1913 as '. . . a relatively stable rate of growth

---

[1] Higonnet, 'Bank Deposits in the United Kingdom 1870–1912'. The quotation is on p. 332.

[2] Phinney, 'Gold Production and the Price Level: the Cassel Three Per Cent Estimate'. The quotation is on p. 677.

[3] See Higonnet, op. cit., pp. 354–8.

[4] 'Explanations of the Great Depression', in Rostow, *British Economy of the Nineteenth Century* (London), pp. 145–60. Higonnet comments: 'Rostow's differences of opinion with Sir Robert Giffen, whom he criticizes, are not, as he believes, those of "men observing honestly the same set of data", but those of men observing honestly different sets of data and Sir Robert Giffen's set of data is far superior to Rostow's.' Higonnet, op. cit., pp. 353–4. For a refutation of Rostow's thesis regarding a relative cessation of foreign lending during 'The Great Depression', see my *Migration and Economic Growth*, p. 188.

[5] Schumpeter, *Business Cycles*, Vol. II, p. 473.

[6] Robertson, 'New Light on an Old Story', p. 297.

interrupted by two monetary episodes from which the system rebounded to approximately its initial path'.[1] However, they do add that

> . . . it is worth emphasizing here that there is an alternative interpretation which could designate 1879 or thereabouts as the trough of a long cycle, some date in the 1880s as the peak and in the mid-1890s as a second trough, and something like 1906 as the next peak. And this interpretation is based not alone on the evidence of these four decades, but also on data that suggest the existence of swings of roughly the same duration for a much longer period before and since. On this alternative interpretation, the monetary difficulties are in part the product of the underlying cyclical process. . . . We have described these interpretations as if they were mutually exclusive. Of course, they are not. One can regard the monetary events partly as shocks that trigger a cyclical reaction mechanism; partly as consequences of prior cyclical reactions . . . for the United States, the movements of capital from and to the outside world played an important role in monetary changes, and they too can be regarded as moving in long swings and as reflecting the fundamental factors giving rise to coordinated long swings in a variety of economic activities.[2]

This is a scrupulously fair statement of the fundamental issues and it serves as an excellent starting-point for this reappraisal.

OUTLINES OF AN INTERACTION MODEL

We regard the Atlantic economy of the second half of the nineteenth century as comprising, on the one hand, Great Britain, highly industrialized with growing population pressure on a small land area, and on the other, a periphery of under-populated developing countries with extensive land and natural resources. Britain practised free trade, London was the financial centre of the system and the gold standard was virtually a sterling standard.

[1] Friedman and Schwartz, op. cit., p. 187.
[2] Ibid., pp. 187–8.

The following hypotheses may be put forward about the inter-action between the creditor country (C) and the factor-importing 'country' (D) (representing the whole periphery).[1]

(*a*) Each is divided into two sectors, home construction and export.

(*b*) C exports capital goods and D food and raw materials.

(*c*) Migration depends on the difference in real wages which can be approximated by the difference in real incomes.

(*d*) Export capacity is generated through population-sensitive capital formation, i.e. the building of infrastructure – railways, roads, land-clearing, ports, houses, public utilities, etc. – and this investment has a relatively long gestation period. There is an intertemporal relation between a country's infrastructure invest-ment in one period and its export capacity in the next period.

(*e*) The level of activity of a country's export sector depends on the expected marginal efficiency of investment in the construc-tion sector of the other country. The marginal efficiency of investment is the marginal physical product of capital multiplied by the ratio of the price of output to the price of capital input. Applied to exported output, this means that the marginal efficiency of investment depends on the expected future purchas-ing power per unit of factor input, i.e., the 'single factoral terms of trade'.

(*f*) A major fraction of total capital formation is population-sensitive, i.e. varying with the rate of change in population growth and internal migration.

(*g*) The population growth rate is a function of population structure (i.e., a vector showing proportions of population in various age and sex groups) and the external migration balance.

(*h*) The countries are linked by a gold standard with specie currency.

These assumptions imply a complicated see-saw movement in which both 'real' and monetary factors are at work. The popula-tion cycle, with migration as a crucial element, determines the time-shape of capital formation in C and D respectively. The

[1] A formal presentation of the model is given in Appendix C at the end of this chapter.

demographic variables, through their impact on the course of investment which in turn is conditioned by the gestation lag, create a state of high sensitivity in which monetary shocks can effectively change the direction of things. A monetary cobweb[1] is superimposed on the real instability inherent in the interplay of the real magnitudes.

The task is to take the basic relationships and build an econometric model. An important constraint on the form of the functions is the long infrastructure gestation period. Another crucial factor is that population structure in each country has a cyclical element in it and that at any moment it is a function of an earlier population structure and of intervening migration. The ability of the model to generate long swings would seem to depend very much on population structure and the infrastructure lag. What is required is an experimental simulation of a complete model, to try out various types of functions with different numerical values of the parameters and different lags to discover what effects these different functions have on the simulated values of the endogenous variables.[2]

TESTING THE ASSUMPTIONS

We shall now consider the evidence for the basic assumptions of the model.

(A) *Export capacity is generated through population-sensitive capital formation; there is an intertemporal relation between a country's infrastructure investment in one phase of the long swing and its export capacity in the next.*

For the United States this is amply confirmed in fig. 4.1 (the short cycle being eliminated by plotting average reference-cycle standings, peak to peak and trough to trough). The upswing in immigration and construction in the late 1860s is followed in the 1870s by an upswing in exports and a downswing

---

[1] For an explanation of this term see p. 98 below.
[2] For a mathematical model of inverse long cycles indicating population as a key variable in their determination see Parry Lewis, 'Growth and Inverse Cycles: a Two-country Model', pp. 109–18.

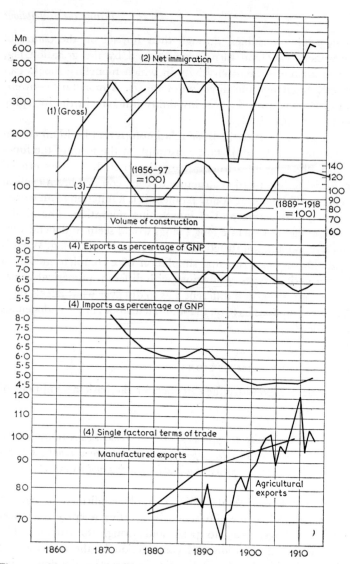

Figure 4.1 United States: long swings in immigration, construction and foreign trade, 1858–1913 (average reference-cycle standings).
Sources: (1) Ferenczi and Willcox, *International Migrations*, Vol. I, p. 377; (2) Kuznets and Rubin, *Immigration and the Foreign Born*, p. 95; (3) Abramovitz, *Evidences of Long Swings in Aggregate Construction since the Civil War*, pp. 166–7; (4) Lipsey, *Price and Quantity Trends in the Foreign Trade of the United States*, pp. 430–1 (annual data plotted).

in imports (each as a proportion of gross national product). A similar process is repeated in the 1880s and 1890s. Finally, in the 1900s the steep rise in immigration and construction is accompanied by a sharp fall in exports and a mild rise in imports as a proportion of GNP. It is interesting to note that imports, unlike exports, show a secular fall between 1870 and 1913 from 8 per cent to 5 per cent of GNP, but the long swing is clearly marked. Fig. 4.1 also gives an estimate of the single factoral terms of trade for agricultural and manufactured exports for the period 1880–1913. The purchasing power of agricultural factors of production increased only slightly in the 1880s, dipped in the early 1890s, and then rose very rapidly in the second half the 1890s and early 1900s, when America's export sector was booming.

Another test may be made by using Kuznets' figures of changes in population-sensitive capital formation and net changes in claims on foreign countries over the long swing. The last two columns of Table 4.1 clearly demonstrate the see-saw movement between the construction and export sectors. An upswing in infrastructure in one phase of the long swing was followed by an upswing in the export sector in the next.

Statistics for other countries of the periphery tell the same story. In the years 1881–90, when the net inflow of capital to Australia was £174 million, the value of merchandise exports was £230 million, or two-thirds of the value of merchandise imports. In the downswing of the investment cycle, 1891–1900, net capital inflow was reduced to £48 million, while exports rose to £322 million, practically equal to imports (£326 million). The evidence for Argentina can be seen in A. G. Ford's authoritative work,[1] and for Canada on pp. 88–91 below.

(B) *A major fraction of total capital formation is population-sensitive, i.e., varying with the rate of change of population growth and internal migration.*

Kuznets has pointed out how difficult it is to get a comprehensive estimate of population-sensitive capital formation. Non-farm residential construction and capital expenditure by railroads in the United States comprised about 40 per cent of total capital

[1] Ford, *The Gold Standard 1880–1914: Britain and Argentina*, Statistical Appendix, p. 195.

TABLE 4.1

United States: Population-sensitive capital formation and net changes in foreign claims, 1874–1917

Changes per year during successive phases of long swings

Phase of long swing	Period	Additions to population	Non-farm gross residential construction	Gross capital expenditure by railways	Total population-sensitive capital formation	Net changes in claims against foreign countries
		Million	Billions of dollars in 1929 prices			
Trough to Peak	1874–90	+0·23	+0·90	+0·14	+1·01	−0·05
Peak to Trough	1890–99	−0·06	−0·32	−0·29	−0·62	+0·64
Trough to Peak	1899–1909	+0·34	+0·62	+0·67	+1·29	−0·33
Peak to Trough	1909–17	−0·34	−0·80	−0·46	−1·30	+2·67

Source: Kuznets, Capital in the American Economy, pp. 330 and 339.

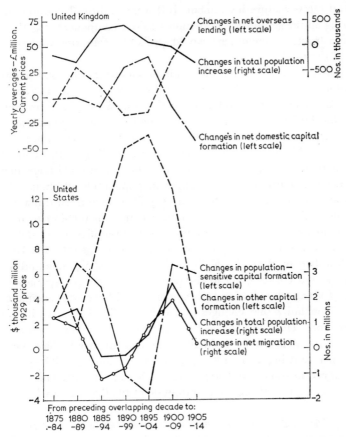

Figure 4.2 United Kingdom and United States: population change and capital formation.
Source: Brinley Thomas, in Adler (ed.), *Capital Movements and Economic Development*, pp. 21 and 31–2.

formation in the 1870s, but these are not the only items which should be included. For example, the construction of stores, local transport facilities and service establishments are population-sensitive, but these are lumped in Kuznets' 'other' private construction and producer durables.[1] What we need is a measure of

[1] Kuznets, *Capital in the American Economy*, p. 340.

total infrastructure investment. If it were statistically possible to bring all the genuinely population-sensitive components together, infrastructure investment would probably comprise well over half the total.

Fig. 4.2 shows the parallelism between changes in total population increase and changes in net domestic capital formation in the United Kingdom and in population-sensitive capital formation in the United States. The inverse relation between population-sensitive and 'other' capital formation in the United States and between home investment and overseas lending in the United Kingdom is clearly shown. In both countries internal migration moved in harmony with changes in population additions.[1] In other countries of new settlement, e.g. Canada and Australia, the magnitude of investment in infrastructure in relation to total capital formation was considerable.[2] The significance of demographic variables in the economic growth of Australia has been quantified by Allen C. Kelley.[3] He calculated the demand for residential construction in the period 1861–1911 on the basis of the 1881 age distribution and compared it with the actual demand, and concluded that changes in age distribution had a significant influence. He found that if the age structure had remained constant the demand for residential construction would have been 80 per cent higher in 1865–70, 26 per cent lower in 1880–5, unchanged in 1890–5 and 20 per cent higher in 1900–05. This factor largely explained the wide amplitude of the fluctuations.[4]

(C) *The population growth rate is a function of population structure (i.e., a vector showing proportions of population in various age, sex and marital status groups) and external migration.*

Evidence for Great Britain and the United States is found in

[1] See Thomas, 'Long Swings in Internal Migration and Capital Formation', pp. 398–412.
[2] For Canada see Urquhart and Buckley (eds.), *Historical Statistics of Canada*, pp. 511–15. For Australia see Butlin, *Investment in Australian Economic Development 1861–1900*, pp. 47–8.
[3] Kelley, 'Demographic Change and Economic Growth: Australia, 1861–1911'. See also Hall, 'Some Long-period Effects of the Kinked Age Distribution of the Population of Australia, 1861–1961'.
[4] Kelley, op. cit., p. 245.

Chapter 2, which concentrates on the growth rate in the house-hold forming age group, 20–44.[1] In discussing Irish emigration I have already shown how a kinked age distribution and the heavy incidence of emigration among young adults can lead to a self-generating cycle.[2] Kuznets and Easterlin, in their studies of American experience, have explored the demographic factors behind the long swing in fertility. Easterlin found that

. . . while the fertility of the total white population declined substantially from the latter part of the nineteenth century to the mid-1930s, there was significant variation in the rate of change over time and among component population groups. Even after averaging data so as to eliminate or substantially reduce variability due to the business cycle, marked fluctuations – Kuznets cycles of fifteen or more years duration – stand out in the patterns for the total, native, and foreign-born white populations.[3]

The analysis is necessarily complicated, comprising the effects of immigration, mortality and fertility rates, labour force participation, the headship rate, and echo effects. Easterlin concluded that

. . . the fertility trend for the *total* white population has been subject to substantial variation as a result of major fluctuations in the fertility of the foreign-born and rural white components. The fluctuations for these groups in turn appear to have been caused by the impact of the rise and fall of immigration on the age, sex, and nationality composition of the foreign-born, and of major swings in agricultural conditions on the economic condition of the farm population.[4]

Clear evidence can be seen in the history of Australia where population cycles originated in the heavy immigration of the 1850s; subsequent immigration waves tended to reinforce and accentuate these cycles. This has been demonstrated by Allen

[1] On Great Britain see also Parry Lewis, *Building Cycles and Britain's Growth*, Chapters 3, 7 and 10.
[2] See *Migration and Economic Growth*, p. 81.
[3] Easterlin, *Population, Labor Force and Long Swings in Economic Growth*, pp. 89, 90.   [4] Ibid., p. 99.

C. Kelley by taking the size and age- and sex-composition of the population of Australia at 1861 and then calculating what would have been the shape of population growth if Australia had had no net migration thereafter. Special attention was given to the cohorts 20–4, 25–9 and 30–4. 'In *both* the total (including migration) and the net-of-migration cases the rate of age-specific demographic change occurring within selected cohorts of the Australian population exceeded by three to nine times the rate of change of the respective aggregate population for all ages.'[1] Moreover:

> ... the timing pattern in the three cohorts results in a remark- ably consistent tendency for net-of-migration cycles to precede the population change including the impact of migration. ... The conclusion thus emerges that with respect to the three most important cohorts of total population change (as measured by their role in key economic activities – labor force entrance, residential demand, and saving), the wave-like movements may be *initiated* by influences deriving from the demographic shock, and subsequent migration follows and lengthens each move- ment.[2]

Kelley's work provides a detailed Australian counterpart to the analysis in Chapter 2 of the demographic determinants of the long swing in construction in Britain.

LONG SWINGS IN CANADA AND AUSTRALIA

We shall now summarize the long swings pattern for Canada and Australia.

Canada

The relevant time series for Canada in the period 1870–1913 are given in fig. 4.3.[3] Canadian long swings have the same time-shape

---

[1] Kelley, op. cit., p. 250. [2] Ibid., p. 253.
[3] Our understanding of Canadian long swings owes much to the pioneer- ing researches of Buckley ('Urban Building and Real Estate Fluctuations in Canada'; *Capital Formation in Canada 1896–1930*; and *Population, Labour Force and Economic Growth, 1867–1962*) and the work of Daly ('Long Cycles and Recent Canadian Experience').

as those of the United States, but their amplitude is greater. There is a close correspondence between net capital imports and gross immigration, and the latter leads urban building and transport investment, as in the United States.

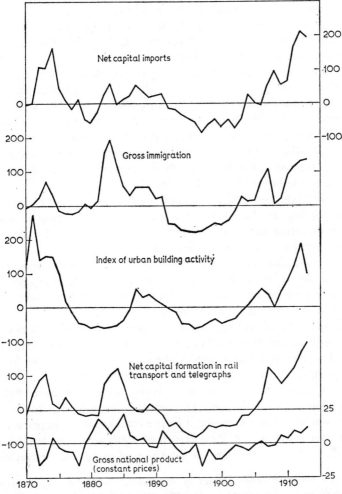

Figure 4.3 Long swings in Canada, 1870–1913 (% deviations from trend). *Source:* Bloomfield, *Patterns of Fluctuation in International Investment before 1914*, p. 25.

Canada had a close economic involvement with Great Britain, and in view of its small size the interplay of forces had a powerful effect. The hypotheses of our model of the Atlantic economy are well borne out. From a peak in the early 1870s there was a decline to a trough at the end of the decade. The long swing pattern for the rest of the period was briefly as follows.

The 1880s. The years 1878–89 saw an upswing in immigration with a prominent peak in 1883 and a mild one in 1889; capital inflow was similarly well above trend. In the early part of this decade there was a boom in railway construction and later on in urban building. Meanwhile, the value of exports to Britain fell from $42·6 million in 1881 to 33·5 million in 1889, whereas imports from Britain rose sharply in the early years (from 30·9 million to 51·7 million) and then settled down at about 40 million. In 1881–8 the terms of trade moved in favour of Canada, and real exports *per capita* fell. In Britain during those years home construction was falling and capital exports rising.

The 1890s. From 1889 to the end of the 1890s there was a severe downswing in Canadian immigration, capital imports, and infrastructure investment, whereas Britain experienced a strong construction boom and declining foreign lending. Between 1889 and 1901 Canada's imports from Britain remained stationary, while her exports to Britain increased threefold. The sharp rise in real exports *per capita* was accompanied by a shift in the terms of trade against Canada in the years 1895–1901.

1900–1913. What happened in this period is a classic case of the growth process during a Kuznets cycle upswing in a new country. It has been well documented.[1] The net capital balance rose from $30 million in 1900 to $542 million in 1913, immigrant arrivals from 42,000 to 401,000, total home investment from $123 million to $628 million. The sectoral price levels, 1900–12, moved as follows: domestic +62 per cent, export +39 per cent, import +13 per cent. Real exports *per capita* after 1903 tended to fall. In the decade 1902–12 the value of exports to Britain in-

---

[1] See Viner, *Canada's Balance of International Indebtedness, 1900–1913*; Cairncross, 'Investment in Canada, 1900–13', in *Home and Foreign Investment 1870–1913*, pp. 37–64. For a critique of Viner's analysis see Stovel, *Canada in the World Economy*, pp. 127–213.

creased by 35 per cent, while the value of imports from Britain increased by 139 per cent; the terms of trade moved in favour of Canada from 111 to 122.

The evidence amply confirms the inverse relation between long swings in Britain and in the periphery as well as the intertemporal relation between infrastructure investment in one period and export capacity in the next. Up to the turn of the century exports had very little causal role,[1] but in the last great upswing the shift in the demand curve for Canadian wheat was an important factor. The course of events in Canada in the 1900s reflected a change of direction in the flow of men and money into the periphery, partly induced by the stage of development which the United States had reached by the turn of the century.

Australia

The inverse relation between fluctuations in home investment in Britain and railway investment in Australia from the 1870s to 1913 was demonstrated in *Migration and Economic Growth*.[2] It is true that the span of the upward and downward phases tended to be longer in Australia than in other countries. This can be explained on demographic grounds: it does not mean that the interaction mechanism was essentially different from what it was in the rest of the periphery.

Clear evidence of the alternation between swings in infrastructure investment and in export capacity has already been cited. By ignoring this basic intertemporal relationship, Arthur I. Bloomfield has erroneously argued that the Australian economy for most of the period 1861–1913 '. . . appears to have followed a relatively independent orbit'.[3] He is here echoing Noel Butlin's thesis on which we have already expressed doubt (pp. 6–7). The nature of Bloomfield's argument can be seen in the following quotation. 'Indeed, real exports, when adjusted for trend, appear to have undergone a long-swing contraction from the early 1870s to the mid-1880s, when the other Australian series were in

[1] See Buckley, *Capital Formation in Canada 1896–1930*, pp. 48–50.
[2] p. 115.
[3] Bloomfield, *Patterns of Fluctuation in International Investment before 1914*, p. 29.

the expansion phase; and the peak in real exports in the mid-1890s came well after the other series had begun to turn down.'[1] This is exactly what one would expect to happen in a country of new settlement. These facts are evidence of the inverse relation

TABLE 4.2

Australia: Peaks and troughs of effects of age-composition on average household savings, labour-force additions, and residential demand, 1861–1911

	Peak	Trough	Peak	Trough	Peak	Trough
Average savings		1862*	1872	1888	1906	1910*
Work-force additions		1862*	1876	1892	1905	1910*
Residential demand	1862*	1870	1883	1900	1910*	

* Determined as the initial or terminal date in the series.
Source: A. C. Kelley, 'Demographic Change and Economic Growth: Australia 1861–1911', p. 264.

between infrastructure investment and the export sector: far from showing that Australia was in an independent orbit, they confirm that she was in the same orbit as other countries of the periphery. She was involved in the same process of interaction with the British economy.[2]

Further proof is found in the demographic determinants of the Australian long swing, with changes in external migration and population structure as the primary variables. Kelley has broadened the analysis by bringing in the effects on additions to the labour force and household savings. His chronology of peaks and troughs, indicating changes due *solely* to variations in the age structure of the population, is given in Table 4.2.

[1] Ibid., footnote 61.
[2] See Hall's article, 'Capital Imports and the Composition of Investment in a Borrowing Country', in Hall, ed., *The Export of Capital from Britain 1870–1914*, pp. 143–52, in which he concludes that '. . . the only fruitful way to view the process of British capital inflow to Australia is to regard it as one of interaction between conditions in Australia and in Britain' (p. 152).

Like H. J. Habakkuk on English building cycles, Noel Butlin attempted to show that Australia did not experience the usual kind of building cycle.[1] He thinks Australia had a long fifty-year cycle punctuated by short-period disturbances. Kelley's conclusions, based on a rigorous demographic analysis, are as follows.

> On the basis of these tests we would propose that each argument in the Butlin thesis is subject to modification. (1) Speculative excesses, as measured by either positive deviations of residential capacity from trends in long-run demand or by the provision of housing ahead of demand, are not generally prominent in Australia in the 1880s; (2) the impact of change in the age-structure of the population has been under-estimated; and (3) the relative importance of age-compositional effects, vis-a-vis rapid urbanization, points to the former as the more powerful explanatory variable.[2]

The weight of quantitative evidence on the United Kingdom, the United States, Canada and Australia justifies the proposition that, with population structure and international migration as crucial variables, the demographic cycle (and its concomitant, infrastructure investment) in the United Kingdom was inverse to the corresponding cycles in the periphery.

THE INTERACTION PROCESS: REAL AND MONETARY FACTORS

We shall now explore the nature of the interaction between the creditor country (C) and the factor-importing 'country' (D) representing the whole periphery, paying particular attention to the interplay of real and monetary factors.

The upswing in emigration and lending

Let us assume a large flow of young migrants from C to D, with consequent opposite impacts on the countries' population structure and internal migration. This increases population-sensitive

[1] Butlin, *Investment in Australian Economic Development*, pp. 224–7, 231.
[2] Kelley, op. cit., p. 246.

capital formation in the receiving country and reduces it in the sending country. There will be an accompanying flow of lending from C to D attracted by the higher marginal efficiency of investment in D's construction sector. We distinguish between *ex ante* lending, i.e. the purchase of D securities by C residents, and *ex post* capital exports, i.e. the balance on current account minus gold imports. This *ex ante* lending can be considered in terms of periodic stock adjustments by C investors. The optimal portfolio of diversified home securities held by the 'representative' investor in country C is necessarily subject to the risk of a change in the general level of activity. When he sees the prospect of a construction slump at home coinciding with a boom abroad, he can reduce this risk by substituting foreign securities for some of his domestic securities. In the words of C. H. Lee,

> . . . given the expected rate of return, variances and co-variances of return of individual securities, there is a unique optimal composition of the securities in a portfolio, and this portfolio can be considered a composite good. Likewise, an optimal portfolio is derived for foreign securities only and this portfolio forms a second composite good. In the second stage, then, the investor makes a choice concerning the allocation of his total wealth between the two composite goods.[1]

When the actual amount of D securities held by the C residents is less than the optimum portfolio of D securities, an outflow of capital takes place, and this can occur even if the rate differential is unchanged.

The increased purchase of D securities (*ex ante* foreign lending) is followed by a rise in the demand for C exports, and the export sector in country C gets a boom at the expense of infrastructure investment. During this upswing the induced investment in C will be in export-sensitive producer durables, e.g. shipbuilding; but this is more than counterbalanced by the decline in population-sensitive construction.

---

[1] Lee, 'A Stock-Adjustment Analysis of Capital Movements: the United States–Canadian Case', pp. 514–15.

Thus, in this first phase there is an infrastructure boom in D and an export sector boom in C. In country D there is an internal shift of labour and resources from the export sector to construction, and vice versa in C. The effect of the upswing on D's price structure is seen mainly in a rise in the price level of domestic goods; next come export prices, and the price level of imports rises least. An important determinant of the latter is the fact that country C, in the early stage of the upswing, can draw factors easily into its export sector owing to declining activity in the construction sector. A rise in measured productivity enables its expansion to proceed for some time without a rise in costs. During this phase the net barter terms of trade (the ratio of export prices to import prices) move against C and in favour of D.

With regard to the course of the upswing in D, it is relevant to note that in an infrastructure boom we have not only *income-induced* accelerator investment but also *investment-induced* investment. The latter is of a complementary nature and is in a fixed relation to the primary investment.[1] This introduces an additional lag into the process and helps to account for the length of the construction upswing.[2]

There are three main determinants of the duration of the upswing in D: first, the course of the demand for additional infrastructure induced by the change in the population structure and the life-cycle spending decisions taken by the household-

[1] For example, for a given increase in residential building, additional investment is required in public utility services, schools, hospitals, etc. For orders of magnitude see Mattila and Thompson, 'Residential-Service Construction: a Study of Induced Investment'. Writing of the United States in the period 1946–54, these authors point out that '. . . housing, which unassisted accounts for only 37 per cent of all new construction activity, when bundled up with what we intend to show to be complementary construction, has constituted almost 64 per cent of all new construction activity in the postwar period'. Ibid., p. 467.

[2] Following Hicks, we could regard the upswing of population-sensitive capital formation as a hump in autonomous investment. In the early phase of the boom in country D the hump in autonomous investment, via the 'super-multiplier', raises the equilibrium line, but not above the ceiling. See Hicks, *A Contribution to the Theory of the Trade Cycle*, pp. 120–3.

forming age groups; secondly, the interaction between the multiplier and the accelerator (with lags); and thirdly, the transfer problem.[1] The financing of the lending by country C has multiplier effects on the balance of trade. When these are allowed for, the question is whether the financing and use of the transferred funds changes the demands for goods so that the improvement in C's balance of trade equals the amount lent.[2] We must note that

---

[1] The essence of the transfer problem can be explained in a simple example. When the British invest £1 million in America by buying shares in American railway companies, there is a transfer of money (or purchasing power) from Britain to America. Purchasing power is reduced at home and increased in America. If the recipients of the money in America use it all to buy British steel rails, then the gap in expenditure at home is exactly filled by the orders from America for increased British exports, and income and prices are not affected. The transfer has been fully effected in real terms. Another way in which it could be done would be for £1 million worth of new British exports to go to America to replace goods which used to be produced there, thus releasing the labour and capital which formerly produced those goods to enable them to work on American engines for the railways. In this way the £1 million paid by the British to acquire the U.S. railway shares is transformed into real railway capital in America. When the transfer is 'under-effected', it means that the amount of the purchasing power coming back as orders for increased British exports is less than the amount of money subscribed by the British investors in buying the American shares, and this gap has to be filled by Britain sending out gold.

[2] Harry G. Johnson's elegant formulation can be summarized as follows:

Let m' and s' be the changes in demand for imports and saving respectively caused by the financing and use of the transfer, expressed as proportions of the amount lent. Let M be the marginal propensity to import and S the marginal propensity to save. Then, the transfer will be under-effected if $m'_e + m'_d$ (the sum of the proportions of the amount lent by which expenditure on imports is changed by the financing and

use of the loan) is less than $1 + \dfrac{M_e}{S_e} s'_e + \dfrac{M_d}{S_d} s'_d$ i.e. $1 +$ the sum of the

proportions of the transfer by which saving is changed (with expenditure unchanged) by the financing and use of the loan, each weighted by the ratio of the marginal propensity to import to the marginal propensity to save in the country concerned. See Johnson, 'The Transfer Problem and Exchange Stability', in *International Trade and Economic Growth*, p. 179.

the flow of interest payments involves wealth effects which should not be left out, as they usually are in the literature on the transfer problem. As we shall see, the flow of interest and dividends on foreign investment from the periphery to Britain was a very large item.

Johnson has shown how the analysis can accommodate the proportions in which changes in saving are divided between holdings of domestic and foreign assets. '. . . if the transfer is treated as an income change, it will be under-effected or over-effected, according as the sum of what may be described as "the marginal foreign investment ratios" is less or greater than unity; in other words, the transfer will be under-effected if there is a bias (at the margin) in each country towards investment in domestic assets – such as would result from additional ignorance and uncertainty about foreign conditions, or from exchange control, but not from difference in yields as such – and vice versa'.[1]

In the early part of the upswing in D there is not likely to be trouble. To simplify, let us ignore saving and postulate that the lending is entirely at the expense of home investment in C and that the borrowings are entirely spent by D; then the transfer will be effected without price or income adjustment if the marginal propensities to import add up to unity. A moderate degree of under-effected transfer will entail adjustments which will slow down the boom in D, but the infrastructure investment projects already launched are unlikely to be much curtailed.

In the later stage of the boom the situation changes. As the export upswing gathers momentum in C, a turning-point is reached. Investment induced by the growth of exports increases rapidly and at the higher level of employment marginal costs rise, while demand is running high in construction activity in D. Productivity in C's export sector has ceased to go up and may be falling, and export prices rise relatively to import prices. Meanwhile, C investors are receiving an increasing flow of interest and dividends on their foreign securities. This wealth effect is likely to promote further *ex ante* lending which now reaches a very high level. The population variable, emigration, is also at a high level but its rate of growth is already declining for demographic reasons, and after

[1] Ibid., p. 183.

97

a short lag this entails an upturn in construction from the low point reached in C.

At this stage transfer becomes seriously under-effected; the growth of the current trade balance cannot keep up with the *ex ante* lending. The monetary authority in C is faced with an external drain of gold to D and an internal drain due to a combination of export-induced investment and a revival in construction. This means severe monetary instability. The Central Bank must take drastic action to replenish its reserves and raises the interest rate to a punitive level. This attracts a large flow of short-term balances and gold from D, and there is a fall in purchases of D securities. The representative investor in C, impressed by the increasing risk attached to D securities and attracted by the marginal efficiency of investment in home construction, will now optimize by increasing his stock of domestic securities at the expense of his foreign portfolio.

The monetary cobweb[1] thus set in motion breaks the infrastructure boom in D. The large loss of gold reduces D's money supply or sharply reduces its rate of growth and this precipitates a downturn.

The downswing in emigration and lending

We now have the reverse process – a decline in emigration and lending, an expansion in C's construction sector and D's export sector. Given absolute confidence in the ability of the creditor country to maintain convertibility, the action taken by C, with its curb on foreign lending, quickly restores C's balance of payments

---

[1] The 'cobweb' theorem was developed to explain self-reinforcing fluctuations where it takes a certain period of time for supply to be adjusted in response to a movement in price. Strictly speaking, the theorem requires three conditions to be satisfied: (*a*) output is determined by suppliers' response to price in a competitive market in which producers plan on the basis that present prices will hold for the future; (*b*) once plans are fixed, it needs a full period to elapse before output can be changed; (*c*) price is determined by the available supply. For an excellent account of the theorem see Ezekiel, 'The Cobweb Theorem', *Readings in Business Cycle Theory*. For its application in the present context see Hicks, op. cit., Chapters XI and XII.

equilibrium through a deflation of effective demand. The incidence of the adjustment, however, is felt mainly in the periphery which gets the full force of the monetary contraction and the reversed accelerator-multiplier process. Prices fall in D much more sharply than in C. The vigorous upswing in construction accompanied by a downswing in the export sector in the borrowing country had made its economy much more vulnerable to monetary contraction than the economy of the creditor country, which had been through a phase of declining construction combined with expanding exports. The degree of credit restriction applied to restore monetary equilibrium in C necessarily overshoots the mark and inflicts on D a steep fall in investment and income.

Under the gold standard D's money supply is a variable dependent on outside forces. The causal sequence runs from the balance of payments and the gold flow to the money stock and then to the level of prices which is consistent with the fixed exchange rate. If the debtor country is to remain on the gold standard, the correction of under-effected transfer by the creditor necessarily entails a reduction in the debtor's money supply and a fall in its price level relatively to the creditor's.

Infrastructure investment in D responding to the population variable declines rapidly, and there is a rise in the output of the export sector geared to the expanding activity in C's construction sector. The productivity of D's export sector is directly related to the expansion which took place in infrastructure in the previous period; a substantial supply of primary produce is exported at falling prices. D's net barter terms of trade are declining; but the significant fact is that its 'single factoral terms of trade' (the net barter terms corrected for the rise in physical productivity in the production of exports) are rising. This is similar to what occurred in C during the early stage of the boom in its export sector in the previous period. Each country, debtor as well as creditor, in its infrastructure boom period, lays the foundations for the performance of its export sector in the following period; and during export upswings there is a shift away from home construction to investment in producer durables, the demand for which is a function of the level of activity in the export sector.

In C substantial internal migration takes the place of

99

emigration; and population-sensitive capital formation sets the pace for the economy. *Ex ante* foreign lending falls and the price of domestic stocks rises. With the supply schedules of labour and loanable funds facing the construction sector moving to the right, the multiplier-accelerator process draws in a growing volume of imports of primary produce. Since the export sector is in decline, the balance on current account shrinks.

It is possible for a monetary crisis to occur before the lags in the real process in C dictate a downturn. The rapidly rising current account balance of country D causes a continuing gold outflow from C and an acceleration of the rate of growth of the money supply in D. This means that sooner or later the price of D's exports will begin to rise. This will increase the strain in C where infrastructure investment has reached a high level and unemployment is at a minimum. The monetary authority in C is now facing a double strain – a continued outflow of gold together with a rapidly increasing interior demand. The representative investor in C, worried by the increasing risk attached to his domestic portfolio and attracted by the expected profitability of investment in construction abroad, will optimize by switching into D securities. This rise in *ex ante* lending adds to the instability. The reserves of the system reach the danger level, and the Central Bank raises its interest rate enough to replenish its reserves. Gold will then flow in from D with a consequent deceleration of the growth of the money supply in that country, and the stringent credit restriction will precipitate a downturn in C's construction sector. This downturn brings D's export boom to an end. The stage is now set for a new upswing in infrastructure investment and a downswing in exports in D and an emigration-lending upsurge with falling infrastructure investment in C.

In this model, country D stands for the periphery of countries of new settlement in the second half the nineteenth century. The critical turning points in the long swing are attributable to monetary instability occurring in the lending country, the financial centre of the system. The see-saw movement arises fundamentally out of the inverse demographic cycles and the alternation of infrastructure and export upsurges, but the whole thing is played according to the rules of the gold standard game, with the monetary authority in the creditor country as referee. This mechanism of interaction offers an explanation of the fact that the overseas countries of new settlement in the pre-1913 period experienced *simultaneous* long swings in capital formation which were inverse to those of the United Kingdom.

HISTORICAL EVIDENCE

The main phases of the inverse long swing, 1862–1913, will now be examined in the light of historical evidence.

1862–79

It is necessary to look separately at the period 1862–79, before the United States returned to the gold standard. After the Civil War the upsurge of investment in the United States gathered strength, reached a peak in 1871-2, from which there was a sharp descent to a very low level at the end of the 1870s. A major factor in this period was the political objective to resume specie payments at the pre-Civil War parity; this entailed a considerable fall in American prices. The average price level in 1865 was over twice what it had been in 1861; the index (1910–14 = 100) fell from 185 in 1865 to 86 in December 1878.[1]

Friedman and Schwartz, in their account of this period, point out that

> . . . for some five or six years after the Civil War, the dollar price of sterling was less than might have been expected from commodity price movements alone. The explanation is a sizable capital inflow from abroad for investment – up to 1870, particularly in U.S. government securities, and after that, in railway bonds. When the capital inflow declined sharply, as it did in 1873–79, the dollar price of sterling first rose by comparison to the ratio of U.S. to British prices, then moved in accord with that ratio.[2]

These authors suggest that, in the decade after the Civil War, America's competitive power in exports increased more than its

[1] See Friedman and Schwartz, op. cit., pp. 80–1.
[2] Ibid., p. 86.

demand for imports and this favourable shift in comparative advantage raised the value of the dollar in terms of foreign currencies at which trade would balance.[1] This needs to be carefully interpreted.

Fig. 4.1. above shows that it was in the downward phase of the long swing in the 1870s that exports rose and imports fell; this was a sequel to the increase in capacity built up in the upward phase culminating in 1871. The rest of the picture can be seen in the series given in fig. 4.7 below. There was a very steep fall in net capital inflow and in the ratio of American to British prices (partly the result of resumption policy); this was accompanied by a marked expansion in the export sector – exports as a proportion of GNP rising from 6 per cent to 9 per cent and as a proportion of imports from 80 per cent to 140 per cent. This boom in exports was mainly geared to the upswing in home investment in the United Kingdom[2] (see fig. 4.4 below), the upturn of which had led the downturn in capital inflow to the United States. Friedman and Schwartz point to the apparent contradiction between the National Bureau's evidence of a protracted and severe slump from 1873 to 1879 (the longest in the U.S. record) and the fact that physical volume series indicate that output was rising in the last part of the contraction. They see the obvious explanation in '. . . the behaviour of prices, which unquestionably fell sharply from 1877 to early 1879, and the continuing state of monetary uncertainty up to the successful achievement of resumption. . . . Observers of the business scene then, no less than their modern descendants, took it for granted that sharply declining prices were incompatible with sharply rising output.'[3] There is no contradiction when it is realized that an upswing in the export sector coexisted with a downswing in immigration, capital inflow and infrastructure investment, the long swing peak of the former and the trough of the latter occurring in 1877–8.

We shall now glance at the behaviour of the monetary variables. In fig. 4.7 we plot the annual rate of change in the United States money stock (5-year moving average), the net external gold flow

[1] Ibid., p. 78.
[2] In the period 1861–78 over one half of America's exports went to Britain. See ibid., p. 64.　　　　　　[3] Ibid., pp. 87–8.

(5-year moving average), and the Bank of England reserve as a percentage of liabilities. In the first half of the 1870s there was a considerable net outflow of gold from America and the curve of the rate of change in money stock was falling, with an absolute decline in 1876; the Bank of England reserve moved inversely and peaked in 1876. Then the U.S. money stock rose sharply as the Government sold bonds to build up a reserve before resuming specie payments in 1879, and the export boom created a very favourable trade balance. At the same time other countries were absorbing gold. The net imports into France in the five years 1874–9 were £83 million, of which £14,500,000, came from Britain; and Germany absorbed £20 million. The result of all this was a steep fall in the Bank of England reserve. The Bank rate was raised to 5 per cent and 6 per cent in 1878 and this reversed the flow. The downswing in the construction cycle in Britain was already gathering momentum before the upturn in the export sector had really begun: indeed the shipbuilding cycle reached a low trough in 1879. In the words of Hawtrey, 'It was the stringency and crisis of 1878 that at last brought British industry to a sufficient state of prostration to free the Bank of England from anxiety in regard to its reserve. The Bank cheerfully watched its reserve fall from £21,372,000 in July 1879 to £12,578,000 in January 1881 before raising the rate to 3½ per cent.'[1]

An interesting feature of this early period is the severe amplitude of the investment downswing in the United States in the 1870s, only partially offset by the export boom pivoted on the construction boom in Britain. Prices fell partly in response to the productivity-raising investment in the previous period but mainly as a result of monetary policy. The exchange rate had to come back within the range determined by the gold points. In the words of Friedman and Schwartz, 'any attempt to return to the pre-war parity before the greenback price of the pound sterling had fallen to that level would have meant a "pound shortage" strictly comparable with the post-World War II "dollar shortage" associated with the maintenance by other countries of official exchange rates that overvalued their own

---

[1] Hawtrey, *A Century of Bank Rate*, p. 102.

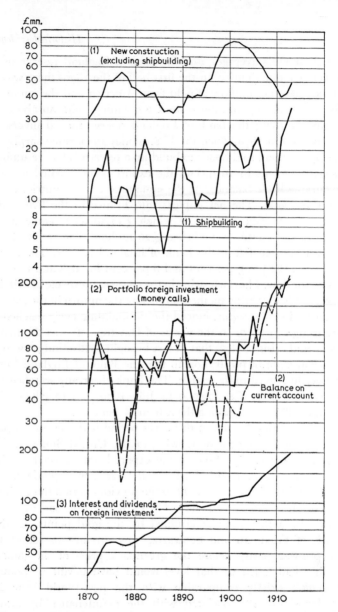

Figure 4.4 United Kingdom: long swings in construction, portfolio foreign investment, balance on current account, and income from foreign investment, 1870–1913.

Sources: (1) Cairncross, *Home and Foreign Investment 1870–1913*, p. 169; (2) M. Simon in Adler, ed., *Capital Movements and Economic Development*, pp. 52–3; (3) Imlah, *Economic Elements in the Pax Britannica*, pp. 72–5.

currencies'.[1] There was a close interaction both in real and monetary terms between the United States and Great Britain.

1879–1913

Between 1879 and 1913, with the international gold standard established, the money supply of the countries of the periphery was a dependent variable determined by outside influences. Predominant among these influences was the Bank of England's policy as guardian of its reserves. Under these circumstances a one-sided interpretation of the fluctuations in the United States is not valid. As Phillip Cagan has pointed out,

> . . . one might argue – about the pre-1914 period at least – that U.S. cycles frequently stemmed from foreign influences and were not usually transmitted abroad. This country's economy during the nineteenth century could not have counted heavily with most foreign economies, while world trade clearly affected U.S. exports. Their irregular cyclical pattern, as noted, reflected the ups and downs of foreign business activity, which often moved counter to domestic business.[2]

Fig. 4.4 shows for Great Britain the course of new construction, excluding shipbuilding (population-sensitive capital formation), shipbuilding (export-sensitive capital formation), British purchases of foreign securities (*ex ante* foreign lending), the balance on current account minus gold imports (*ex post* capital exports), and interest and dividends received on foreign investment.

[1] Friedman and Schwartz, op. cit., p. 80.
[2] Cagan, op. cit., p. 110. Friedman and Schwartz have estimated that '. . . at the time of resumption the U.S. held just over 5 per cent of the world's monetary gold stock, and perhaps 8 per cent of that part of the gold stock which served as monetary reserves; a year later these percentages were 9 and 13; and for the rest of the century both percentages were probably below 20. This is one rough measure of the relative importance of the U.S. economy in the gold standard world and one that almost surely overstates its importance since both the unit banking system in the U.S. and the absence of a central bank probably worked to make the ratio of the gold stock to the money stock higher than in most other important gold-standard countries.' Op. cit., footnote 2, p. 89.

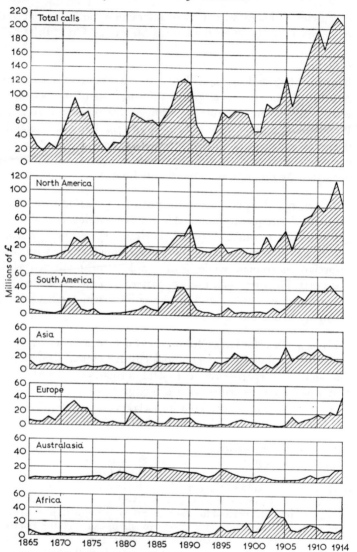

Figure 4.5 Geographical distribution of British portfolio foreign investment, 1865–1914.

Source: M. Simon in Adler, ed., *Capital Movements and Economic Development*, pp. 55–6.

With shipbuilding excluded from the construction index, the long swing stands out very clearly in the raw data, and so does the short shipbuilding cycle. The ups and downs in shipbuilding correspond to the minor and major fluctuations in the export sector. For example, in the first phase of the upswing of the 1880s there was a minor peak in foreign lending in 1881 with a peak in shipbuilding in 1882. After a short recession in foreign lending accompanied by a sharp fall in shipbuilding, the upswing proceeded to a long swing peak in 1889, with a matching peak in shipbuilding.

The portfolio investment and current account series give a rough indication of whether there is over- or under-effected transfer. The annual amount of interest and dividends on foreign investment rises from £30 million in 1870 to as much as £200 million in 1913, and, as expected, it traces out a mild long swing corresponding to that of foreign investment. The distribution of British foreign lending by geographical area is given in fig. 4.5. There is strong evidence that the upward and downward phases were simultaneous in different parts of the periphery. North and South America clearly swing together, and they dominate the total. The upswing of the early 1870s is very evident in Europe as well as North and South America. The bulge in investment in Asia in the late 1890s and in Africa in the early 1900s reflects the activity of colonial powers.

The balance on current account (*ex post* capital exports) lags behind portfolio foreign investment, indicating that the causal sequence ran from the purchase of foreign securities to the trade balance.[1] The money was first raised and then a great deal of it was spent on British goods and services. Fig. 4.4 shows that when foreign lending was rising the current account balance kept in step with it remarkably well: there was no serious transfer problem until the final stage of the boom. The propensity to spend funds borrowed from Britain on British exports, however high it

[1] See Ford, 'Overseas Lending and Internal Fluctuations 1870–1914' in Saville, ed., 'Studies in the British Economy, 1870–1914', pp. 19–31. '. . . it is of great interest that deviations in overseas issues exhibited a marked cyclical pattern but *led* fluctuations in exports and in world trade by one or two years' (p. 27).

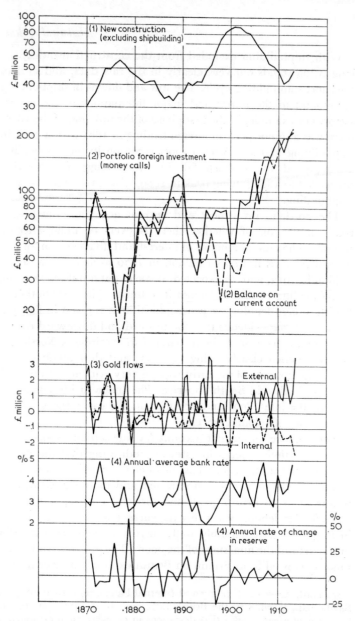

Figure 4.6 United Kingdom: gold flows, Bank rate and Bank of England reserve, 1870–1913.

Sources: (1) and (2) as for Figure 4.4; (3) – 1869 to December 1880, Hawtrey, *A Century of Bank Rate*, pp. 297–8; July 1881 to July 1913, Beach, *British International Gold Movements and Banking Policy*, pp. 52–3, 66–7: (4) Hawtrey, op. cit., pp. 297–300.

might be, was by no means the whole story.[1] The cumulative upsurge in infrastructure investment in the periphery, associated with inflowing capital and population, entailed a big shift in demand curves for British goods and services, and in view of Britain's primacy as an exporter of capital goods and manufactures[2] and the fact that the downswing in her home investment had a depressing effect on imports, it was possible to generate a current balance equal to the flow of foreign lending, except in certain critical phases.

In fig. 4.6 we plot for Great Britain the external and interior gold flows, the annual rate of change in the reserve, and the average level of Bank rate each year. When these data are read in relation to the course of foreign lending, *ex ante* and *ex post*, and home construction, we can gauge the pressures which built up in the course of each boom.

The upswing in overseas investment 1879–89

This vigorous upswing was interrupted at an early stage in 1881 when, as shown in fig. 4.6, there was already under-effected transfer, with a gold outflow accompanied by an internal drain. By February 1882 the reserve was down to £9,175,000, a loss of £7,856,000 since a year before, intensified by the failure of the Union Générale in Paris in January 1882. The Bank of England raised its rate to 5 per cent in October 1881 and 6 per cent in January 1882. This had the required effect in a sharp reaction in foreign lending and a reflux of gold; by 1884 the transfer difficulty had disappeared.

The impact on the periphery can be illustrated by what happened in the United States, where the stock of gold had risen from $210 million in June 1879 to $439 million in June 1881. This increase in the money supply raised the American price level in relation to the British from 89·1 in 1879 to 96·1 in 1882. The Bank of England's intervention, through its impact on foreign lending and prices, reversed the gold flow. This was the classic

[1] See Brown, 'Britain in the World Economy 1870–1914', in ibid., pp. 51–4.
[2] In 1880 she supplied 63 per cent of world exports of capital goods and 41 per cent of world exports of manufactured goods. See p. 12 above.

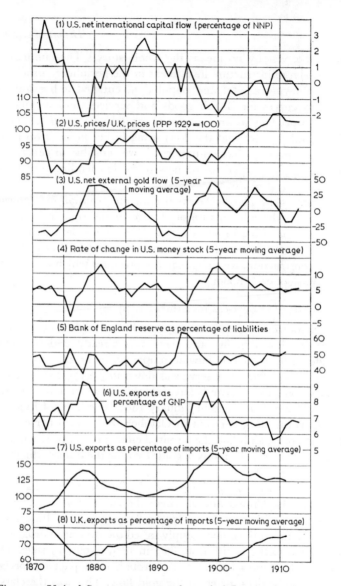

Figure 4.7 United States: money stock, capital flows and other indices 1870–1913.

Sources: (1) Friedman and Schwartz, *A Monetary History of the United States*, pp. 769–70, Table A–4, col. 4; (2) U.S./U.K. prices (PPP = 100), ibid., col. 1; (3) ibid., Table A–4; (4) ibid., pp. 704–7; (5) Pigou, *Industrial Fluctuations*, p. 369; (6) Lipsey, *Price and Quantity Trends in the Foreign Trade of the United States*, p. 430; (7) ibid., pp. 154–5; (8) Imlah, *Economic Elements in the Pax Britannica*, pp. 96–8.

gold standard mechanism in action. If the United States was to retain its fixed exchange rate, a fall in her income and price level was unavoidable. British investors, fearing that the United States would not be able to stay on the gold standard, began to sell American securities, leading to a further outflow of gold which helped to cause a panic in May 1884. Because British prices fell 12 per cent between 1882 and 1885, the achievement of a 1 per cent decline in American prices relative to British necessitated an absolute fall of 13 per cent in the American price level over these three years.[1]

The rate of growth in the U.S. money stock fell sharply from 1881 to 1885 (see fig. 4.7) from 16 per cent a year to 3 per cent, and that of real output declined from 7 per cent a year to 1 per cent. Severe though the recession was, it was only an interruption in the infrastructure investment upswing which was resumed in 1885, with a further strong inflow of capital from Britain. By 1888, as fig. 4.6 clearly indicates, there was serious under-effected transfer; the flow of *ex ante* foreign lending exceeded the current balance by a large margin. The situation in Britain at the peak of portfolio investment in 1889 was as follows: there was an external and an internal drain of gold; the shipbuilding cycle was at a peak; overseas migration had already begun to turn down; the upturn in home construction had already begun; and a shift in British investment away from the United States to Argentina had started. The Bank of England alarm bells were ringing loudly; the rate went up to 5 per cent in October 1888 and to 6 per cent at the end of December 1889, in response to which gold began to flow back. At the end of 1890 there was a further spell of dear money. The result was a huge reflux of gold.

The repercussions were felt throughout the periphery. With the shock of the Baring crisis in November 1890, Argentina experienced a severe reaction.[2] The effect in the United States is shown by the parallel movement of net capital imports and the purchasing power parity index (see fig. 4.7). The ratio of U.S. to British prices began falling in 1887. Looking at this from the

[1] On this episode see Friedman and Schwartz, op. cit., pp. 100–1.
[2] For a detailed account of the boom and collapse in Argentina see Ford, *The Gold Standard 1880–1914: Britain and Argentina*, Chapter VIII.

British end, one can interpret the course of events as follows. Between 1880 and 1887, the first phase of the lending-export boom, British prices fell by 30 per cent while money wages remained constant; this gives a strong suggestion of rising productivity in the export sector which did not lead to higher money wages. There was a high elasticity of supply of factors for the export sector due to the downswing in home construction. As the boom gathered momentum, a turning-point was reached; marginal costs began to rise because of bottlenecks at the higher level of employment in the export trades and export-sensitive investment, while demand was running high in overseas construction activity. The turning-point came in 1887; from that year to 1890 British export prices rose by 18 per cent and money wages by 8 per cent; we may infer that in those years physical productivity fell. After 1887 there was a shift in the supply schedule of capital against the United States. Because of the rise in British prices, the absolute fall required in American prices was moderate.

Nevertheless, this ushered in a phase of great difficulty for the United States, with substantial gold outflows, a fall in the rate of growth of money stock, and a banking panic in 1893. The maintenance of the gold standard once again necessitated a drastic deflation of prices and income. Meanwhile, the gold stock of the Bank of England rose to a record of £49,000,000 in February 1896. Bank rate fell to 2 per cent and was ineffective; for much of the time the market rate of discount was under 1 per cent.[1]

The upswing in U.K. home investment 1890–1901

The upswing in home construction in Great Britain which began in 1889 was halted in 1891–3 and then developed into an intense boom which reached its peak in 1901. In the periphery conditions in the early part of the decade were bordering on collapse; British portfolio investment dropped sharply from £120 million in 1889 to just over £30 million in 1893, and the current balance receded to a low trough of £22·9 million in 1898.

---

[1] For a well documented account of the London money market during the 1890s, see Beach, *British International Gold Movements and Banking Policy, 1881–1913*, pp. 122–36.

In the United States the reaction from the investment boom of the 1880s was intensified by lack of confidence in the stability of the dollar. The Sherman Silver Purchase Act and the McKinley Tariff Act of 1890 helped to increase the uncertainty, the years 1890–4 saw large outflows of gold (see fig. 4.7), and net capital inflows declined to a trickle – foreign investors selling $300 million of American securities. The effect of the gold outflow on the money stock was strengthened by the public tending to hold a higher ratio of currency to deposits. In the first half of the decade there was a steep decline in the rate of growth of the money supply; and, in view of falling prices abroad, America had to experience a severe prices and income deflation if convertibility was to be maintained. The long crisis of confidence did not end until the triumph of the Republicans in the election of 1896: from then on there was a dramatic change in the fortunes of the American economy, aided by the powerful effect of the gold discoveries in South Africa, Colorado and Alaska.

Similar depressive influences dominated the rest of the periphery, e.g., Argentina, Canada and Australia, in the first half of the 1890s. Whereas the export capacity of all these countries had been greatly increased by the infrastructure boom of the 1880s, their export sectors did not have a real income expansion until the second half of the decade when the fall in world prices was reversed and the home construction boom in Britain really got going. Argentina is a good example of the cobweb-type instability to which the periphery was exposed because of the lag between infrastructive investment and the subsequent phase when it matured in increased exports. In the years 1885–9 Argentina absorbed £60 million of British portfolio investment and a net total of 640,000 foreign immigrants, and by 1890 the annual servicing of the foreign debt, which had to be made in gold or sterling at a fixed rate, took 60 million gold pesos, or 60 per cent of the export proceeds.[1] According to Ford, 'the slow maturing of investment projects for which the service charges were immediate was a main cause of the Baring crisis'.[2] The *volume* of exports of wheat and wool increased substantially after 1890, but export

[1] Ford, *The Gold Standard 1880–1914*, pp. 140–1.
[2] Ibid., p. 142.

values did not show a marked rise until 1898. As in the United States, there was a strong export upswing in real terms in the late 1890s, pivoted to a large extent on the home investment upsurge in the United Kingdom. Similarly in Canada the index of the value of exports between 1895 and 1900 rose from 114 to 192 and in Australia total exports rose from £36·5 million to £49·2 million.

Even when full allowance is made for special political and other circumstances in the overseas countries, there was undeniably a basic common factor. Their economies were seriously destabilized in the wake of the corrective measures taken by the Bank of England in 1890; when Britain caught a cold, the periphery caught pneumonia. There is no clearer demonstration of the process of interaction than the monetary series for the 1890s (fig. 4.7). Gold flowing out of the United States and other countries went into the coffers of the Bank of England. Between June 1892 and June 1896 there was actually an absolute fall of 5 per cent in the U.S. money stock, the first such decline since the 1870s, whereas the Bank of England reserve increased spectacularly from £15 million to no less than £49 million (February 1896). When America was struggling desperately to stay on the gold standard, Britain was enjoying such a surfeit of liquidity that the market rate of discount was below 1 per cent. In the second half of the 1890s the reverse happened (fig. 4.7), the Bank of England reserve as a proportion of liabilities fell almost as rapidly as it had risen, while the money stock of the United States increased by 52 per cent.

The demographic determinants of the inverse construction cycle have been fully demonstrated in Chapter 2. The upturn of the cycle in Britain preceded the downturn in the export sector. Detailed research has established the primacy of residential construction in the home boom of the 1890s.[1] 'This is the major single item of home investment which begins a decade's rise gradually but steadily as early as 1891–2, preceding all other types of home investment by several years.'[2] Its progress was

[1] The subject has been admirably explored by Sigsworth and Blackman, 'The Home Boom of the 1890s', in Saville, ed., op. cit., pp. 75–97.
[2] Ibid., p. 78.

accelerated by two powerful forces—abnormally cheap money and the high peak in internal migration and the natural increase component of the 20–44 population curve in the second half of the decade.[1]

The ability to borrow money at abnormally low rates had been, according to *The Economist*, the most important cause behind the rising prices of Stock Exchange securities, having 'enabled enterprising investors to carry large blocks of securities with loans obtained from the banks. While money could be obtained upon Consols at 1 per cent and under, and while the banks were willing to lend at but little over that figure upon home railway stocks . . . it was obviously good business to enter into such transactions'. . . . The favourable cost structure of the building industry in a period of cheap money and of increasing demand for new and better quality houses made housing a particularly attractive field for speculative investment; and it was this sector which dominated the expansion of the 1890s.[2]

This strong investment upswing in Britain was the foundation of the export sector boom in the periphery. American exports as a proportion of imports rose from 105 per cent early in the decade to 165 per cent at the end (fig. 4.7), and net gold imports to the United States from mid-1896 to mid-1899 amounted to $201 million or 40 per cent of the initial stock. With domestic mines producing at the rate of $60 million a year, the monetary gold stock had reached $859 million by the middle of 1899, a rise of 90 per cent in three years.[3]

In 1898 and 1899 there were signs of strain in the British economy. Construction was at a very high level, and shipbuilding was nearing a peak. The Bank of England up to 1890 had regarded a reserve of about £10 million as a sign that the rate should go up; after 1896 the critical level was held to be about £20 million. In April 1898, when the reserve had fallen to £18·3 million, the rate was raised to 4 per cent; there was a sizeable reflux and then a

[1] See fig. 2.4.   [2] Sigworths and Blackman, op. cit., p. 96.
[3] Friedman and Schwartz, op. cit., p. 141.

further loss, so that the rate was again raised to 4 per cent in October 1898, and gold again flowed in. Fig. 4.6 shows how the internal drain was rising rapidly at the height of the boom; gold imports had to accommodate this demand and so did not strengthen the Bank's stock. The outbreak of the South African war led to the rate being raised to 6 per cent in November 1899. For the second half of 1900 it was at 4 per cent, and it was put up to 5 per cent in January 1901.

The peak of the boom had been reached in 1899 when unemployment was as low as 2 per cent, interior demand for gold was running at over £10 million, and the index of share prices touched its highest point. Meanwhile in the United States the demographic cycle had already turned upwards; net immigration had begun to recover in 1898 and rose from 121,000 in that year to 201,000 in 1899, accompanied by a 20 per cent jump in real construction. This was happening at the very time when the steam had gone out of the demographic cycle in Britain. The London stock market was signalling a downturn in 1900 and unemployment rose to 2·5 per cent; total construction reacted in 1901, unemployment rose to 3·3 per cent, and in 1902 a vigorous upswing in portfolio foreign investment was in progress, with the index of share prices 9 per cent down from the top. The British investment boom of the 1890s was over, and the final infrastructure upswing in the periphery was under way.

Friedman and Schwartz, in their analysis of this period, are baffled by what they regard as the 'puzzle' of '. . . why should the United States have been a net exporter of capital during 1897–1906, let alone on so large a scale?'[1] They are intrigued by the fact that '. . . the whole level of the capital movement series for the period after 1896 seems lower compared with the relative price series than the level before 1896 does . . .'[2] (see fig. 4.7); and after several attempts they end up by saying that they can find no satisfactory explanation – '. . . we are inclined to believe that there are either some other important economic factors at work or some errors in the figures that we have been unable to discover'.[3] There *are* indeed some other important factors at work and they have

[1] Friedman and Schwartz, op. cit, p. 142.
[2] Ibid., p. 147.   [3] Ibid., p. 148.

been the main subject matter of this chapter; once these are recognized, the puzzle disappears.[1]

There is a marked parallel between America's export upswing of the late 1890s and that of the late 1870s. In both periods net capital exports were substantial, a large net inflow of gold was accompanied by a sharp rise in money stock, and an upturn in U.S. prices relative to British preceded the reversal in net capital outflow. The slump in investment in America in the 1890s coincided with a strong boom in Britain; and it was natural that some of the U.S.-owned foreign balances created by the export upsurge should have been invested abroad. At the long swing turning-point in 1900 net capital outflow sharply declined and by 1906 there was again a net inflow.

When we compare the 1900s with the 1880s, the only difference is that the rate of absorption of foreign capital by the American economy had declined; in fig. 4.7 the level of the capital flow series with respect to the relative price series in the 1900s is much lower than in the 1880s.[2] The reasons for this are fairly clear. First, America had become the world's largest manufacturing country, producing 30 per cent of the world's output in 1896–1900 as against Britain's 20 per cent; she was already emerging as an exporter of capital[3] and was soon to become the world's biggest creditor. Secondly, the 1900s saw a change in the direction of British investment in the periphery, with less going to the United States and much more to Canada and South America.

[1] In their treatment of export upswings, Friedman and Schwartz attach far too much significance to episodes such as the bumper harvests in America (coinciding with bad harvests in Europe) in 1880–1 and 1897–8 (ibid., pp. 97–9 and p. 140). Their interest is to see how the gold standard mechanism worked; they found that it worked beautifully in 1880–1 but not so well in 1897 and after. Hence the puzzle. A glance at fig. 4.7 will show that the moving average of the series of U.S. exports as a percentage of imports, 1870–1913, traces a definite long swing which reduces the quirks of the weather to insignificance.

[2] This reflected the growth in the industrial strength and competitive power of the United States.

[3] See my *Migration and Economic Growth*, pp. 120–1. For details of the growth of American foreign investment see Lewis, *America's Stake in International Investments*, pp. 335–40, and Dunning, *American Investment in British Manufacturing Industry*, pp. 19–36.

The upswing in overseas investment 1902–13

Fig. 4.6 brings out the similarity between the periods 1902–13 and 1879–89 in the United Kingdom, with domestic capital formation falling and foreign investment rising. As in the 1880s there were two well-defined phases, each of which culminated in strong pressure on the reserves of the Bank of England. From 1902 to 1907 there was a vigorous upsurge in capital formation in the United States where immigration reached the unprecedented level of over 1 million a year in 1905–7; American prices rose at an average rate of 2 per cent a year and the money stock at 7 per cent a year. There was a sharp increase in the ratio of American to British prices. In Britain domestic capital formation was declining and the purchase of foreign securities was resumed on a large scale, so much so that in 1905 the level of *ex ante* foreign investment was well above the current surplus in the balance of payments; under-effected transfer coincided with a large interior demand for gold induced largely by the peak in export-sensitive investment, e.g. shipbuilding, in 1906 (see fig. 4.6). This is reminiscent of what happened in the early 1880s. Gold was flowing to the United States and by October 1906 the reserve of the Bank of England was at the danger level of £18·3 million. Bank rate was raised to 5 and then 6 per cent in October 1906, and this succeeded in inducing a reflux of gold.

The boom in the United States had generated dangerous speculation, and the failure of the Knickerbocker Trust, the third largest trust company in New York, on 22 October 1907, caused a serious panic and a general suspension of cash payments. Huge exports of gold took place from England to America, and Bank rate reached 7 per cent in November 1907, the first time it had gone above 6 per cent since 1873. This drastic action brought in gold to the value of £19 million, of which £6½ million came from the gold-producing countries, South Africa and Australia, £7 million from Germany and £3½ million from France. To quote W. E. Beach,

> . . . England became a clearing center through which gold passed from the rest of the world to the United States. . . . This

achievement was heralded as the acme of success of the English banking system under the Act of 1844. But, in fact, the Bank rate of 7 per cent drew gold only because of the action of the Bank of France and the Reichsbank in permitting specie to be drawn from their hoards. . . . In other words, the high Bank rate brought gold merely because the two Continental banks preferred to aid the Bank of England, rather than suffer higher discount rates in their own countries. Otherwise, the English Bank rate might have had to go to untold heights to keep their Reserve up, and the trade of the country would have suffered severely.[1]

The impact of the crisis on the United States was severe but short-lived. In the words of Friedman and Schwartz, '. . . in the 1907–8 episode, the climax occurred early before the banking structure had been seriously affected and, if our analysis is correct, served to prevent widespread bank failures, to cut short a possible major deflation, and to keep the maximum decline in the stock of money to less than 8 per cent'.[2]

After the violent setback the reserves of the Bank of England were replenished and the upswing in foreign lending continued with tremendous vigour, with capital going to all parts of the periphery, especially Canada. This second phase ran into trouble in 1909–10 when gold was again flowing out, particularly to the United States; again there was under-effected transfer (see fig. 4.6). The double strain of heavy foreign lending and renewed interior demand for bullion (the approach of another shipbuilding peak) endangered the reserve, and the Bank rate was raised to 5 per cent in October 1910. As we saw in Chapter 3, the Edwardian climax in 1907–13 saw foreign investment at a level one-third higher than domestic fixed investment, equivalent to no less than 9 per cent of net national income. There can be little doubt, however, that the parameters affecting both Britain and the United States had undergone a profound change by that time; the outbreak of war brought the cycle to an abrupt end.

[1] Beach, op. cit., pp. 145–6.
[2] Friedman and Schwartz, op. cit., p. 167.

LONG SWINGS IN PRODUCTIVITY AND REAL INCOME

This chapter is to be regarded as an interim report designed to pave the way for a more rigorous econometric demonstration. With the aid of fig. 4.8 (showing rates of change from one overlapping decade to the next), we can summarize briefly what the analysis suggests about the growth and fluctuations of productivity and real income *per capita*.

(*a*) Both in the United Kingdom and the United States the rates of change in fixed capital formation are inverse to those in exports as a percentage of imports; in other words, export performance in any one period correlates with the movement of fixed investment in the previous period.

(*b*) In the United States there is a strong positive correlation between rates of change in 'other' capital formation (which includes producer durables), exports as a percentage of imports, and changes in additions to the real flow of goods to consumers *per capita*. The course of these three variables is reflected (after a short lag) in the rate of change of real gross national product *per capita*. In other words, in the upward phase of the long swing in population-sensitive capital formation, the economy is investing in capacity to produce more output per unit of input in the future. *Ex post*, the high rate of growth in real national income *per capita* is the pay-off on the population-sensitive capital formation of the previous phase; *ex ante*, it is the inducement to a further round of fixed investment in the next phase. It is in the pay-off phase that the balance of payments is strong, the rate of growth of the

Figure 4.8 Long swings in real national product and related variables in the United Kingdom, 1856–1913, and the United States, 1870–1913 (rates of change from one overlapping decade to the next).
Sources: (1) Feinstein's estimates in Mitchell and Deane, *Abstract of British Historical Statistics*, pp. 373–4; (2) ibid., p. 367; (3) Imlah, *Economic Elements in the Pax Britannica*, pp. 96–8; (4) Kuznets, 'Long Swings in the Growth of Population and in Related Economic Variables', p. 49, Table 13; (5) ibid., p. 50, Table 15; (6) Lipsey, *Price and Quantity Trends in the Foreign Trade of the United States*, pp. 154–5; (7) Kuznets, op. cit., p. 48, Table 11; (8) ibid., p. 49, Table 13.

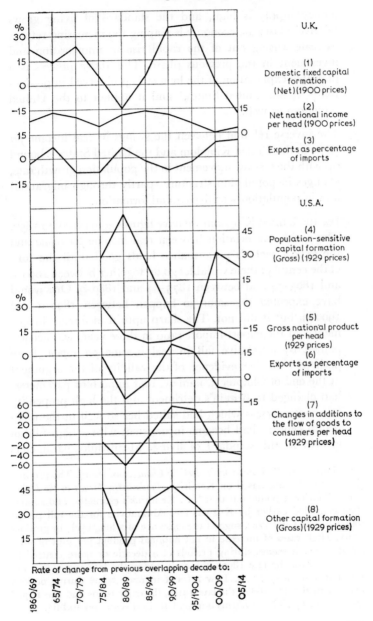

U.K.

(1)
Domestic fixed capital
formation
(Net)(1900 prices)

(2)
Net national income
per head (1900 prices)

(3)
Exports as percentage
of imports

U.S.A.

(4)
Population-sensitive
capital formation
(Gross)(1929 prices)

(5)
Gross national product
per head
(1929 prices)
(6)
Exports as percentage
of imports

(7)
Changes in additions to
the flow of goods to
consumers per head
(1929 prices)

(8)
Other capital formation
(Gross)(1929 prices)

Rate of change from previous overlapping decade to:

1860/69 65/74 70/79 75/84 80/89 85/94 90/99 95/1904 00/09 05/14

money supply is high, and the standard of living grows relatively fast; the economy is reaping the increasing returns to scale arising out of the rapid rise in immigration and investment in the previous phase. The above process is a plausible explanation of the long swings observed in productivity in the United States,[1] and it applies to the United Kingdom as well.

(c) The inverse relation between the swings in real income *per capita* in the United Kingdom and the United States is bound up with the see-saw movement in the population growth rate, changes in population structure (partly through migration) and in population-sensitive capital formation.

(d) For the United Kingdom we have figures going back to 1856. The positive association between real income *per capita* and the export sector's performance holds good until the turn of the century; these variables go up together between 1860–9 and 1865–74 and between 1875–84 and 1880–9. One would have expected the same to happen between 1890–9 and 1900–9, but it did not. The sharp upturn in foreign investment and the export-import ratio in those years was accompanied by a relative fall in real income *per capita*. Here perhaps is further evidence of the validity of the argument at the end of Chapter 3, namely, that important parameters had changed to Britain's detriment and the high propensity to invest overseas which had suited her so well in the nineteenth century had become inconsistent with a high rate of growth in the standard of living. Meanwhile, parameters

---

[1] See Fabricant, *Basic Facts on Productivity Change*, pp. 16–17. The productivity estimates are based on Kendrick, *Productivity Trends in the United States*. Fabricant points out that '. . . Kendrick's estimates, and similar data compiled earlier by Kuznets and Abramovitz for the full period following the Civil War, suggest the existence of a long cycle in productivity. High rates of increase in net national product per unit of total input came, it seems, during periods of a decade or more centred in the late 1870s, the late 1890s, the early 1920s, the late 1930s, and the late 1940s or early 1950s. Low rates of increase came during periods centred in the late 1880s, the late 1910s, the early 1930s and the 1940s' (op. cit., p. 17). This confirms our analysis in this section and fig. 4.8.

affecting the United States had also changed; she had built up a large and highly productive manufacturing sector (accounting for 35 per cent of world output in 1906–8) and had become a net creditor country; the share of manufacturing producer durables in gross domestic capital formation increased from 31 per cent in 1869–78 to 57 per cent in 1899–1908.[1] In 1834–43 American income *per capita* was probably lower than the British. 'Between 1834–43 and 1944–55 American GNP increased at an exceptionally high rate of 42 per cent per decade, a rate perhaps never equalled elsewhere for such an extended period. GNP *per capita* also increased at a high rate, compared with British and French growth.'[2]

CONCLUSIONS

The main results can now be summarized.

(*a*) United States experience in the period 1870–1913 can best be interpreted within the ambit of the inverse long swing relationship between the periphery and Great Britain, with an alternation of infrastructure and export upsurges. An interaction model fits the facts better than the notion of '. . . a relatively stable rate of growth interrupted by two monetary episodes from which the system rebounded to approximately its initial path'.[3] It also has much more explanatory power than the one-sided models based on fluctuations in the 'pull' of the United States economy.[4] (See Chapter 1.)

(*b*) Home investment was dominated by population-sensitive capital formation, and inverse long swings in the latter were associated with (and probably attributable to) inverse swings in the demographic variables – population structure and migration – in Great Britain and the periphery.

[1] Gallman, 'Gross National Product in the United States, 1834–1909' in *Output, Employment and Productivity in the United States after 1800*, p. 15. In this important paper, Gallman has shown that the movements of the real GNP series and the main components conform well to the chronology of long swings as established by Abramovitz (ibid., pp. 21–3).
[2] Ibid., p. 23.
[3] Friedman and Schwartz, op. cit., p. 187.
[4] Regression analysis bears this out. Jeffrey Williamson did a univariate

(c) The fact that the United States, Canada, Argentina and Australia had simultaneous swings cannot be fully explained without recognizing the constraints of the gold standard and the effect of the Bank of England's reserve policy. This is not meant to imply that the Old Lady 'managed' the pre-1914 international gold standard system; on the contrary, according to her lights, she minded her own business and on critical occasions this was very much at the expense of all the borrowers.[1]

---

test, with net expenditure on railroads in the United States as a variable, to explain net capital imports in the period 1871–1914.

The best fit occurs when net capital imports ($\check{K}$) lag Ulmer's net expenditure in the railroads (I_{US}) by one year ($\bar{R}^2 = 0.624$) where the coefficient is positive and significant:

$$(1871–1914)\ \check{K}^t = 6.7487 + 1.0189\ I_{US}^{t-1},\ \bar{R}^2 = 0.624$$
$$(0.1271)$$

When, however, we add the Cairncross series of British home investment (I_{GB}), an extraordinary thing happens. Not only does the fit improve only slightly, but also the coefficient of I_{US} becomes insignificant.

$$(1871–1914)\ \check{K}^t = 914.45 - 0.0303\ I_{US}^t - 8.8473\ I_{GB}^t,\ \bar{R}^2 = 0.654$$
$$(0.2000)\qquad (0.1556)$$

It would seem that Ulmer's series does not add much to the explanatory power of the Cairncross series. Over the long swing, and statistically, it seems that the rate of British home investment is inversely related to the rate of net capital inflow and that conditions in the American railroad industry are somewhat unimportant. This holds true, incidentally, under all reasonable lead-lag conditions. (*American Growth and the Balance of Payments 1820–1913*, pp. 147–8.)

Reference should also be made to an econometric analysis by Maurice Wilkinson, 'European Migration to the United States: An Econometric Analysis of Aggregate Labor Supply and Demand' (mimeographed), presented to the European Meeting of the Econometric Society, Brussels, September 1969. His conclusion refutes one-sided interpretations of American long swings. He found that 'European migration to the U.S. prior to World War I was significantly influenced by both employment opportunities in the particular European country (as represented by changes in domestic output) and the gain in real income to be achieved by migration to the U.S.' (p. 19).

[1] In Jacob Viner's words, '. . . it may be that the need of the Bank for income for dividend-paying purposes was an adequate justification for

(*d*) It is very difficult in the present state of knowledge to sort out the parts played by real and monetary elements in the long swing interaction. Fig. 4.7 suggests some interesting clues. The course of the rate of change in the growth of the U.S. money stock (5-year moving average) traces out a long swing corresponding to that of net external gold flows (5-year moving average), with the former showing a short lag. The gold stock accounted for most of the large changes in high-powered money in the United States up to 1913.[1] The swings in net gold flows correspond to and lag behind the swings in U.S. exports as a percentage of imports. There was an inverse relation between the swings in the rate of change in the growth of the U.S. money stock and the swings in the Bank of England reserve as a percentage of liabilities. Fluctuations in net capital flows were related to those in the ratio of U.S. to U.K. prices (purchasing power parity, 1929 = 100).

It is clear that the U.S. trade balance determined the gold flow, and the latter determined the rate of growth of the money supply. There is no basis for the notion that investment upswings, by generating excess demands, attracted net capital inflows which

---

the Bank's failure to accumulate larger gold reserves from its own capital resources. But there were many ways in which the Government could have made it possible for the Bank to acquire adequate gold reserves without depletion of its revenues. As far as England as a whole was concerned, it managed to operate its part of the international gold standard throughout the nineteenth century on an investment in gold stocks pitiably small in relation to the benefits which would have accrued to it and to the world if there had been less parsimony in this connection.' ('Clapham on the Bank of England', p. 63.) See also Bloomfield, *Monetary Policy under the International Gold Standard: 1880–1914*, pp. 23–6.

[1] See Cagan, op. cit., pp. 50–1. 'High-powered' money is '. . . the total amount of hand-to-hand currency held by the public plus vault cash plus, after 1914, deposit liabilities of the Federal Reserve System to banks.' (Friedman and Schwartz, op. cit., p. 50.) It is called 'high-powered' because for every dollar of it which banks hold as reserves they can create several dollars of deposits. Other things being equal, when the volume of high-powered money goes up the money stock rises in the same proportion.

more than offset the unfavourable trade balance, thereby inducing gold inflows.[1] Gold inflow, and as a consequence the money
stock, rose most rapidly in the phases of the long swing when exports were surging upwards and infrastructure investment and imports were declining. Moreover, it was in these periods that upswings
in additions to the labour force and to gross national product took
place.[2] In these phases Britain was having a home investment
boom, her exports as a proportion of imports were falling, and
gold flowed from the Bank of England to the periphery. When the
United States had its investment upswing, the trade balance
deteriorated and gold tended to flow out, with the result that the
rate of growth of the money stock tended to fall.

There can be no such thing as a purely monetary theory of the
inverse long swing; but it seems to be equally true that no explanation will be satisfactory if it leaves out important monetary
forces. First, in the words of Milton Friedman, '. . . the major
source of long-period changes in the quantity of money in the
United States has been changes in high-powered money, which,
until 1914, reflected mostly changes in the amount of gold'.[3]
Secondly, Cagan, after a careful analysis, reached the following
conclusion:

> Severe contractions are an important exception . . . to the . . .
> statement that fluctuations in business activity seem to produce
> the cycles in the money series. For severe contractions, this
> effect may explain the timing, but apparently a deep depres-
> sion cannot account for the sharp decline in the rate of change
> in the money stock associated with it. . . . Panics made ordinary
> business contractions severe when they led to substantial
> decline in the rate of monetary growth, and not otherwise. . . .
> The variety of reasons for decline in monetary growth during
> severe depressions rules out any single cause and rules out, in

---

[1] This is the thesis argued by Jeffrey Williamson, op. cit.: 'The rate of
net gold flow over United States borders . . . is predominantly caused
by income movements and excess demands for real-money balances'
(p. 183).
[2] Kuznets, *Capital in the American Economy*, pp. 342–6.
[3] Foreword to Cagan, op. cit., p. xxv.

particular, a sharp fall in business activity as the main reason for the associated decline in monetary growth. The evidence is therefore consistent with, and taken as a whole, impressively favors emphasis on the decline in the rate of monetary growth as the main reason some business contractions, regardless of what may have initiated them, became severe.[1]

This conclusion is in line with our analysis of the impact of changes in the money stock when long swing expansions came to their usually severe end. In short, our view of the pre-1913 Atlantic economy is that the inverse cycle was propelled by real determinants but that, in the crucial phases when expansion gave way to contraction, changes in the stock of money played a significant independent part in influencing the course of the economy.

(*e*) Our analysis of the mechanism by which productivity and real income grew in the Atlantic economy has a close affinity with the results obtained by George H. Borts and Jerome L. Stein in their investigation of the causes of differential regional rates of growth in the United States. In order to explain the convergence of *per capita* personal incomes among States between 1880 and 1950, these authors found it necessary to discard simple aggregative theory and use a model with two sectors, one providing construction of all kinds and the other producing goods traded among regions. Their analysis led to the conclusion that the fastest economic growth occurs in those regions of a free market economy where the supply of labour increases most rapidly; they stress the crucial role of shifts in labour supply functions (via intra- and inter-regional migration) in determining differences in regional growth rates.[2]

Similarly, there is a link with the thesis propounded by Nicholas Kaldor in his analysis of the causes of slow growth in the United Kingdom,[3] in which he stresses the dynamic relationship

[1] Ibid., p. 267.
[2] Borts and Stein, *Economic Growth in a Free Market*, especially Chapters 3, 4 and 5, pp. 48–100.
[3] Kaldor, *The Causes of the Slow Rate of Growth of the United Kingdom.*

between rates of change of productivity and output, based on the work of P. J. Verdoorn and others. The following quotation is highly relevant:

> The rate of growth of industrialization fundamentally depends on the exogenous components of demand (a set of forces extending far beyond the income elasticities of demand for manufactured goods). The higher the rate of growth of industrial output which these demand conditions permit, the faster will be the rate at which labour is transferred from the surplus-sectors to the high productivity sectors. It is my contention that it is the rate at which this transfer takes place which determines the growth rate of productivity of the economy as a whole. The mechanism by which this happens is only to a minor extent dependent on the *absolute* differences in the levels of output per head between the labour-absorbing sectors and the surplus-labour sectors. The major part of the mechanism consists of the fact that the *growth* of productivity is accelerated as a result of the transfer at both ends – both at the gaining-end and at the losing-end; in the first, because, as a result of increasing returns, productivity in industry will increase faster, the faster output expands; in the second because when the surplus-sectors lose labour, the productivity of the remainder of the population is bound to rise.[1]

This passage describes the essence of the growth process in the Atlantic economy which has been explored in this chapter. Kaldor stresses that the relationship between the rate of growth of productivity and of output is a phenomenon peculiar to the secondary rather than the primary and tertiary sectors of the economy. In our analysis we have seen how essential it is to split this secondary sector into construction, public utilities etc., on the one hand, and manufacturing, on the other. In this way one can observe how a high rate of growth of population and construction is a prelude to a high rate of growth of labour supply and manufacturing output, thereby entailing a high rate of growth of productivity mainly through increasing returns.

[1] Kaldor, 'Productivity and Growth in Manufacturing Industry: a Reply', p. 386.

THE PROCESS IN REVERSE: AMERICA AND HER
PERIPHERY, 1946-71

The experience of Britain since World War II is in marked
contrast to the alternation of capital formation and export
upsurges characteristic of her growth up to 1913. Because of the
balance of payments constraint, increases in home investment
have been frequently nipped in the bud by deflationary measures;
there were balance of payments crises in 1949, 1951–2, 1956,
1957, 1959, 1961, 1964, 1966, and 1969, and the pound was
devalued twice. If her international margin had been wide
enough, and the labour supply elastic enough, to allow her to
have sustained upswings in capital formation as a basis for major
upswings in exports, her average growth rate since 1945 would
have been higher. Successive governments concentrated on
the regulation of internal demand, entailing 'consumption-led'
rather than 'export-led' growth.[1] Ironically enough, the latter
was precisely what West Germany and Japan, with copious aid
from the victors, were able to achieve after the war.

The course of events since World War II can be regarded
as the nineteenth-century story in reverse, with the United States
in the role of financial centre providing funds (though not, of
course, migrants) for her periphery and presiding over an international 'dollar standard' with fixed exchange rates. There have
been three long swing phases and the beginning of a fourth. The
first, between 1946 and the early 1950s, was marked by an enormous flow of Government loans and grants from the United
States to Europe – exports of public capital to enable the Old
World to recover from the impact of the war. During these years
the American economy advanced vigorously, while European
countries suffered balance of payments difficulties at a time of
'dollar scarcity'. From the mid-1950s to the beginning of the
1960s there was a tremendous economic upsurge in the periphery,
a retardation in the United States, and a 'dollar glut' appeared.
In the second half of the 1960s America was in an upward phase

---

[1] See Kaldor, 'Conflicts in National Economic Objectives' in Kaldor
(ed.), *Conflicts in Policy Objectives*, pp. 1–19.

of the long swing, whereas the rate of advance in Western Europe and Japan was less than in the previous phase. Meanwhile, fundamental changes had taken place in the economic balance of power, culminating in the suspension of the dollar's convertibility in August 1971.

Post-war reconstruction

In the first phase the United States was in a particularly strong economic situation. The Federal Government had absorbed no less than 40 per cent of the gross national product during the years of all-out war effort, 1942–4; personal consumption had been restricted to 75 per cent of disposable personal incomes in this period. Only an insignificant amount of residential construction had been carried out, and gross business investment was only two-fifths of gross business savings. The productive capacity of the economy had expanded to an unprecedented extent; the real gross national product in 1946 was double that of 1940; and this enormous productive potential was ready for the transition to peacetime demands to be exercised by a population holding very large liquid balances. Moreover, since the productive capacity of several of the other major industrial countries, particularly in Europe, had been seriously reduced by the ravages of war, there was bound to be an abnormally high demand for American products for some years. In these circumstances it was natural that the United States should be poised for a phase of rapid economic growth in the immediate post-war period. Between 1947 and 1955 gross national product in real terms increased by 39 per cent, an average annual rate of growth of 4·2 per cent. Industrial production rose by 47 per cent, an annual growth of nearly 5 per cent. Residential construction in real terms went up by 90 per cent, and real expenditure on fixed investment in durable goods manufacturing (to 1957) by 58 per cent.

The key to the reconstruction of the international economy after the war is to be found in the massive export of *public* capital from the United States. Between 1946 and 1952 total *gross* movements of public capital and grants amounted to $75,500 million, 58 per cent of which came from the United States and Canada in 1948; these transfers were equal to 20 per cent of the aggregate value of world imports in that year.[1] The net amount of public funds supplied by the United States was $33,800 million, of which $22,800 million went to Europe. The latter was five times larger than the entire net volume of $4,400 million of American private direct investment (i.e. investment by United States companies in their subsidiaries and branches abroad) throughout the world in the same period. Thanks to this generous aid, the exhausted economies of Europe were able not only to cover their large trade deficits but also to operate a considerable measure of multilateral trade and resume capital exports and emigration to overseas countries within their orbit. There was very little American *private* investment in Western Europe in this period: it comprised only 8 per cent of total United States direct foreign investment in 1946–52. However, there was a large flow of American private capital to Canada and Latin America, and this helped the resumption of European emigration to these countries while the outer Sterling Area was strengthened. Such was the triangular mechanism which in the early post-war years put new life into the world economy; it was based on the European Recovery Programme, and it made possible a rapid revival of commercial relations between North America, Europe and the developing countries overseas. The beneficiaries have been too apt to forget what they owe to the unparalleled statesmanship which inspired the Marshall Plan, with which the name of its chief architect, the late Dean Acheson, will always be associated.

Economic resurgence of Western Europe

The 1950s saw a remarkable economic revival in Western Europe. Between 1953 and 1961 industrial production in the European Common Market countries went up by 82 per cent as against an increase of 20 per cent in the United States and 30 per cent in the United Kingdom. One is reminded of the nineteenth-century pattern of development when Great Britain was the world's

[1] See Weiner and Dalla-Chiesa, 'International Movements of Public Long-term Capital and Grants, 1946–50', p. 116, and Barnénas, 'International Movement of Public Long-term Capital and Grants, 1951–2', p. 110.

leading creditor; phases of heavy British investment in countries of recent settlement overseas were followed by phases in which the production and export capacities of these countries showed a rapid increase. The extraordinary upsurge in production and export capacities in Western Europe and Japan in the 1950s would not have been possible without the basic capital formation and renewal of resources brought about by the inflow of public capital in the years 1946–52.

Between 1953 and 1961 the volume of industrial production in Germany rose by 90 per cent and productivity per manhour by 63 per cent; the labour force increased by no less than 5,000,000, i.e. by one-third, the volume of exports expanded by 169 per cent, and the Central Bank's gold reserve grew from 1,368 million to 14,427 million D.M. One of the necessary conditions of this 'economic miracle' was the absorption of immigrants on a unique scale. The population of the Federal Republic increased by one-third in twelve years. Between May 1945 and July 1959 Western Germany absorbed 3·2 million refugees from the Soviet zone and 9·4 million from beyond the Oder–Neisse, from the Sudeten area and from South-eastern Europe. These newcomers included a high proportion of skilled manpower and qualified personnel: they spoke the same language and had the same background as the people of the host country. Highly adaptable and mobile, these immigrants found little difficulty in being assimilated. At a later stage many workers were recruited from Southern Europe, particularly Italy, Spain, Greece and Turkey. This massive inflow of labour into an economy with an advanced industrial technique provided the basis for a rapid increase in productivity; and Government policy concentrated on the promotion of a high rate capital of accumulation and the introduction of the most modern methods of production.

Retardation of growth in the United States, 1955-61

Between the middle of the 1950s and 1961–2 the rate of growth in the United States was much slower than in the previous high phase, 1947–55; and it was in sharp contrast to what was happening in continental Europe. For example, real expenditure on automobiles and parts in the years 1956–61 averaged 16 per cent below the peak of the previous upward phase. Even in 1962 real expenditures on plant and equipment in manufacturing and public utilities were 15 per cent below the previous peak. In the years 1955–62 expenditures on residential construction rose on an average by about 1 per cent per annum, which was far less than the rate of advance before 1955. The relative stagnation shown by these strategic economic variables was reflected in the movement of the gross national product in real terms which showed an average annual increase of only 2·7 per cent between 1955 and 1962.

The emergence of Western Europe as a strong power in the world's market was bound to lead to a redistribution of monetary reserves. Between 1953 and the end of 1961 the official gold and foreign exchange holdings of the European countries belonging to OECD rose from \$11,200 million to \$26,800 million, whereas those of the United States fell from \$22,000 million to \$17,000 million. From the point of view of the working of the international economy this was a salutary development and it was not necessarily harmful to the United States. As an American writer pointed out in 1960,

> . . . Whatever difficulty the United States may be having in maintaining its previous relative position in world trade is not due to the higher relative prices of our export goods, but to the ability of the Western European countries to offer far larger supplies than formerly at the same relative prices as the United States. Even so, the payments position of the United States would not be adversely affected by the greater increase in production and exports in Western Europe, if these countries would increase their imports and foreign investment to an equivalent extent. This balance of payments difficulty apart, and for which an appropriate remedy can be found, the United States clearly benefits from the growth in European productivity and would benefit from the growth in output in the underdeveloped countries.[1]

The continental European countries which absorbed monetary reserves on such a large scale did not, however, increase their

[1] Bernstein, *International Effects of U.S. Economic Policy*, p. 35.

imports and foreign investment to anything like an adequate extent. Meanwhile, in addition to a very considerable outflow of United States government funds for defence purposes, there was an appreciable increase in private foreign investment, both direct and portfolio. In 1958 American military *expenditure* abroad amounted to $3,416 million, of which $1,852 million was incurred in Western Europe. The fact that the latter was the equivalent of over half the exports of Western Europe to the United States is an indication of its size in relation to the balance of payments. About three-quarters of these military expenditures were incurred by the Defence Department for supplies, services and construction in the countries where American forces were located. The total of United States military *grants* to foreign countries in 1958 was $2,522 million, of which $1,154 million went to Western Europe. The aggregate of all foreign transfers and payments by the United States Government in 1958 was equal to 45 per cent of aggregate private outlay on imports of goods and services plus the net outflow of American private capital.[1]

With the sharp change in relative growth rates in America and Western Europe in the period 1955–62, 'dollar shortage' gave way to 'dollar glut'. The deficit in the overall payments of the United States amounted to $3,400 million in 1958 and $4,000 million in 1959. An important factor in this situation was the growth in American private foreign investment superimposed on the politically determined outflow of government loans and grants. The value of United States direct investment in Europe in 1962 was more than double what it was in 1957 ($8,843 million as against $4,151 million). The increase in the European Common Market countries was from $1,680 million to $3,671 million, and in the United Kingdom from $1,974 million to $3,805 million. There was also a considerable growth in American private investment other than direct investment, i.e. purchases of foreign dollar bonds, other foreign securities and short-term assets; this category of private investment in Western Europe increased from $3,386 million in 1957 to $5,617 million in 1962. American policy to reduce the payments deficit included an investment equaliza-

[1] See Thomas, 'Recent Trends in American Investment in Western Europe', p. 19.

tion tax designed to discourage portfolio investment abroad, and some reductions were made in foreign aid and military expenditures overseas. The weakness of the dollar and the high price of gold on the London market prompted the American authorities to bring into existence in 1961 the gold pool agreement between leading central banks; concerted buying and selling by this official consortium helped to stabilize the gold market.

The end of an epoch

In the third phase, beginning in the early 1960s, the pace of activity was strong in the United States, and the deficits in her balance of payments, aggravated by the effect of the Vietnam War on the capital account, became much worse. Meanwhile, the receiving countries, particularly Germany and Japan, went on expanding their share of world exports and adding to their already huge stock of dollar assets. Between 1959 and 1969 the combined gross national product of the European Economic Community and Japan grew from 49 per cent of that of the United States to 61 per cent. By the first half of 1971 the gold and foreign exchange reserves of Germany ($16·9 billion) and Japan ($10·4 billion) were together well over double those of the United States ($12·5 billion). The periphery's performance had been too much of a good thing. On 15 August 1971, President Nixon made his historic announcement, 'I have directed Secretary Connolly to suspend temporarily the convertibility of the dollar into gold and other reserve assets', and he levied a temporary surcharge of 10 per cent on imports. This momentous change of policy ushered in a new era.

It had been evident for some time that the United States dollar was overvalued in terms of other currencies and that the fundamental disequilibrium was due in part to the piling up of excessive payments surpluses by the periphery, particularly Germany and Japan. It was a glaring example of the basic truth emphasized by Lord Keynes when he presented his plan for an International Clearing Union in 1943. He pointed out that

. . . the world's trading difficulties in the past have not always been due to the improvidence of debtor countries. They may

135

be caused in most acute form if a creditor country is constantly withdrawing international money from circulation and hoarding it, instead of putting it back again into circulation, thus refusing to spend its income from abroad either on goods for home consumption or on investment overseas.[1]

The drastic action by the United States on 15 August 1971 led to an upward revaluation of the major currencies of Europe and that of Japan, and the American dollar was devalued in terms of gold. This introduced a new phase in which it was expected that the official reserve transactions deficit of at least $9·8 billion in the American balance of payments would be substantially reduced and the rate of economic growth in the United States would tend to be higher and that of the periphery lower than in the previous phase.

[1] Lord Keynes, speech delivered in the House of Lords, 18 May 1943, quoted in Harris, ed., *The New Economics: Keynes' Influence on Theory and Public Policy*, p. 362.

Appendix C

Formal statement of the model

Notation

Y	real income
N	population
C	creditor country
D	debtor country
I	investment
r	population growth rate
m	migration
h	population structure (vector)
E	exports (supply)
M	imports (demand)
P	home prices
P_E	export prices (import prices)
g	investment gestation period

We first give a simple version of the model which can later be elaborated.

INVESTMENT AND POPULATION GROWTH FUNCTIONS FOR EACH COUNTRY

In each country, creditor and debtor, investment is a function of population growth rate and population structure, and the population growth rate is a function of migration and population structure, h, which is a vector whose elements are the numbers in various age, sex and marital status groups.

$$I_C = f_1(r_C, h_C) \tag{1}$$

$$I_D = f_2(r_D, h_D) \tag{2}$$

$$r_C = f_3(m, h_C) \tag{3}$$

$$r_D = f_4(m, h_D) \tag{4}$$

This system can be closed if we make assumptions about migration and population structure. We can write migration as a function of relative real income per head and population structure.

$$m = f_5\left(\left[\frac{Y_D}{N_D} - \frac{Y_C}{N_C}\right], h_C, h_D\right) \quad (5)$$

Population structure (h) in each country has a cyclical element in it; at any moment it is a function of an earlier population structure and of intervening migration. Thus,

$$h_C^t = f_6(h_C^{t-\tau}, m_t, m_{t-1}, \ldots m_{t-\tau}) \quad (6)$$

$$h_D^t = f_7(h_D^{t-\tau}, m_t, m_{t-1}, \ldots m_{t-\tau}) \quad (7)$$

We can define N in terms of structure.

Thus,

$N_C = \Sigma\, h_C^i$ where h_C^i is the ith element of the vector h_C (8)

$N_D = \Sigma\, h_D^i$ where h_D^i is the ith element of the vector h_D (9)

Let us forget income for the time being. Export supply depends on investment lagged by the infrastructure gestation period (g), while import demand depends on investment in the importing country. We make P home prices and P_E export prices (import prices). We can write exports as an increasing function of the ratio of export prices to home prices. Then,

$$E_D = f_{10}\left(I_D\left\{t - g_D\right\}, \frac{P_{ED}}{P_D}\right) \quad (10)$$

$$E_C = f_{11}\left(I_C\left\{t - g_C\right\}, \frac{P_{EC}}{P_C}\right) \quad (11)$$

We now make imports (M) an increasing function of real income and a decreasing function of the relevant price ratio.

$$M_D = f_{12}\left(Y_D, \frac{P_{EC}}{P_D}\right) \quad (12)$$

$$M_C = f_{13}\left(Y_C, \frac{P_{ED}}{P_C}\right) \quad (13)$$

Still leaving income aside, we can close this part of the model. We have the identities

$$E_C \equiv M_D \quad (14)$$

$$E_D \equiv M_C \quad (15)$$

As a first approximation, home prices can be written simply as a function (possibly a weighted average) of export and import prices:

$$P_D = f_{16}(P_{ED}, P_{EC}) \tag{16}$$

$$P_C = f_{17}(P_{ED}, P_{EC}) \tag{17}$$

This leaves income which can be written as a function of investment and exports. To handle it properly we should include lags, but as a simplification we may write:

$$Y_C = f_{18}(I_C, E_C) \tag{18}$$

$$Y_D = f_{19}(I_D, E_D) \tag{19}$$

This version of the basic relationship can now be taken a little further. We need the accelerator effect which can be introduced by Y or ΔY. The marginal efficiency of investment is the marginal physical product times a price ratio, i.e. P_E/P. Thus, we rewrite the investment functions as:

$$I_C = f_{1a}\left(r_C, h_C, \Delta Y_C \frac{P_{EC}}{P_C}\right) \tag{1a}$$

$$I_D = f_{2a}\left(r_D, h_D, \Delta Y_D \frac{P_{ED}}{P_D}\right) \tag{2a}$$

Then we have to add:

$$\Delta Y_C = f_{20}(Y_C^t, Y_C^{t-1}, \ldots) \tag{20}$$

$$\Delta Y_D = f_{21}(Y_D^t, Y_D^{t-1}, \ldots) \tag{21}$$

In this model capital formation is 'population-sensitive' not just 'migration-sensitive'. Its ability to generate long swings would seem to depend on g and h, the infrastructure lag and population structure. There are a number of different possible forms of the investment function, particularly with respect to lags, which are conceivable, and the best empirical form can be found only by experimenting. It is proposed as a future development of this work to simulate a complete model, to try out various functions with different parameters and lags so as to see what effects they have on the simulated values of the endogenous variables.

5 Negro Migration and the American Urban Dilemma

After the Civil War the best thing that could have happened to the black workers of the United States would have been a fair opportunity to contribute to satisfying the great demand for labour in the rapidly growing cities of the North and West. They could have participated alongside the millions of European immigrants in each upswing of the long cycle in urbanization; this would have materially raised the real income of the black migrants themselves and conferred benefits indirectly (e.g. through remittances) on those left in the South. The Negroes as an ethnic group could have earned their place like the Irish, the Scandinavians, the Germans, the Jews and the Italians in an expanding economy which permitted a continually changing equilibrium between a succession of very different ethnic groups. That this did not happen is part of the tragic history of racial intolerance.

Gunnar Myrdal, in his classic study published in 1944, pointed out that there was '. . . enough industrial activity, and there could be opportunity for anonymity, as well as a low level of race prejudice, in many of the smaller centres of the North to permit a significant immigration of Negroes. That Negroes have not migrated to these places is as much of a mystery as the relative absence of migration to the West.'[1] He concluded that '. . . much in the Great Migration after 1915 is left unexplained if we do not assume that there was before 1915 *an existing and widening difference in living conditions between South and North which did not express itself in a mass migration simply because the latter did not get a start and become a pattern*'.[2] Since Myrdal wrote, the findings of research on

[1] Myrdal, *An American Dilemma: the Negro Problem and Modern Democracy*, pp. 189–90.   [2] Ibid., p. 193.

140

internal migration have yielded important clues to the solution of the mystery. This chapter presents evidence that in the period between the Civil War and the Immigration Restriction Act of 1924 the ability of the Negro to establish himself in the North was conditioned by the volume of immigration. The outflow of the blacks from the South exhibited a time-pattern which was the opposite of that of the inflow of Europeans and the internal migration of native whites.

THE PATTERN OF NEGRO MIGRATION, 1870–1950

When I examined this subject in an earlier work,[1] my object was to test the general hypothesis that swings in external migration were inverse to swings in internal migration in countries of immigration as well as those of emigration. I happened to use the statistics for Negro migration in the United States as a proxy for

TABLE 5.1

The United States: decennial rates of change in foreign-born population and internal migration of Negroes, 1870–1930

Decade	Rate of increase in foreign-born population* %	Rate of increase in number of Negroes enumerated in the North† %
1870–80	20	36
1880–90	39	14
1890–1900	12	26
1900–10	31	17
1910–20	3	44
1920–30	3	67

Sources:
* U.S. Department of Commerce, *Historical Statistics of the United States, 1789–1945,* p. 32, and † U.S. Department of Commerce, *Negroes in the United States, 1926–1932,* p. 5.

[1] *Migration and Economic Growth,* pp. 130–4.

total internal migration, and I thought I had verified my hypothesis when I found that swings in Negro internal migration were inverse to those in immigration.[1] However, as critics pointed out, in the United States total internal migration (dominated by the movement of whites) moved harmoniously with immigration[2] and so the hypothesis was refuted. Negro migration, far from being a proxy, was itself inverse to the internal migration of whites. This striking fact opened up a promising area of inquiry.

My original thesis rested on the relationship brought out in Table 5.1. The inference from Table 5.1 is that when immigration of foreign workers was in full spate the northward movement of Negroes was at a low ebb and vice versa. The rate of increase in the foreign-born population rose sharply from 20 per cent in 1870–80 to 39 per cent in 1880–90, whereas the growth in the Negro population in the North fell from 36 per cent to 14 per cent. The opposite occurred when we compare 1890–1900 with 1880–1890. During the period 1910–30, when immigration was drastically reduced, first by the World War and then by the Immigration Restriction Act of 1924, an extraordinary increase took place in the number of Negroes enumerated in the North, 44 per cent in 1910–20 and 67 per cent in 1920–30.

Foreign immigrants distributed themselves over the United States very unevenly; there was a marked variation in the degree of concentration in various States over the period 1850–1920. In 1850 the foreign-born comprised 22 per cent of the population of the Pacific States and only 11 per cent in New England: by 1920 New England ranked highest with a proportion of 26 per cent and the Pacific States were third with 20 per cent. The Mountain States began in 1850 with a modest foreign-born element of 6 per cent; in 1870 it had reached 28 per cent, and in 1920 it was down to 14 per cent. These changes over time in the proportion of foreign-born in the populations of different regions reflect important phases in the economic growth of the United States. If we take the spatial distribution over the 48 States as shown in the census of 1920, there is a clear inverse correlation between the

---

[1] *Migration and Economic Growth*, p. 131.
[2] For a criticism see Dorothy S. Thomas's chapter on international migration in Hauser, ed., *Population and World Politics*, p. 152.

proportion of Negroes and that of foreign-born whites in the population.[1]

So far I have merely summarized the argument in *Migration and Economic Growth*. Its validity can be tested by looking at the results of the major research project on population redistribution and economic growth, 1870–1950, which was carried out at the University of Pennsylvania.[2] The data illustrated in fig. 5.1, based on an exhaustive analysis of census sources, leave no doubt about the pattern of Negro migration. Hope T. Eldridge and Dorothy S. Thomas reach the following conclusion about regional rates of urban growth.

> The rates for native whites are closely similar to those for the population as a whole. It is the contrapuntal movement of rates for foreign-born whites and Negroes in the northern regions that is of particular interest. For the North-east, the pattern of fluctuation in the rates of foreign-born whites is inverse to that of Negroes up to 1910–20; there is evidence of some opposition also in the rates of the North Central. *It would be difficult to interpret these findings in terms other than a tendency for the movement of the foreign born into urban areas to have a repressive effect upon the movement of Negroes into the same areas.*[3]

A closer examination reveals that the Negro migrants tended to go to certain specific areas in the North; it was not until the 1940s that the big movement to California took place. The favourite States were New York, New Jersey and Pennsylvania (sub-region N3), Ohio, Indiana, Illinois, Michigan and Wisconsin (sub-region CI) and the District of Columbia. The proportions of all States' gains contributed by the migration of blacks to the above destinations were 76 per cent in 1910–20, 79 per cent in 1920–30, 68 per cent in 1930–40 and 70 per cent in 1940–50, the

[1] For the data on the 48 States see Carpenter, *Immigrants and their Children*, Table 145.
[2] American Philosophical Society, *Population Redistribution and Economic Growth, United States 1870–1950* (Philadelphia), Vol. I (1957) by Lee, Ratner Miller, Brainerd and Easterlin; Vol. II (1960) by Kuznets, Ratner Miller and Easterlin; Vol. III (1964) by Eldridge and Thomas.
[3] Eldridge and Thomas, op. cit., Vol. III, *Demographic Analyses and Interrelations*, p. 224. My italics.

fall in the last two percentages being a reflection of the increasing pull of California. Net migration rates for the native white, the Negroes and the foreign-born white in sub-regions N3 and CI, 1870–1950, are given in Table 5.2.

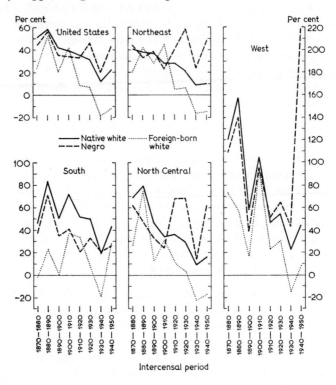

Figure 5.1 Percentage change in urban population, by race and nativity, for the United States and regions, 1870–80 to 1940–50.
Source: Eldridge and Thomas, *Population Redistribution and Economic Growth*, III, p. 223.

In interpreting Table 5.2 we must bear in mind that the migration rate of Negroes is on a much higher *level* than that for foreign-born whites because it is based on the average Negro population whereas the other rate is based on the average *total* population. These figures again demonstrate the inverse relation and the breakthrough of the blacks to the North as from

TABLE 5.2

United States: Net migration rates, sub-regions N₃ and CI, 1870–80 to 1940–50

Decade	Sub-region N3[1]			Sub-region CI[2]		
	Native White *Per 1,000 average native white population*	Negro *Per 1,000 average Negro population*	Foreign-born white *Per 1,000 average total population*	Native white *Per 1,000 average native white population*	Negro *Per 1,000 average Negro population*	Foreign-born white *Per 1,000 average total population*
1870–80	−37	135	45	−65	146	50
1880–90	−20	212	95	−55	91	77
1890–1900	4	382	78	—	195	43
1900–10	−8	272	123	−38	187	60
1910–20	−9	388	43	24	564	41
1920–30	1	485	43	19	524	26
1930–40	−6	169	2	−5	128	−4
1940–50	−33	290	7	−9	407	3

[1] New York, New Jersey and Pennsylvania.
[2] Ohio, Indiana, Illinois, Michigan and Wisconsin.
Source: Eldridge and Thomas, *Population Redistribution and Economic Growth, United States 1870–1950*, Vol. III, pp. 72 and 101.

1910–1920. Significant also is the net outflow of native whites from these areas shown in Table 5.3.[1]

Most of these Northern States were losing white and gaining black population; this was true of Pennsylvania in every decade between 1870–80 and 1940–50, of Ohio, Indiana, Illinois and Wisconsin in at least six decades and of New York in five decades.[2] In contrast, the Southern States of Texas and Virginia had large

TABLE 5.3

United States: decennial net migration of native whites and Negroes, sub-regions N3 and CI, 1870–1950

Decade	Native whites Thousands	Negroes Thousands
1870–80	−815	47
1880–90	−720	64
1890–1900	44	156
1900–10	−644	153
1910–20	256	428
1920–30	396	779
1930–40	−233	324
1940–50	−977	1040

Source: Eldridge and Thomas, op. cit., p. 93.

gains of native whites and large losses of Negroes. There are two factors to be noted here. First, the westward movement was composed largely of native whites. Secondly, immigrants' children born in the United States were an addition to the native population and the size of this element varied from region to region; on the other hand, there was hardly any influx of blacks from abroad. Thus, since the immigrants were to be found mainly in the eastern regions of America and the migration to the West was predominantly native white, the children of the foreign-born tended to

[1] Eldridge and Thomas, op. cit., Vol. III, *Demographic Analyses and Interrelations*, p. 93
[2] A similar process can be seen in the conurbations of England, 1961–6. See Chapter 6, pp. 193–7.

reduce the degree of redistribution of native whites below what it would have been otherwise.[1]

Immigration which had been running at an average of over a million a year between 1910 and 1914 was practically stopped by World War I and there was a dramatic rise in the movement of Negroes into the Northern States. So severe was the shortage of labour that many recruiting agents were sent to the South; for example, the Pennsylvania Railroad could not have carried out its essential maintenance work without bringing to the North many thousands of Negro workers. In the decade 1910–20 net migration into New York, Pennsylvania and New Jersey was 388 per 1,000 of the black population there as compared with 272 per 1,000 in the previous decade, and in Ohio, Indiana, Illinois, Michigan and Wisconsin the increase was even more spectacular, from 187 per 1,000 to 564 per 1,000 (see Table 5.2). When the war was over immigration was resumed on a large scale, and in the five years, 1920–4, no less than 2,775,000 arrived. This last great upsurge was brought to an abrupt end by the passing of the Immigration Restriction Act of 1924.

In contrast to 1901–10 when an average of 600,000 Southern and Eastern Europeans came to America every year, the number admitted between 1925 and 1928 was a mere trickle of 34,000 a year. At last there was a vacuum in the mines, steel works, stock-yards and factories of the North which only the black workers from the South could fill; the number of Negroes enumerated in the North-centre and North-east rose by a million between 1920 and 1930. This tendency has continued ever since and received another powerful impetus during World War II.

What the evidence suggests is that in the sixty years after the end of the Civil war the strong competition of white workers from abroad in a society where the dice was loaded against the Negro set a stern limit to the number of blacks who could obtain employment in the booming urban areas of the North and West, and consequently they suffered relative impoverishment during an era of record advance in the average standard of living of Americans. The invisible hand of the market was no match for the

[1] For a detailed analysis of this see Eldridge and Thomas, op. cit., pp. 98–100.

all too visible hand of discrimination. Hemmed in between the poor whites in the South and the poor whites from Europe in the North, the Negroes found that their only chance of making any headway was at times when the immigration tide was going out. It was not until World War I that they got their first real break, and then came the 1924 Immigration Restriction Act which was to prove of lasting benefit to them.

FERTILITY AND MORTALITY

Since the migration experience of the blacks differed so much from that of the whites, one wonders whether there was also a significant contrast between the course of the fertility and mortality of the two groups. Kuznets found it '. . . particularly noteworthy

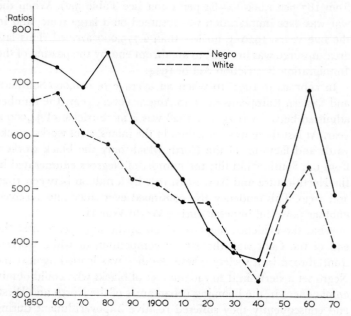

Figure 5.2 Ratio of children 0–4 to women 15–44 in the white and Negro population of the United States, decennially, 1850–1970.
Source: Reynolds Farley, *Growth of the Black Population: a Study of Demographic Trends*, Figure 3–2; U.S. Department of Commerce, Bureau of the Census, *Census of Population 1970*, PC (V2)–I, Table 2.

that additions to the non-white population do not show a rise from the 1890s to the first decade of the twentieth century similar to those in the additions to other sections of the population'.[1] Moreover, '. . . the long swings in the births of non-white population also show a markedly different pattern from those in white population – the former missing the second swing, viz., the larger additions to births during the first decade to decade and a half of the twentieth century'.[2] Finally, '. . . fluctuations in the deaths of the non-white population differ substantially from those of the white, the former declining and the latter rising during the 1890s and the early twentieth century. The difference in the timing pattern is most pronounced after the 1870–1880s and until about World War I.'[3] Kuznets referred to my analysis in *Migration and Economic Growth* and suggested that it might be a key to the explanation of the deviant movement of non-white births, deaths and net increase during the pre-World War I period, since the upswing of the immigration cycle made life harder for the blacks and the downswing of the cycle was an alleviation. In Kuznets' words '. . . this would explain an *inverse* relation between the long swings in the net increase of non-white population and those in the net increase of both native white and foreign-born. The disappearance of this inverse relation during and after World War I would then be associated with the marked drop in the flow of immigrants from abroad.'[4]

To understand these intriguing patterns, we must look at the long-run picture. For fertility this is given in fig. 5.2, based on the number of children 0–4 per 1,000 women 15–44 at each census. For mortality there is no reliable composite index for the nineteenth century, but various estimates have been made from the partial information which does exist.[5] Annual growth rates in

[1] Kuznets, 'Long Swings in the Growth of Population and in Related Economic Variables', p. 26.
[2] Ibid., pp. 26–7.   [3] Ibid., p. 27.   [4] Ibid., p. 31.
[5] Life tables for Negroes were not calculated until the beginning of this century, and at first they were confined to people enumerated in the Death Registration Area comprising ten northern cities and the District of Columbia. The Negroes in that area were nearly all urban dwellers, whereas in the United States as a whole in 1910 as many as 77 per cent of Negroes were country dwellers.

TABLE 5.4

United States: white and Negro population at each census and annual growth rate, 1790–1970

Dates	Population (000) White	Negro	Average annual growth rates for interdecennial period White %	Negro %	Proportion of total Population Negro %
1790	3,172	757	–	–	19
1800	4,306	1,002	3·06	2·80	19
1810	5,862	1,378	3·08	3·19	19
1820	7,867	1,772	2·94	2·51	18
1830	10,537	2,329	2·92	2·73	18
1840	14,196	2,874	2·98	2·10	17
1850	19,553	3,639	3·20	2·36	16
1860	26,923	4,442	3·20	2·00	14
1870	33,589	4,880	2·22	·94	13
1880	43,403	6,581	2·56	2·99	13
1890	55,101	7,389	2·39	1·25	12
1900	66,809	8,834	1·92	1·79	12
1910	81,732	9,828	2·01	1·07	11
1920	94,821	10,463	1·48	·63	10
1930	110,287	11,891	1·51	1·28	10
1940	118,215	12,866	·70	·79	10
1950	134,942	15,042	1·33	1·56	10
1960	158,832	18,871	1·63	2·27	11
1970	177,612	22,673	1·12	1·84	11

Sources: U.S. Department of Commerce, Bureau of the Census, *Historical Statistics of the United States: Colonial Times to 1957*, Series A, 95–122; *Census of Population: 1960*, PC(1)–1B, Table 44; *Census of Population, 1970*, Table 2.

decennial periods for the white and the black population from 1790 to 1970 are shown in Table 5.4. Intensive research by demographers suggests the following interpretation.[1]

[1] I have benefited greatly from the authoritative work of Farley, *Growth of the Black Population: a Study of Demographic Trends*. My thanks are due to the author and publisher for their kind permission to reproduce Table 5.4 and fig. 5.2.

In the initial stage, which covered most of the nineteenth century up to the 1870s, the mortality of the Negroes was very high but their fertility was even higher, and it is estimated that the population grew by well over 2 per cent per annum (see Table 5.4). The censuses of 1910 and 1940 contain information on the number of live children born to women who had at some time been married. On the basis of the information relating to Negroes, Reynolds Farley found that '. . . two-thirds of the women who survived to be enumerated bore at least five children and, on the average, each had seven children. Such high numbers of children support the view that Negro fertility was near a biological maximum during much of the nineteenth century.'[1] Fig. 5.2 shows that the ratio of children 0–4 to women 15–44 for Negroes fell steeply from a very high level of 750 in 1880 to well under 400 in 1940; the decline in the ratio for whites was more gradual and by the 1920s and 1930s there was very little difference between the fertility of the two groups. The evidence about mortality shows that the expectation of life for blacks in the South in 1930 was only slightly higher than it had been in 1860. The annual rate of growth of the black population in the decade of the Great Depression was only 0·79 per cent.

Here we have a demographic cycle different from C. P. Blacker's 'high stationary' phase (high birth rate and high death rate) followed by the 'early expanding' phase (high birth rate and lower, or falling, death rate) and then the 'late stationary' (declining birth rate and death rate, with the latter consistently lower than the former).[2] Why did the Negro population have this unique experience up to the 1940s? Reynolds Farley made a thorough analysis of this fundamental question, and reached significant conclusions. The steep decline in the fertility of the blacks between about 1880 and the 1930s cannot be attributed to changes in family patterns or to the practice of birth control.[3] It is only since the beginning of the 1940s that contraceptives have been widely used by Negroes, and yet between 1940 and 1960 their fertility went up sharply (see fig. 5.2). A factor which appears to explain much of the long-period fall in fertility is a

[1] Ibid., p. 57.   [2] Blacker, 'Stages in Population Growth'.
[3] See Farley, op. cit., Chapters 6 and 8.

change in the physical ability of Negroes to have children, i.e., their fecundity. Farley demonstrates the high incidence of foetal deaths and fertility-inhibiting diseases such as pellagra, gonorrhoea and syphilis in the South up to the 1930s,[1] and he suggests that the '. . . fluctuations in childlessness reflect changes in fecundity rather than intentional changes in planned family size'.[2]

The demographic cycle which we have outlined cannot be explained except in terms of what was happening to the Southern economy. For several decades after the Civil War the South-east of America was seriously over-populated and the living conditions of many blacks were deteriorating. After the early 1890s the deprivations of the boll weevil had a calamitous effect. In the sixty years before the Great Depression of the 1930s, the acreage devoted to agriculture in the South-east contracted and the yield of cotton and tobacco per acre was stationary, but the labour force on the farms almost doubled. The south was in the grip of a creeping Malthusian crisis,[3] and there was hardly any safety-valve. The inability of blacks in large numbers to escape to gainful employment in the North, except to some extent when immigration was waning, condemned them to languish in an over-populated depressed area; this led to intensified population pressure in the South, increasing poverty with consequent high mortality and lower fecundity.[4]

The way it worked out was that, when the safety-valve of out-migration was opening, the forces keeping up the death rate and reducing fecundity in the South were weakened; the fact that the mortality of blacks was greater and their fertility lower in the North than in the South could not have much countervailing effect because the national rates were dominated by the vast majority who were in the rural South.[5]

[1] Ibid., pp. 208–33.
[2] Ibid., p. 226.　　　　　　　　　[3] See Myrdal, op. cit., pp. 230–50.
[4] Alan Sweezy, in an interesting paper, has attempted to refute the proposition that fertility varies positively with economic conditions. He argues that changes in fertility have been mainly determined by changes in attitudes. 'The Economic Explanation of Fertility Changes in the United States', pp. 255–67. The evidence for the Negro population runs contrary to his argument.
[5] This is borne out by components of difference in an analysis of the

Migration to the North was a necessary but not sufficient condition for an improvement in the living standard and prospects of Negroes. There also needed to be fair competition in the labour market, adequate welfare provision (including education), and an effective social ladder. It was not likely that these conditions could be fulfilled quickly and so the growing movement of blacks to the cities in the 1940s and 1950s was accompanied by a big increase in broken families, high unemployment and general disillusion-

TABLE 5.5

United States: decennial net migration of native whites and Negroes, sub-regions N3 and CI, 1870–1950

Education level attained	Number of children ever born to all women (married or unmarried) 35–9 years old, by level of education (based on the 1960 census)	
	Non-white	*White*
Completed elementary school	3·0	2·8
4 years of high school	2·3	2·3
4 years of college	1·7	2·2
5 years or more of college	1·2	1·6

Source: New York Times Company, *Report of the National Advisory Commission on Civil Disorders*, p. 239.

decline in the ratio of children 0–4 to women 15–44 for the black population, 1910–40, from 519 to 368. Farley shows that this total change of −151 was attributable as follows: fertility rates in North and West −3, fertility rates in urban South −11, fertility rates in rural South −80, change in distribution of population −78, and interaction of factors +21. (Farley, op. cit., p. 113.) Farley comments: 'The decrease in childbearing by rural Southern Negroes played a role every bit as important as urbanization in bringing down the national fertility rate. Had there been no shift to urban residence, there still would have been a large decline in Negro fertility. This means that the long term decline in Negro fertility must have been the result of the reduced childbearing of those Negro women who remained on the farms of the South.' (Ibid., p. 114.)

ment.[1] Nevertheless, real progress has been achieved, as we shall see in the next section. The Negro infant mortality rate, which was as high as 83 per 1,000 births in 1937, was down to 42 by 1956, and it was further reduced to 35 by 1967. Between 1937 and 1956 the overall Negro death rate, adjusted for age composition, fell from 19 per 1,000 to 10, but there was hardly any change in the 1960s.

TABLE 5.6

United States: regional distribution of black population, 1940–1970

Region	1940		1950		1960		1970	
	Thousand	%	*Thousand*	%	*Thousand*	%	*Thousand*	%
North-East	1,370	10·6	2,018	13·4	3,028	16·0	4,342	19·2
North-Central	1,420	11·0	2,228	14·8	3,446	18·3	4,572	20·2
West	171	1·3	571	3·8	1,086	5·8	1,695	7·5
South	9,905	77·0	10,225	68·0	11,312	59·9	12,064	53·2
United States	12,866	100·0	15,042	100·0	18,872	100·0	22,673	100·0

Source: United States Population Censuses, 1940–1970.

In the 1950s the fertility of the blacks rose far more than that of the whites, and their population grew by 2·3 per cent per annum – almost as fast as it did in the 1840s; in the 1960s, with the widespread use of the pill, the Negro birth rate declined with that of the whites, but less sharply (fig. 5.2), bringing the annual rate of growth down to 1·7 per cent in 1967–9. A most significant portent in its bearing on the future is that Negro women with several years of college education are having fewer children than white women with similar education, as seen in Table 5.5.

As far as fertility and mortality are concerned, it looks as if the forces making for convergence between the experience of the two groups will become stronger as time goes on.

THE IMPACT ON THE CITIES

The regional distribution of the rapidly growing black population, 1940–1970, is set out in Table 5.6 (to the nearest thousand).

[1] See Moynihan, *The Negro Family: the Case for National Action.*

In these 30 years the number of Negroes went up by 77 per cent, making it just over 11 per cent of the population of the United States; in 1970 53·2 per cent of the 22,673,000 Negroes were in the South, 39·4 per cent in the North and 7·5 per cent in the West.

TABLE 5.7

Estimated Negro population of large American cities, 1970 (nearest thousand)

City	Total Population	Negro Population	Negro %	Ranking according to F.B.I. crime index (*August 1970*)
	(1)	(2)	(3)	(4)
New York	8,100,000	1,500,000	19	New York
Chicago	3,610,000	1,150,000	32	Los Angeles
Los Angeles	3,000,000	700,000	23	Chicago
Philadelphia	2,200,000	700,000	32	Detroit
Detroit	1,700,000	800,000	47	Washington D.C.
Houston	1,140,000	310,000	27	Baltimore
Baltimore	920,000	432,000	47	Houston
Cleveland	805,000	305,000	38	San Francisco
Washington D.C.	840,000	574,000	68	Cleveland
Milwaukee	800,000	146,000	18	St Louis
Dallas	800,000	200,000	25	Dallas
San Francisco	750,000	126,000	17	Philadelphia
St Louis	700,000	320,000	46	Boston

Sources: Congressional Quarterly Inc. and Federal Bureau of Investigation. The material in this table is taken from the *New York Times Encyclopedia Almanac 1971*, pp. 276 and 290, by kind permission of the New York Times Co., New York.

The net migration out of the South was 1,599,000 in 1940–50, 1,456,000 in 1950–60, and 1,400,000 in 1960–70; and yet, because of high fertility in the South, its population went up by just over 2 million.

The effect on the large cities of the North and West is vividly apparent from the figures in Table 5.7. The largest totals of Negroes are in New York (1,500,000), Chicago (1,150,000), Detroit (800,000), Los Angeles (700,000), and Philadelphia

(700,000); the highest proportions of the population are in Washington D.C. (68 per cent), Detroit (47 per cent), Baltimore (47 per cent), St Louis (46 per cent) and Chicago and Philadelphia (32 per cent). Column 4 of Table 5.7 ranks the cities in accordance with the crime index of the Federal Bureau of Investigation.

Amid the welter of discussion on the crisis of the cities, one is staggered by the complexity of what is happening. I propose merely to refer to one or two findings of expert research which refute some popularly held beliefs. How much and what kind of displacement of population has taken place in the cities? This question can be answered by examining the census results,[1] and this has been thoroughly done by Karl and Alma Taeuber for the period 1955–60. They examined the figures for the Standard Metropolitan Statistical Areas (SMSAs), which correspond to conurbations in Britain; each of these is divided into the Central City and the Outer Ring. The data are based on the answers to the question regarding place of residence on 1 April 1955 and at the time of the census in April 1960.

We shall first deal separately with the movements of the white population set out in Table 5.8.

According to expectations, there was a massive efflux of whites from central cities to the outer rings; in eight of the cities, for every six persons who moved out only one came in. New York City stands out by having a huge influx of immigrants from abroad (e.g. Puerto Ricans). There was also a considerable movement into all outer rings from other metropolitan areas.

Among the striking things revealed is that movements of young men joining the armed forces have a considerable influence in exaggerating the outflow to the suburbs in some metropolitan areas. For example, '. . . one-third of men in the labor force among migrants (regardless of origin) to the rings of Philadelphia,

[1] Unfortunately, even the census statistics have serious deficiencies. It has been estimated that 10 per cent of the Negroes were not counted in 1960, and in 1950, according to Ansley J. Coale, as many as one in five of the non-white males were not covered ('The Population of the United States in 1950 classified by Age, Sex and Color – a Revision of Census Figures', p. 44). Many of these would have been migrants. There is also the high number of those who failed to answer the questions on socio-economic characteristics.

TABLE 5.8

White population of U.S. Metropolitan Areas by migration status, 1955–60
(Numbers in thousands)

Receiving Area	Total population ages 5 and over	In-migrants from:				Movers, 1955 residence not reported
		Ring to central city	Other SMSA	Non-metro. area	Abroad	
(1)	(2)	(3)	(4)	(5)	(6)	(7)
Central Cities						
New York	6,096·1	54·6	124·8	40·3	211·8	116·3
Los Angeles	2,172·5	172·8	256·6	88·0	66·0	57·3
Chicago	2,462·6	47·3	71·1	56·9	57·7	67·5
Philadelphia	1,337·8	23·6	34·7	13·3	14·3	24·4
Detroit	1,079·3	39·0	24·4	17·5	13·3	15·6
San Francisco	813·6	37·4	73·5	32·1	28·4	23·0
Boston	573·0	24·8	25·5	12·4	10·7	19·1
Pittsburgh	456·8	20·2	11·8	6·9	3·2	8·8
St Louis	484·6	15·2	13·3	22·5	3·3	13·8
Washington	324·1	14·1	38·5	21·6	14·2	14·7
Cleveland	558·7	19·8	25·7	24·6	12·1	8·6
Baltimore	555·6	13·8	18·4	13·0	4·7	12·0
		Central city to ring				
Rings						
New York	2,456·5	410·9	91·6	33·5	34·7	48·2
Los Angeles	3,320·6	348·7	418·2	191·6	69·9	63·9
Chicago	2,268·2	355·5	146·8	105·9	21·3	38·2
Philadelphia	1,940·9	167·5	139·4	56·9	21·3	21·2
Detroit	1,730·5	260·2	77·6	52·7	17·5	20·2
San Francisco	1,383·6	124·4	180·0	93·8	33·1	23·3
Boston	1,669·4	80·6	87·7	42·9	20·8	26·4
Pittsburgh	1,550·4	61·8	50·1	37·4	6·7	14·1
St Louis	1,077·0	130·1	54·6	58·2	7·5	16·9
Washington	1,002·0	88·2	143·2	83·0	41·4	16·3
Cleveland	812·0	142·6	49·9	26·7	7·4	6·1
Baltimore	644·0	106·2	48·9	32·1	8·8	11·3

Source: Karl and Alma Taeuber, 'White Migration and Socio-economic Differences between Cities and Suburbs', p. 720.

Washington and Baltimore were in the armed forces in 1960'.[1] Moreover, the classification of the migrants by socio-economic categories disproved the commonly held notion that those who go from cities to suburbs are people of high status while those who move the other way have a low status. The three basic findings of the authors are important.

> City-to-ring and ring-to-city migrants are highly similar with regard to average measures of educational and occupational status. Migrants of a given origin going to the city tend to resemble those going to the ring. Migrants, whether to city or ring, tend to be of higher educational and occupational status than the non-migrant population.[2]

We now turn to a similar analysis of the non-white population, and since nearly all these migrants went to the central cities the SMSA totals will serve the purpose (see Table 5.9). The important point emerging is that in the northern metropolitan areas half the in-migrants come from other similar areas where they have had urban experience: this is true of only one in three in the South. The picture of the black migrant as the poor oppressed rural proletariat escaping to the city hardly applies any longer to the majority. A special analysis of city-to-ring movements brings out once again the side effect of the military draft in creating a phoney rise in suburbanization; '. . . about half of the men in the labor force moving from our SMSAs to the suburban ring of another metropolitan area were in the armed forces. Military-connected migration also accounts for much of the movement from metropolitan to non-metropolitan places.'[3]

Most striking are the findings on occupational and educational characteristics; recent non-white migrants from the South living in the North had median educational levels on a par with those of non-whites born in the North. Contrary to what is usually believed, Negro in-migrants in 1955–60 had a much higher average socio-economic status than the Negroes living in a number of the big

---

[1] Karl and Alma Taeuber, op. cit., p. 725.   [2] Ibid., p. 727.
[3] Karl and Alma Taeuber, 'The Changing Character of Negro Migration', p. 435.

TABLE 5.9

United States: non-white population by migration status, 1955–60 (In thousands)

Standard metropolitan statistical areas	Total population age 5+	Total in-migrants	In-migrants from: Other SMSAs	Non-metro-politan areas	Abroad	Total out-migrants	Moved 1955, residence not reported
New York	1,129·7	101·7	37·5	39·4	24·8	50·0	48·6
Chicago	777·8	68·1	28·2	35·9	4·1	39·7	59·4
Detroit	486·6	25·5	13·6	10·4	1·4	30·1	16·3
Cleveland	222·8	19·9	10·7	8·3	0·8	12·0	7·1
Philadelphia	589·9	37·4	18·3	15·8	3·4	22·6	18·5
St Louis	252·7	14·1	5·5	7·9	0·6	14·7	10·9
Washington	429·5	44·5	18·4	20·6	5·5	22·2	21·6
Baltimore	328·3	21·6	8·8	11·3	1·5	13·2	12·8
New Orleans	228·1	11·2	3·0	7·6	0·6	14·3	5·2
Atlanta	199·1	10·8	3·1	7·4	0·4	11·5	4·5
Birmingham	190·1	8·9	3·0	5·7	0·3	15·3	1·8
Memphis	193·2	12·7	2·4	10·1	0·2	15·8	3·0
Houston	210·6	20·5	6·8	13·1	0·6	13·1	6·5

Source: Karl and Alma Taeuber, 'The Changing Character of Negro Migration', p. 431.

conurbations. Our authors' general conclusion is worth quoting in full.

> Very likely a high status intermetropolitan stream of Negro migrants always existed, but its relative importance has increased substantially in recent years owing to the rapid urbanization of the Negro population. We have found that it is in-migrants of non-metropolitan origin who most nearly resemble the stereotype of the socioeconomically depressed migrant. It seems reasonable that, as this component declines and the inter-metropolitan component increases in relative importance, the status of the total in-migrant group would rise. As the character of the Negro population has changed from that of a disadvantaged rural population to a largely metropolitan population of rising social and economic status, Negro migration should increasingly manifest patterns similar to those found among the white population.[1]

Thus, we may conclude that trends in migration as well as fertility and mortality for the Negro population may be converging towards those for the whites. If this is so, it has important implications for the future.

ASSIMILATION OR POLARIZATION?

Chronologically, the wave of Negro in-migrants to the North and West after World War II is the sixth in a succession of immigration waves since the Irish-German one in 1845–54. The fundamental question is whether it is so different in kind from its predecessors that the mechanism of absorption can no longer work.

Nathan Glazer and Daniel P. Moynihan, in the introduction to the second edition of their remarkable book, *Beyond the Melting Pot*, found reason for doubt and disappointment when they looked back in 1970 at the basic hypothesis of their first edition (1963). They had assumed that in New York City '. . . the larger American experience of the Negro, based on slavery and repres-

[1] Karl and Alma Taeuber, 'The Changing Character of Negro Migration', p. 442.

sion in the South, would be overcome, as the Negroes joined the rest of society, in conflict and accommodation, as an ethnic group'.[1] But they had to admit that it didn't happen.

The experience of Negroes in New York since the great migration fifty years ago has had a great deal in it, good and bad. If one compared it with the first fifty years of the Irish, the Italians, and the Jews, we are convinced that there would be enough in that comparison to justify an ethnic rather than a racial or an 'internally colonized' self-image. But the arts of politics, as exercised in the nation and the city, were insufficient to prevent a massive move toward what must be, for the nation and the city, a more damaging entity. The failure is a complex one.[2]

The mills of ethnic absorption, like the mills of God, grind slowly, but they don't grind exceeding small; a long sense of historical perspective is needed to judge their effectiveness. After well over a century of assimilation, the differences between, say, the Irish Americans and the WASPs (the white Anglo-Saxon Protestants) are not insignificant, so much so that the analogy of the melting pot seems hardly appropriate. Indeed, before considering the prospects of the Negroes, one might look at the experience of the millions of destitute Irish who came to America after the great famine. Like the Negroes, they were escaping from a caste system and an agricultural economy undergoing a long-drawn-out Malthusian crisis; they knew from bitter experience what it meant to be 'internally colonized' and, according to J. E. Cairnes, 'not far from one in five of the multitudes who swarmed across the Atlantic had been driven by positive physical violence from his home'.[3] In their new country these post-1845 immigrants found a big generation gap between themselves and the old stock going back to the Revolution; in New York there had been a long tradition of keeping Irish Catholics out of

---

[1] Glazer and Moynihan, *Beyond the Melting Pot: The Negroes, Puerto Ricans, Jews, Italians and Irish of New York City*, p. xiii.

[2] Ibid., p. xiv.

[3] Cairnes, 'Fragments on Ireland' (1866), in *Political Essays*, p. 193.

political life. They had to face their full share of discrimination[1] and, as with all ethnic groups, there was a great deal of residential segregation.

Very few of the Irish-born managed to obtain jobs of high status. The proportion in the professional class was as low as 0·8 per cent in 1870 and 1·3 per cent in 1890, and even by 1900 it was still only 1·6 per cent as compared with 4·3 per cent of the British-born. At the other end of the social scale the proportion of the Irish-born who were servants was 15·1 per cent in 1900 as against 4·1 per cent of the British-born.[2] In some occupations the Irish had a very strong footing; in 1910 they accounted for 18 per cent of America's coachmen and footmen, 12 per cent of the labourers in public service, and 11 per cent of the policemen.[3] For half a century the progress of the first-generation Irish up the social ladder had been extremely slow; it was their sons and daughters who found the doors of opportunity opening to them. In 1900 4·8 per cent of the second-generation Irish were in the professions, not much lower than the 6·6 per cent of the second-generation British, whereas the proportion in the servant class was down to 4·8 per cent, not much above the 3·2 per cent of the second-generation British. At the turn of the century, as the second-generation Irish and other Northern Europeans were occupying the better-class occupations, the great influx of Italians and Eastern Europeans was entering the unskilled sector of the labour market, and in the long run many of their children would rise in the social scale.

The history of successive ethnic groups shows how American society was able to evolve a remarkable social device for maintaining a tolerable equilibrium in situations which often looked impossible; '. . . there are many groups; coalitions form and reform; positions in the pecking order shift; there is a rhetoric of

[1] Brown, *Social Discrimination against the Irish in the United States* (mimeographed).
[2] The full analysis from which the figures in this paragraph are taken is to be found in my *Migration and Economic Growth*, Chapter IX, 'The Social Ladder in the United States', pp. 147–52.
[3] Ibid., p. 152. In New York City it was recently estimated that 54 per cent of the Catholics in Brooklyn have relatives or close friends in the police force. (Glazer and Moynihan, op. cit., p. lxxiv.)

civility and celebration'.[1] Is this system going to fail now that the turn of the Negro has come? The overriding threat is the age-old powerful force of racial discrimination, different in kind from ethnic antagonism. W. E. B. Du Bois, describing conditions in Philadelphia in 1899, declared that

> . . . the industrial condition of the Negro cannot be considered apart from the great fact of race prejudice – infinite and shadowy as that phrase may be. It is certain that, while industrial cooperation among the groups of a great city population is very difficult under ordinary circumstances, here it is rendered more difficult and in some respects almost impossible by the fact that nineteen-twentieths of the population have in many cases refused to cooperate with the other twentieth, even when the cooperation means life to the latter and great advantage to the former. In other words one of the great postulates of the science of economics – that men will seek their economic advantage – is in this case untrue, because in many cases men will not do this if it involves association, even in a casual and business way, with Negroes. And this fact must be taken account of in all judgments as to the Negro's economic progress.[2]

If market forces had been allowed to work, real gains would have accrued both in the middle- and high-status groups and to the Negroes in the lowest stratum, even though there was marked residential segregation. Race prejudice was in direct conflict with the American creed and the principles of free enterprise, and this forced the Negro to turn in upon himself. In the words of a historian of Negro thought, '. . . urbanization served as the chief basis of the new group life which Du Bois and others perceived as developing and which formed the basis of the Dream of Black Metropolis in Chicago and elsewhere; which created a new race consciousness, a new racial solidarity and self-reliance, a new middle class that depended for its support upon the Negro community, and ultimately the cultural flowering of the Harlem Renaissance.'[3]

[1] Moynihan, 'On Ethnicity'.
[2] Du Bois, *The Philadelphia Negro*, pp. 145–6.
[3] Meier, *Negro Thought in America, 1880–1915*, p. 276.

TABLE 5.10

Occupational distribution of non-white males and females in the United States (outside the South), 1940 and 1960

Occupational Grade	Non-white males in U.S.A. (outside the South)			
	1940 (000)	1960 (000)	1940 (%)	1960 (%)
Total labour force	1,030	2,023		
Unemployed	327	210		
Total employed	702	1,812	100·0	100·0
Professional	21	83	3·1	4·8
Farmers	35	19	5·2	1·1
Managers	27	50	4·0	2·9
Clerical	37	165	5·4	9·4
Craftsmen	48	195	7·1	11·2
Operatives	115	444	16·9	25·5
Private household workers	25	12	3·7	0·7
Service workers	178	269	26·2	15·4
Farm labourers	44	32	6·5	1·8
Other labourers	144	271	21·1	15·6
Not reported	5	203	0·7	11·7

	Non-white females in U.S.A. (outside the South)			
Total labour force	501	1,261		
Unemployed	125	124		
Total employed	375	1,137	100·0	100·0
Professional	14	82	3·7	7·2
Farmers	3	2	0·9	0·2
Managers	5	13	1·2	1·2
Clerical	14	180	3·8	15·9
Craftsmen	1	11	0·4	0·9
Operatives	44	206	12·0	18·1
Private household workers	212	259	57·5	22·8
Service workers	59	236	16·1	20·8
Farm labourers	2	5	0·6	0·4
Other labourers	11	12	2·9	1·0
Not reported	3	130	0·8	11·4

Source: Horace Hamilton, 'The Negro leaves the South', pp. 288–91.

The race factor is important but it is by no means the whole story. Even if it had been absent, the Negroes would still have faced formidable handicaps. By the time their turn came, there was much less demand for unskilled and blue-collar labour than there had been in the pre-1913 era when millions of unskilled European immigrants had built the infrastructure of American cities. There has been a marked shift towards craft and white-collar skills which the vast majority of the Negroes have been unable to acquire. Circumstances had also changed in that there was no longer much scope for economic advancement through political patronage. When the big cities were being built, powerful political machines held out substantial economic prizes to members of the older ethnic groups in exchange for support at the polls. 'By the time the Negroes arrived, the situation had altered dramatically. The great wave of public building had virtually come to an end; reform groups were beginning to attack the political machines; the machines were no longer so powerful or so well equipped to provide jobs and other favors'.[1] In many cities the areas where the blacks are concentrated are dominated by politicians belonging to the older ethnic groups, and this is a cause of bitter conflict.

In these unpromising circumstances, what progress has the Negro been able to make in scaling the socio-economic ladder? The record for the non-white population in the United States outside the South between 1940 and 1960 is shown in Table 5.10.

One of the snags about these figures is that there is no information on over a tenth of those enumerated in 1960. Nevertheless, they are the best source available and we can draw some firm inferences. Starting at the bottom, we can group private household and service workers, labourers, and the 'unknown', and the comparison with the whites outside the South and in the South is as seen in Table 5.11.

Non-white females outside the South have been the most successful in moving out of low-status occupations, even though more than half of them still remained there in 1960; similarly, non-white males have done relatively better than whites outside the

[1] New York Times Company, *Report of the National Advisory Commission on Civil Disorders*, p. 279.

165

South and much better than non-whites in the South. In the North and West the non-white population is clearly involved in the national shift away from unskilled labour, whereas in the South this tendency is much less evident.

The number of non-white males employed in skilled jobs as craftsmen went up three-fold, bringing the percentage up to 11·2 as compared with 20·5 for the whites, and the increase in the middle-class white-collar occupations (mainly clerical) was as

TABLE 5.11

United States: Proportion of whites and non-whites classified as unskilled in the South and the rest of the country, 1940 and 1960

	South		Outside the South	
	1940 %	1960 %	1940 %	1960 %
White male	21·8	16·3	21·2	17·8
Non-white male	55·9	53·6	58·2	45·2
White female	23·9	21·3	26·7	24·0
Non-white female	85·1	76·8	77·9	56·4

Source: Horace Hamilton, op. cit., p. 293.

much as seven-fold, the percentage for non-white males reaching 9·4 with that of whites being 14·6. At the top of the pyramid, in the professional, technical and kindred grades, the proportion of non-white males rose from 3·1 per cent to 4·8 per cent and that of females from 3·7 per cent to 7·2 per cent. Undeniably there *was* vertical mobility between 1940 and 1960, but it was only a beginning; it is consistent with the observed rise in the average socio-economic status of Negro migrants. In the North and West in this period the amount of total new employment was 14·5 million, of which non-whites accounted for 13·8 per cent; 5·3 million of these new jobs were in the unskilled category and a quarter of these were occupied by non-white workers; additional employment in the professional grades amounted to 8·3 million, of which non-whites accounted for only 6·2 per cent.

It must be noted that the extent to which Negroes have been able to enter professions where they are competing with whites is more apparent than real. In examining the situation revealed in the 1930 census, Myrdal observed that '. . . the poverty of the Negro people represents a general limitation of opportunity for Negro businessmen and professionals. Since they are excluded from the white market, it becomes important for them to hold the Negro market as a monopoly. The monopoly over the Negro market of teachers, preachers, undertakers, beauticians and others is generally respected.'[1] In 1960 the picture had not changed very much.[2] Of the 115,683 Negro males classified as professionals 30 per cent were teachers in schools or colleges, 11 per cent clergymen, 5 per cent musicians or music teachers, and just under 3 per cent funeral directors: only 3·6 per cent were engineers as against 19·4 per cent of the white professionals and 15·7 per cent of those of Japanese origin. In the case of Negro females classified as professionals, as many as 60 per cent were teachers in schools or colleges as compared with 44 per cent of white female professionals. Of the latter, it is interesting to find that 21 per cent were professional nurses, the corresponding proportion for Negro females being 18 per cent. As the black population has grown relatively to the white and its average standard of living has risen, the scope for inside employment of certain classes of professionals has become comparatively larger: a significant breakthrough into the white economy has yet to take place.

A summary view of the distribution of the American population by race and socio-economic status is given in Table 5.12 on the basis of the new socio-economic measures used in the 1960 census.[3] In the top quartile are 20 per cent of the whites, 3·2 per cent of the blacks, and 13·8 per cent of other races: in the bottom quartile are 12·9 per cent of the whites, 45·4 per cent of the blacks and 25·2 per cent of other races.

No one who has read the Report of the National Advisory

[1] Myrdal, op. cit., pp. 304–5.
[2] See U.S. Department of Commerce, *U.S. Census of Population 1960. Special Reports. Characteristics of Professional Workers*, pp. 9 and 10.
[3] See U.S. Department of Commerce, *U.S. Census of Population 1960. Special Reports. Socio-economic Status*, p. xiii.

Commission on Civil Disorders (the Kerner Report) can have any illusions about the plight of the cities, with their eroding tax

TABLE 5.12

United States: distribution of whites, Negroes and other races by socio-economic status, 1960

Race	Total, all scores (*thousands*)	Socio-economic status in 1960			
		75–99 (*high*)	50–74	25–49	0–24 (*low*)
Total population	179,311	32,557	62,282	54,987	29,486
Race:					
White	158,814	31,738	59,191	47,365	20,520
Negro	18,859	595	2,599	7,111	8,556
Other races	1,637	226	489	511	411
% Distribution					
Total population	100·0	18·2	34·7	30·7	16·4
Race:					
White	100·0	20·0	37·3	29·9	12·9
Negro	100·0	3·2	13·8	37·7	45·4
Other races	100·0	13·8	29·8	31·2	25·2

Source: U.S. Department of Commerce, *U.S. Census of Population 1960. Special Reports. Socio-economic Status,* p. xiii.

base, mounting cost of welfare, and the increase in crime and racial conflict. At the same time there can be no doubt that a growing number of Negro migrants made a real advance during the 1960s. The Kerner Report found that

. . . the Negro 'upper-income' group is expanding rapidly and achieving sizeable income gains. In 1966, 28 per cent of all Negro families received incomes of $7000 or more, compared with 55 per cent of white families. This was double the proportion of Negroes receiving comparable incomes in 1960 and four times greater than the proportion receiving such incomes in 1947. *Moreover, the proportion of Negroes employed in high-skill, high-status and well-paying jobs rose faster than comparable proportions among whites from 1960 to 1966.*[1]

[1] New York Times Company, *Report of the National Advisory Commission on Civil Disorders,* p. 251. (My italics.)

According to a sample survey of New York adults in 1963,[1] the proportions engaged in professional employment in various groups were as follows: Negroes 9·5 per cent; Puerto Ricans 3 per cent; Italians (first and second generation) 9 per cent; Irish (first and second generation) 9 per cent; foreign-born Jews 10·5 per cent; native-born Jews 21·5 per cent; and white Protestants 22 per cent. The dark side of all this is that the increasing Negro middle class widens the gap between the haves and the have-nots; about two-thirds of the lowest income group – or about a fifth of all Negroes – remain in dire poverty, many of them in the worst parts of the central cities.

It took many decades for the Irish immigrants of the nineteenth century to escape from poverty, and it is only after three or four generations that Eastern and Southern European immigrants from rural backgrounds have been able to make their way out of the lowest occupations. What the Negroes in the North and West have achieved in two or three decades is not to be underrated when we consider the long haul which was the lot of previous ethnic groups.

The evidence reviewed in this chapter suggests that the mass migration of Negroes has begun to bring about a convergence of the trends in their fertility, mortality, internal migration, and occupational distribution towards the white pattern. The black population is much younger than the white; in 1969 the median age of Negroes was 21·1 years as against 29·3 for whites. It is estimated that by 1985 less than a third of the expected increase of 8·7 million in the black population of central cities will have been due to in-migration: from now on the main dynamic will be natural increase. The stage is set in the Northern cities for high growth and strong demographic echo effects in the future. American society, facing human problems of the most appalling complexity, has the resilience to overcome them in the long run. Assimilation according to the ethnic model must triumph over the ideological and other forces making for racial polarization. In Myrdal's phrase, 'separate can never be equal'.

[1] Glazer and Moynihan, op. cit., p. lvi.

6 Migration and Regional Growth in Britain

The new evidence on British regional building cycles in Chapter 2 showed that the two regions which did not conform to the national pattern were London and South Wales. It would be interesting to do a separate analysis of London with reference to long swings in the growth of the Atlantic economy, but this would be a major work in itself. Since the Welsh economy was based entirely on coal exports, its fluctuations were a direct index of those of the British export sector in the period 1860–1913. In this chapter I shall look at this regional cycle in more detail. Then I shall examine the southward shift of population in Britain between 1911 and 1966 with particular reference to urbanization trends in London and the South-east. This will be followed by an analysis of the volume and regional incidence of non-white immigration from the new Commonwealth, mainly India, Pakistan and the West Indies, in the 1950s and 1960s.

WALES AND THE ATLANTIC ECONOMY

Reasonably accurate estimates of regional net losses or gains by migration can be obtained for periods between population censuses by taking the increase in the enumerated population from one census to the next and subtracting from it the excess of births over deaths during the inter-censal period. A net gain by migration is registered when the increase in the enumerated population exceeds the excess of births over deaths, and a net loss when the increase in the enumerated population is less than the excess of births over deaths.

Table 6.1 sets out the record for England, Wales, and Scotland from 1851–61 to 1961–6; the figures are expressed as annual rates per 10,000 mean population and are illustrated in fig. 6.1.

The period 1851–1911, which was not interrupted by major

TABLE 6.1

England, Wales, and Scotland: Annual rate of net loss (−) or gain (+) by migration, each decade, 1851–1966

Period	England	Wales	Scotland
	Annual rate per 10,000 mean population		
1851–61	−16	− 28	−101
1861–71	− 7	− 47	− 44
1871–81	− 5	− 35	− 28
1881–91	−23	− 11	− 58
1891–1901	− 2	− 5	− 13
1901–11	−19	+ 45	− 57
1911–21	−16	− 21	− 50
1921–31	+ 3	−102	− 80
1931–9	+24	− 72	− 8
1939–46 ⎫	+ 6	+ 1	− 3
1946–51 ⎭		− 18	− 92
1951–61	+20	− 11	− 55
1961–6	+18	+ 8	− 75

Note: The figures for 1939–46 exclude non-civilian deaths abroad, and the figures for 1951–61 and 1961–6 exclude movements of armed forces. *Sources:* Population Tables of Census *Reports*, 1851–1961; Carrier and Jeffery, *External Migration: a Study of the Available Statistics, 1815–1950*, Table 2, p. 14; General Register Office, *Registrar General's Quarterly Return for England and Wales*, 4th Quarter, 1968, pp. 42–7; General Register Office, Scotland.

wars, shows some interesting features. The decennial rates of migration exhibit long swings. England and Scotland have a common long swing, with that of Scotland having the greater amplitude: the migration cycle for Wales is inverse to that of England and Scotland. This interesting fact, which could be brought into the open only when the England and Wales total

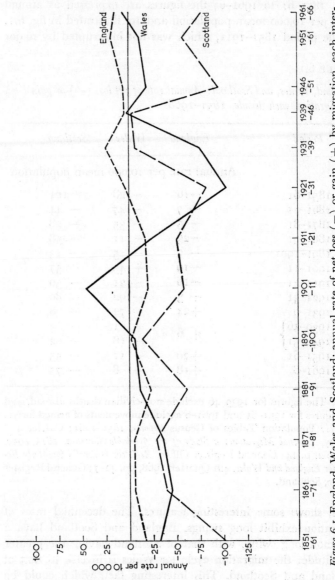

Figure 6.1 England, Wales and Scotland: annual rate of net loss (−) or gain (+) by migration, each inter-censal period, 1851–1966. *Source:* Table 6.1.

was disaggregated, may throw some light on the mechanism of internal migration.

Let us first look at regional rates of long-term growth. In the forty years 1871–1911, Scotland had a net loss by migration of 619,000, whereas Wales had a net gain by migration of 20 000. In this period Scotland, starting in 1871 with a population of

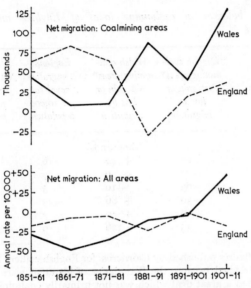

Figure 6.2 Migration balances in coalmining areas, England and Wales, 1851–1911.
Source: Table 6.2.

3,360,000, lost 31 per cent of its natural increase of 2,019,000 through migration, whereas Wales, starting in 1871 with a population of 1,421,000, kept the whole of her natural increase of 986,000 and added 20,000 through net absorption. In England the net loss by migration in the period 1871–1911 was 1,355,000, which was 10 per cent of her natural increase. It is clear that the secular rate of economic growth in Wales in the period 1871–1911 was higher than in England and much higher than in Scotland. It was based mainly on the phenomenal expansion of the steam coal export trade. In the process Cardiff became the world's greatest coal-exporting port, the volume of exports increasing fifteenfold from 708,000 tons in 1851 to 10,577,000 tons in 1913. This phase of secular expansion culminated in the first decade of this century when Wales was a country of new settlement absorbing immigrants at a rate not much less than the

TABLE 6.2

Migration balances in coalmining areas of England and Wales, 1851–1911

Decade	English coal-mining areas* Net gain or loss by migration	Welsh coal-mining areas* Net gain or loss by migration	England Net migration† Annual rate per 10,000 population	Wales Net migration† Annual rate per 10,000 population
	(thousands)			
1851–61	+63	+ 42	−16	−28
1861–71	+82	+ 9	− 7	−47
1871–81	+63	+ 10	− 5	−35
1881–91	−30	+ 86	−23	−11
1891–1901	+18	+ 40	− 2	− 5
1901–11	+35	+126	−19	+45

Note: The figures published by Cairncross for English colliery areas have had to be revised because the boundaries of his areas were such that they included a great deal which was not primarily coalmining. When the boundaries are drawn to cover coalmining areas proper, the migration balance for English colliery areas in 1901–11 changes its sign to +35,000 from the −12,000 shown by Cairncross.

Sources: * Welton, *England's Recent Progress*: Cairncross, 'Internal Migration in Victorian England', and *Home and Foreign Investment 1820–1913*, Chapter IV.
† Thomas, ed., *The Welsh Economy: Studies in Expansion*, Chapter I, p. 7.

United States in the same period (an annual rate of 4·5 per 1,000 as against 6·3 per 1,000).

We shall now examine the inverse relation between the long swings in the migration experience of England and Scotland on the one hand and Wales on the other. This can be done most clearly by concentrating on England and Wales and on the time-shape of coalfield development in the two regions. Table 6.2 and fig. 6.2 set out the annual net absorption of labour decennially in Welsh and English coalfields together with the parallel course of net migration in Wales and England respectively. There is a marked inverse relation between the rate of growth of the Welsh and English coalfields except in the decade 1901–11. In the 1860s and 1870s the main expansion was in England; in the 1880s Wales took the lead, whereas the bulk of the advance in the 1890s took place in England; in the years 1901–11 both were expanding, but the Welsh districts much more than the English.

The interpretation of this inverse relation lies in the fact that Welsh industry was geared almost entirely to the export trade in coal. When we divide Britain into two sectors, home investment and export, the coalmining areas of Wales fall wholly within the export sector. In the period 1861–1911 long swings in the export sector of Britain were inverse to those in home investment. The rate of output of coal in Wales synchronized with fluctuations in the British export sector, whereas the rate of output of English coals consumed on the home market was sensitive to the long swing in home capital construction. Thus, a phase of decline in the rate of expansion of the export-oriented coalfields of Wales would correspond to a phase of increase in the rate of expansion of the domestically-oriented coalfields of England, and vice versa.

We have already seen that Wales experienced a very rapid rate of long-run growth in the period 1851–1911, based on the export multiplier-accelerator effects of the secular expansion of the international demand for steam coal. Wales started with a population of 1,187,000 in 1851, and in the following 60 years the excess of births over deaths was 1,337,000. Only 80,000, or a mere 6 per cent, of this huge natural increase was lost through migration. The net migration balances for the rural and urban areas of England and of Wales separately for 1871–1911 are set out in Table 6.3.

Here we find an interesting contrast between the fluctuations in the rural-urban transfers of population in Wales and in England. In the 1870s practically the whole of the rural exodus in England was absorbed in the urban sector of that country, whereas only one-fifth of the rural exodus in Wales was absorbed internally. In the 1880s, on the other hand, 82 per cent of the rural exodus emigrated out of the country, while in Wales it was almost exactly

TABLE 6.3

England and Wales: decennial net gains or losses by migration in rural and urban areas, 1871–1911

| | Net loss (−) | | Net gain (+) | |
	1871–81 (000)	1881–91 (000)	1891–1901 (000)	1901–11 (000)
England				
Rural	−769	−731	−596	−251
Urban	+673	+132	+551	−346
	− 96	−599	− 45	−597
Wales				
Rural	− 65	−106	− 57	− 38
Urban	+ 13	+ 88	+ 48	+132
	− 52	− 18	− 9	+ 94

Source: Welton, op. cit. and Cairncross, op. cit. (with appropriate revisions for the coalmining areas).

the reverse – 83 per cent of the rural exodus being absorbed in the Welsh urban sector. In the 1890s the flight from the land in England was counterbalanced by an almost equal net intake of population by the urban areas; in Wales the number of rural migrants taken by the home urban sector was only about half of the number in the previous decade and 16 per cent emigrated. At no time was the contrast more evident than in the decade 1901–11. In England there was a net efflux from the urban as well as the rural sector, giving a net emigration of 597,000, or an annual rate of 19 per 10,000 mean population. In Wales a net rural exodus of 38,000 was overshadowed by a net absorption of no less than 132,000 in the urban sector, giving a net immigration of 94,000, or an annual rate of 45 per 10,000 mean population.

Some light on the destination of emigrants from different parts of Britain can be obtained by consulting United States figures. The United States was the major destination of British emigrants, accounting for over two-thirds of them in the period under review.

TABLE 6.4

Immigrants to the United States originating in England, Scotland, and Wales, 1881–1910

Period and country of origin	Mean population of country of origin (000)	Immigrants to U.S.A.	Annual rate per 10,000 mean population
England			
1881–90	25,812	644,680	25
1891–1900	28,861	224,350	8
1901–10	32,061	387,005	12
Scotland			
1881–90	3,881	149,869	39
1891–1900	4,294	60,046	14
1901–10	4,617	133,333	29
Wales			
1881–90	1,677	12,640	8
1891–1900	1,895	11,219	6
1901–10	2,238	18,631	8

Source: Thomas, 'Wales and the Atlantic Economy' in Brinley Thomas, ed., *The Welsh Economy: Studies in Expansion*, p. 11.

Table 6.4 indicates that the rate of gross outflow from Wales to the United States between 1881 and 1911 was negligible as compared with that of Scotland and England, and it did not fluctuate much.

The popular impression that Welsh workers flocked to the United States in the latter half of the nineteenth century is a myth. In the decade 1881–90, when the absorptive power of the United States was at a peak, the effect on Wales was hardly noticeable. In proportion to population, English emigrants to

America (with occupation) were four times as numerous as the Welsh, and the Scots were seven times as numerous. Welsh emigrants were not forced out by the impoverishment of the economy as happened in Ireland and Scotland; it was a complementary export of labour on a very minor scale induced by the export-biased nature of the Welsh economy. In the short cycle, however, emigration, as one would expect, was inverse to fluctuations in income in Wales. Sharp and frequent changes occurred in the price of coal; when the price rose there was prosperity and the incentive to emigrate weakened, and vice versa when the price fell. These short cyclical ups and downs are to be distinguished from the long swing.

The interaction of the long swings for the period 1871–1911 (fig. 6.1 and Table 6.3) may be explained in the following terms. Since the Welsh economy was entirely export-oriented, its upswings coincided with upswings in the English export sector: the latter were accompanied by downswings in the home construction sector of England. During such phases (i.e., 1881–90 and 1901–1911) Welsh economic growth was strong enough to retain nearly the whole of the country's natural increase or even to attract an appreciable net inflow from the rest of the United Kingdom, whereas in England the relatively slow rate of growth of the home construction sector caused a large part of the rural surplus (and in 1901–10 many people from the urban areas) to emigrate overseas. Thus, low emigration from (or immigration into) Wales coincided with high emigration from England. On the other hand, when the Welsh economy was in a downswing relative to trend, the English home construction sector was simultaneously experiencing a rapid upswing, with the export sector declining relative to trend. In this phase the workers displaced from the land in Wales, facing a weak demand for labour in the urban areas of their own country, migrated over the border to England where there was a brisk demand for labour in the flourishing home investment sector. Thus, high emigration from Wales coincided with low emigration from England. The surplus agricultural population in Wales was recruited either for the export-geared urban sector within Wales or for the home construction sector in England: there was comparatively little recruitment for overseas.

A CULTURAL EFFECT OF URBANIZATION

What effect did urban development have on the language and traditions of Wales? It is usually taken for granted – it is certainly a commonplace of the standard textbooks – that industrialization was an anglicizing force which swept over the country leaving the rural areas of the north and west as the last strongholds of the Welsh-speaking tradition.[1] Is it really true that economic development and the accompanying flight from the land undermined the language and culture of Wales in the period 1850–1913? The truth of the matter, which historians do not seem to have noticed, is that the Welsh language was really saved by the growth of industrial towns which enabled most of the people uprooted from the Welsh countryside to be absorbed within the boundaries of Wales.

In the sixty years after 1851 the population of Wales grew from 1,187,000 to 2,421,000 and by 1911 there were 970,000 persons recorded as speaking Welsh, of whom 57 per cent lived in the coalmining counties of South Wales. The vast majority of these people would simply not have been there but for urban development. If Wales had remained completely agricultural like Ireland, the whole of her surplus rural population, which was Welsh to the core (about half a million people up to 1911), would have had to go to England or overseas; these people together with their descendants would have been lost to the land of their birth for ever. Furthermore, the exodus would have been much worse than that, since the Welsh agricultural community, robbed of

[1] A well-known Welsh historian puts it as follows: 'The area which has suffered this depopulation is, of course, the area which is predominantly Welsh in speech, so that the economic forces which have caused depopulation have affected the fortunes of the Welsh language and the cultural heritage of Wales.' (David Williams in Roderick, ed., *Wales through the Ages*, Vol. II, p. 153.) In another reference the same author writes, 'While Wales was isolated geographically, and was almost self-sufficing economically, the influence of England was not strong. But the building of roads and railways, and the enormous growth of Welsh industry as a part of the economic development of Britain, profoundly affected Welsh life; so much so that there is a marked tendency to regard Welsh culture as being in essence the culture of rural Wales and not of the industrial areas.' (Williams, *A History of Modern Wales*, p. 269.)

the purchasing power of the densely populated coalmining areas, would have shrunk into a tiny group of impoverished hill farmers. All this would have been a grievous blow to the Welsh language.[1] The reason why it did not happen was the growth of industrial areas in Wales. Industrial development was on such a scale that Wales was able to provide a good living for the great majority of the native stock displaced from the countryside.[2] The farm labourers from all parts who flocked into mining valleys took the Welsh way of life with them and brought up their children to speak the mother tongue. As we have already noted, the natural increase in Wales in the two generations up to 1911 was no less than 1,337,000, larger than what the population had been in 1851. Describing the Rhondda Valley in 1896, the Report of the Welsh Land Commission said: '. . . speaking broadly, the characteristics of Welsh life, its Nonconformist development, the habitual use of the Welsh language, and the prevalence of a Welsh type of character, are as marked as in the rural districts of Wales'.[3] In 1905, there were in the Rhondda no less than 151 Nonconformist churches with a seating capacity of 85,105; these churches alone could accommodate three-quarters of the entire population of the Rhondda Urban District. Indeed in the whole of Wales in 1905 the seating capacity of Nonconformist churches was equal to 74 per cent of the total population. The mining townships were so Welsh in character that many of the English immigrants – not to mention Italian shopkeepers – became fluent in the Welsh language. And it is worth noting that even in 1951 54 per cent of the 715,000 recorded as Welsh-speaking were in the South Wales industrial areas.

[1] For a more detailed statistical analysis see Thomas, ed., *The Welsh Economy: Studies in Expansion* (Cardiff, University of Wales Press, 1962), Chapter 1, pp. 9–29.

[2] Williams (*A History of Modern Wales*, pp. 290–1) says that the absolute number of those who could speak Welsh went on increasing '. . . because of the natural increase of the population'. This is a misconception. The reason was not the natural increase (which by itself would have been a menace) but the fact that industrialization enabled most of the natural increase to remain in Wales.

[3] *Report of the Royal Commission on Land in Wales and Monmouthshire*, British Parliamentary Papers, 1896, C-8221, p. 176.

No doubt the romantic nationalist will reply that the Welsh heritage would have been much safer in the hands of a small nation of monoglot peasants. But what would have been its fate in the great agricultural crisis which hit the whole of Europe in the 1880s? Given a miracle Wales, like Denmark, might have changed the basis of her agriculture and become a producer of bacon and butter for the English market, but it is much more likely, when we remember the physical disabilities of Welsh agriculture, that she would have been caught, like Ireland, in the vicious circle of mass emigration. Instead of having a population of over $2\frac{1}{2}$ million, modern Wales would have been just a hand-ful of impoverished peasants scratching a meagre subsistence and eking it out with remittances from their kinsmen who had been lucky enough to go to America. It would have been a tiny and much more depressed version of Ireland – without the stimulus which the rise of the House of Guinness meant to the Emerald Isle. It was the massive growth of coalmining which saved Wales from that fate. Instead of bemoaning the rural exodus, the Welsh nationalist should sing the praises of industrial development which gave the Welsh language a new lease of life and Welsh Noncon-formity a glorious high noon.

THE SOUTHWARD SHIFT OF POPULATION, 1911–66

It is very difficult to identify the timing and amplitude of long swings for the half century beginning in 1911, since all time series reflect the profound economic consequences of two world wars. The internal migration picture is summarized in fig. 6.1. The sharpest break took place in the fortunes of Wales where an annual net population inflow of 4·5 per 1,000 in 1901–11 was converted into an annual net loss of 10·2 per 1,000 in the 1920s. Between 1921 and 1939 Wales lost on balance 450,000 people by migra-tion: the natural increase in the period was 259,000, and so the population fell by 191,000. Scotland was also hard hit in the 1920s, with an annual loss by migration of 8 per 1,000, but in the 1930s the rate of outflow was negligible as compared with the exodus from Wales. Most of the migrants from Wales and Scotland settled in England where there was an average annual inflow of 2·4 per 1,000 between 1931 and 1939. The exceptional circumstances of World War II brought a temporary halt in inter-regional population flows.

The outstanding fact about the inter-war period was the heavy incidence of mass unemployment in the coalmining regions and

TABLE 6.5

United Kingdom: the southward drift, 1931–61. Net gain (+) *or loss* (−) *by migration* (thousands)

Region	1931–39	1939–51	1951–61
Northern			
Northern	−149	− 60	− 86
East and West Ridings	− 41	− 90	− 98
N. Western	− 59	− 70	−124
Wales	−182	+ 7	− 49
Scotland	− 32	−247	−255
Southern			
N. Midlands	+ 32	+ 78	+ 65
Midland	+100	+ 88	+ 61
Eastern	+201	+240	+455
London and South-east	+458	−640	−183
Southern	+129	+191	+237
S. Western	+ 36	+236	+ 78

Source: Census, England and Wales, Preliminary Report, 1951, p. xv, 1961, p. 7; Carrier and Jeffrey, op. cit., p. 14.

the redistribution of population in favour of the relatively prosperous areas of Southern England. The extent of the southward shift between 1931 and 1961 is seen in Table 6.5. Much has been written about the alleged imbalance between the old industrial North and the new industrial South, and it is often inferred that it began during the great depression between the wars. This inference is quite correct in the case of Wales where the remarkable export-led secular growth in the period 1860–1913 ended in a collapse in the inter-war years. But it would be wrong to generalize.

No explanation of the deeper factors behind the southward shift can be adequate unless it takes into account the tendencies already evident in the years 1881–1911, as shown in Table 6.6. We recall that the analysis in Chapter 2 (fig. 2.3) revealed a peak in building at the turn of the century in the mainly rural

TABLE 6.6

United Kingdom: the southward drift, 1881–1911, net gain (+) or loss (−) by migration (thousands)

	1881–91	1891–1901	1901–11
Northern England towns			
Eight large towns	+ 21	−144	− 90
Twenty-two textile towns	+ 4	− 41	− 52
Fourteen industrial towns	− 89	− 51	− 81
Seven old towns	− 17	+ 0·3	+ 5
Nine residential towns	+ 22	+ 60	+ 18
Southern England towns			
London	+169	+226	−232
Eleven industrial towns	− 6	+ 25	+ 7
Thirteen old towns	− 24	+ 1	− 35
Twenty-six residential towns	+ 45	+ 83	+129
Sixteen military towns	+ 13	+ 73	+ 8

Source: Cairncross, *Home and Foreign Investment 1870–1913*, p. 70.

counties of the South and South-west. The location of this activity is illustrated in the migration figures for certain towns given in Table 6.7.

Residential building was the most important element in the upswing in domestic capital formation in the 1890s. The composition and geographical distribution of the investment were determined partly by changes in the pattern of consumers' expenditure, which favoured the growth of seaside towns, and by the location of government expenditure on the armed forces. Then there were the powerful spin-off effects of the dominance of London, and these were bound to be felt mainly in the southern part of England. In the period 1881–1911 nearly all towns in northern England were recording net losses by migration, with the exception of the residential towns which showed moderate gains. On the other hand, in the South the residential towns received large net gains of population, as did the industrial towns,

TABLE 6.7

Migration into residential, military and industrial towns in Southern England, 1891–1900

	Net Gain by Migration 1891–1900
Residential towns	
Bournemouth	+10,329
Brighton	+ 5,201
Worthing	+ 4,115
Eastbourne	+ 4,219
Military towns	
Plymouth	+15,838
Portsmouth	+13,145
Weymouth	+ 6,793
Aldershot	+ 2,895
Industrial towns	
Southampton	+20,694
Reading	+ 3,856
Swindon	+ 3,459
Gloucester	+ 2,920

Source: Welton, op. cit., pp. 178–85.

unlike those of the North. The trend in favour of the South which was characteristic of the late Victorian and the Edwardian era continued in the inter-war period, albeit in very different circumstances.

For the period 1939–61 the one exception in the southern part of Britain is the London and South-east region where big net losses by migration were recorded, but this hides some interesting intra-regional flows. The net outflow of 640,000 between

1939 and 1951 was largely the result of the war; the population of Greater London in 1951 was 400,000 fewer than the peak of 8,728,000 in 1939. Between 1951 and 1961 the centrifugal tendency continued, with a net loss of 502,000 in Greater London and a net gain of 319,000 in the rest of the South-east region.

REGIONAL GROWTH OF MANUFACTURING

Regional migration balances for the period 1951–66 are shown in Table 6.8 which ranks the regions according to rate of growth of employment in manufacturing. The contrast between the South and the North is again striking. Between 1951 and 1966 the southern part of Britain absorbed 1,059,000 migrants and the northern part lost 815,000, with Scotland accounting for nearly half a million. The South-west, South-east, East Anglia and the Midlands rank high in rate of expansion of manufacturing and in rate of net in-migration. The northern regions and Scotland have a relatively low rate of advance in manufacturing and heavy net out-migration.

Wales is an exception in having a rate of expansion in manufacturing almost as high as the South-east but without attracting population. It had been more specialized in coalmining than any other region and, apart from its steel and tinplate industry, a virtually new manufacturing sector has developed since the war. Plenty of labour was available from the huge surplus released by mining and other declining industries and through the recruitment of the hitherto untapped supply of women workers. Between 1959 and 1966 employment in manufacturing grew faster in Wales than in any other region, i.e. by 18 per cent as compared with 12 per cent in the South-west, 8 per cent in London and Eastern England, the Midlands and Yorkshire, 6 per cent in the North, 4 per cent in Scotland, and a slight decline in the North-west.

The Board of Trade has published information about the movement of manufacturing establishments in the period 1945–65. For this purpose the United Kingdom was divided into fifty areas, and the survey related to the opening of new manufacturing establishments when the development in question had its origin outside the area in which the new establishment was opened.

TABLE 6.8

United Kingdom: regional migration and growth of manufacturing, 1951–66

Standard region	Mid-year population 1951	Net civilian migration 1951–66	Migration 1951–66 per 1,000 of 1951 population	Mid-year employment in manufacturing		Rate of change in manufacturing employment 1953–66
				1953	1966	
	Thousand	Thousand	Per 1,000	Thousand	Thousand	%
South-west	3,247	+198	+60	333	408	+23
South-east and East Anglia	16,604	+662	+40	2,339	2,791	+19
Wales	2,589	−16	−6	276	326	+18
West Midlands	4,426	+92	+21	1,086	1,259	+16
East Midlands	2,913	+107	+37	546	623	+14
North	3,130	−111	−36	406	458	+13
Yorkshire and Humberside	4,488	−89	−20	855	897	+6
Scotland	5,103	−476	−93	741	740	0
North-west	6,417	−129	−20	1,405	1,364	−3
Great Britain	48,917	+238	+49	7,987	8,866	+11

Sources: General Register Office, *Registrar General's Quarterly Return for England and Wales*, 4th Quarter, 1968, pp. 42–5, and General Register Office, Scotland. Howard, *The Movement of Manufacturing Industry in the United Kingdom 1945–1965*, p. 11.

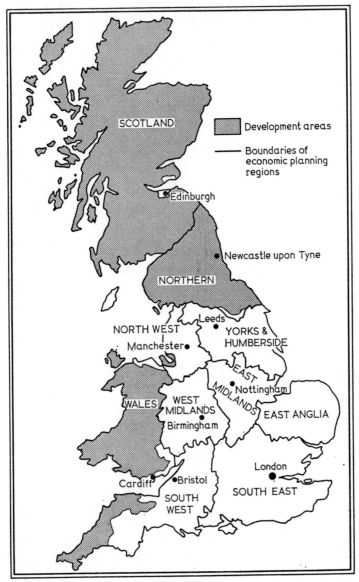

Figure 6.3 Great Britain: Economic Planning Regions and Development Areas.

TABLE 6.9

Contribution of moves of establishments to changes in regional employment in Britain, 1953–66 (figures in thousands)

Region	Total employment in manufacturing mid-1966	Change in manufacturing employment 1953–66	Employment at end-1966 in inward moves taking place in 1952–65	Net change in manufacturing sector 1953–66 other than 1952–65 moves
South-west	408	+ 75	28	+ 47
South-east and East Anglia	2,791	+452	39	+413
Wales	326	+ 50	24	+ 26
West Midlands	1,259	+173	6	+167
East Midlands	623	+ 77	18	+ 59
North	458	+ 52	27	+ 25
Yorkshire and Humberside	897	+ 42	16	+ 26
Scotland	740	− 1	50	− 51
North-west	1,364	− 41	68	−109
Great Britain	8,866	+879	56*	823†

* i.e. employment in moves from abroad. The sum of the regional figures in this column is 276,000 which is total British employment in regional moves.

† i.e. employment change in Britain less employment in moves from abroad. The sum of the regional figures in this column is 603,000 which is the net employment change in Britain excluding employment in inter-regional moves.

Source: Howard, op. cit., p. 11.

Such 'moves' include not only transfers (a new factory in one area replacing a closure in another area) but also branches (an additional factory opened by a firm in an area where it had not manufactured previously).[1] These statistics throw light on trends in regional economic growth in relation to internal shifts of population. A summary is given in Table 6.9.

In 1966 56 per cent of employment in British manufacturing was in the industrial South, i.e. the South-east, East Anglia, South-west and the Midlands, and nearly a third was in the South-east and East Anglia. Between 1953 and 1966 no less than half the increase in manufacturing employment in Britain (452,000 out of 879,000) took place in the South-east and East Anglia, which had an increase in population in this period equal to 47 per cent of the growth in Britain as a whole.

Successive British governments have pursued policies designed to attract industries into the Development Areas which are located mainly in regions where coalmining has been rapidly contracting, i.e. Scotland, the North, the North-west and Wales (see fig. 6.3). The last two columns of Table 6.9 give some indication of the extent to which these measures have succeeded. In Scotland and the North-west the manufacturing sector, apart from the employment gained through inward moves of factories, underwent a sizeable decrease; Wales and the North fared better. It is clear that, without the incentives in favour of the Development Areas, the growth of manufacturing in the industrial South would have been even more pronounced.

One of the chief causes of the difficulties of the older industrial areas is that the British economy is switching from coal to more economical sources of energy, such as natural gas, nuclear power and oil. The country as a whole will gain considerably from the consequent increase in productivity, but the heavy incidence of the transition falls on particular regions such as Scotland, Wales and the North. In the 9 years 1959–68 the decline in employment in mining and quarrying was 53,200 in Scotland, 86,100 in the North and 55,700 in Wales. The increase in employment in manufacturing was 13,600 in Scotland, 16,600 in the North and 51,800 in Wales. Whereas the growth of manufacturing in Wales

[1] For precise definitions see Howard, op. cit., pp. 48–9.

came near to offsetting the contraction of mining and quarrying, in Scotland and the North the increase in manufacturing was only one-fifth of what was lost through mining closures.

The main source of migrating establishments was Greater London, accounting for 43 per cent of the employment entailed by internal moves; but it is significant that the overspill of manufacturing from Greater London to the rest of the South-east and East Anglia was nearly twice as large as the movement to the old industrial North (194,000 as against 115,000 in terms of employment).[1]

The population of the South-east region increased from 15,200,000 in 1951 to 17,100,000 in 1966, i.e. from 34·7 per cent to 35·6 per cent of the population of England and Wales. The growth took place in the outer areas. There was an absolute fall in population in Greater London from 8,200,000 to 7,900,000, a rise in the Outer Metropolitan Area from 3,500,000 to 5,000,000, and a rise in the Outer South-east from 3,500,000 to 4,100,000. Net in-migration accounted for 68 per cent of the population increase of the Outer Metropolitan Area and 72 per cent of that of the Outer South-east.[2]

Post-war government measures to steer manufacturing industry to regions of high structural unemployment, while they have had a moderate success, have been overshadowed by the powerful effect of the inflow of population into the South, particularly the counties surrounding London. In 1966 the value of construction orders received by contractors in the private and public sectors in the South-east region was 36 per cent of the total for England and Wales, which was exactly the region's proportion of the total population. Our analysis has shown that half the increase in manufacturing employment in Britain in 1953–66 took place in the South-east and East Anglia where nearly half the growth in Britain's population occurred. This population upsurge was to a large extent a migration dynamic and, as in similar previous periods, it was associated with a high rate of growth of population-sensitive capital formation, manufacturing, and services.

[1] Ibid., p. 15.
[2] See Ministry of Housing and Local Government, *A Strategy for the South East. A First Report by the South East Economic Planning Council*, p. 70.

The components of population change for the South-east in 1961–6 are shown in Table 6.10. The striking feature is the big net inflow of 302,000 external immigrants (from outside England and Wales) and the net outflow of 136,000 internal migrants. The abnormal number of immigrants in 1961–2 was followed by a sharp rise in natural increase in 1963–5. To interpret this pattern it is necessary to examine a new phase in Britain's migration history – the entry of immigrants from New Commonwealth countries, particularly the West Indies, India and Pakistan, in the 1950s and 1960s.

TABLE 6.10

South-east England region: components of population change 1961–6
(Figures in thousands)

	1961–2	1962–3	1963–4	1964–5	1965–6
Natural increase	95	93	123	121	109
Net migration					
within England and Wales	− 40	− 14	− 17	− 36	− 29
outside England and Wales	+141	+ 42	+ 49	+ 42	+ 28
Net migration	+101	+ 28	+ 32	+ 6	− 1
Total home population change*	+201	+126	+151	+126	+118

* This includes changes in the number of armed forces and minor statistical corrections.
Source: Ministry of Housing and Local Government, *A Strategy for the South East. A First Report by the South East Economic Planning Council*, p. 86

THE NEW IMMIGRATION

The middle of the 1950s saw the beginning of a remarkable inflow into Britain of migrants from the West Indies and Asia. Between 1955 and 1960 net arrivals from the Caribbean, India and Pakistan came to 219,540, of whom 96,180 were from Jamaica and 65,270 from the rest of the Caribbean. Almost as many, 203,470, entered in the year and a half ending in June 1962, and 45 per cent were from India and Pakistan, an abnormal influx caused in large measure by a rush to come in before the restrictions contained in the Commonwealth Immigrants Act came into force on 1 July 1962. From the middle of 1962 to the end of 1967 there was a net inward movement of 231,830 from the West Indies, India and Pakistan; 60 per cent were from the latter two countries, and over two-thirds of the total were dependants.[1]

Controls

Section 2 of the Commonwealth Immigrants Act of 1962 gave immigration officers power to refuse admission, or to admit subject to a condition respecting the period of stay, with or without a condition restricting freedom to take employment. People born in the United Kingdom and certain classes of people holding United Kingdom passports were completely exempt from control. There was no general power to refuse admission to people ordinarily resident in the United Kingdom, to holders of Ministry of Labour vouchers or to wives and children under sixteen accompanying or joining husbands or parents. Returning residents, wives, and children under sixteen could be refused admission only if they were subject to a deportation order. Voucher holders, students and persons of independent means (including visitors) could be refused admission if they were subject to a deportation order, on medical or security grounds, or on account of a criminal record.

A Commonwealth citizen who wished to work and settle in Britain had to have a Ministry of Labour voucher. There were three categories: category A for applications by employers in the United Kingdom who had a specific job to offer to a particular Commonwealth citizen; category B for applications by Commonwealth citizens without a specific job to come to but with certain special qualifications (e.g. nurses, doctors, teachers); category C for all others. Priority was given to the first two categories. The issue of vouchers in category C was subject to the condition that no country received more than a quarter of the vouchers available for issue, and within category C preference was given to

[1] The source of these figures is the Home Office and annual statistics issued under the Commonwealth Immigrants Act, 1962. For details see Rose and associates, *Colour and Citizenship: A Report on British Race Relations*, pp. 82–4.

applicants who had served in the British armed forces. Vouchers were issued to other applicants in category C in the order in which their applications were received in London.

In 1962 and the first months of 1963 a high proportion of the vouchers issued were not taken up and the rate of issue was accordingly stepped up. As time went on a much higher proportion of the vouchers issued came to be used, and the rate of issue was reduced until it settled at about 400 a week, of which about three-quarters were being used. When the scheme was introduced it was thought that most of the vouchers would be for applicants in category C, i.e., mainly unskilled workers. However, between September 1964 and the middle of 1965 the two priority classes of skilled workers, categories A and B, took up the whole issue of 400 a week, so that there was no room for any applicants in category C. There was soon a waiting list of no less than 300,000 persons in this group.

In 1965 government policy became much more restrictive. The White Paper of that year[1] abolished category C and fixed the annual issue of A and B vouchers at 8,500 a year (1,000 of which were reserved for Malta). It specified the kinds of people who would be favoured: doctors, dentists and trained nurses; teachers eligible for the status of qualified teacher in Britain; graduates in science and technology with at least two years' experience in suitable employment since graduation; and non-graduates with at least two years' experience in suitable employment since qualifying. Applicants in category A, whether skilled or unskilled, would be admissible if they had a specific job to come to in Britain. The White Paper stated that '. . . the Government will continue to welcome people who come from other Commonwealth countries on holiday, social or business visits or to follow a course of study'.

Regional Incidence

There is an extensive literature on many aspects of this new immigration.[2] What concerns us particularly in this context is the

[1] *Immigration from the Commonwealth*, Government White Paper, Cmnd. 2739, August 1965.
[2] For a comprehensive inquiry into the whole problem see E. J. B. Rose

regional distribution of the newcomers. According to the 1966 census there were in Britain 2,603,250 persons who were born abroad, including the Irish Republic; 850,600 of these, or nearly a third, came from New Commonwealth countries,[1] and 738,790 were from the Irish Republic. As many as 60 per cent of the New Commonwealth immigrants were in the South-east and East Anglia and 13 per cent were in the West Midlands.[2] Of those in the South-east and East Anglia, 35 per cent were from the Caribbean and 30 per cent from India and Pakistan; the corresponding proportions for the West Midlands were 38 per cent and 50 per cent. The majority of the 850,600 New Commonwealth immigrants had settled in large urban areas and no less than 43 per cent were in Greater London.

Table 6.11 sets out the changes in population and number of immigrants in each region and conurbation between 1961 and 1966. The regions are ranked, as in Table 6.8, according to rate of growth of manufacturing, 1953–66.

The increase of 381,500 in immigrants enumerated in Britain between 1961 and 1966 was dominated by 309,500 from New Commonwealth countries, of whom one in four were in Greater London. If we take the South-east and East Anglia without Greater London, the three regions with the fastest growth in manufacturing employment received an addition of only 61,600 New Commonwealth immigrants between them. As a national average, people born in New Commonwealth countries were 16·3 per 1,000 of the population in 1966: the proportion in the South-west was 10·1, in the South-east and East Anglia (excluding

---

and associates, op. cit. It contains an excellent bibliography. For an authoritative economic analysis see Jones and Smith, *The Economic Impact of Commonwealth Immigration.* An illuminating account of immigration from the West Indies is to be found in Peach, *West Indian Migration to Britain.*

[1] New Commonwealth countries comprise Barbados, British Guiana, Jamaica, Trinidad and Tobago, and other countries in the Caribbean; Ceylon, Cyprus, Hong Kong, India, Malaysia, Pakistan and Singapore; British East and Central Africa, Nigeria, and other countries in West Africa; Gibraltar, Malta and Gozo.

[2] General Register Office, *Sample Census 1966, Great Britain,* Summary Tables, pp. 29–38.

TABLE 0.11
Great Britain: changes in population and number of immigrants, by region, 1961-6

Area	Change 1961 to 1966 in:				New Commonwealth immigrants per 1,000 of 1966 population
	Total Population	Total immigrants	New Commonwealth immigrants	Indigenous Population*	
Regions					
South-West	+ 148·7	+ 17·0	+ 10·2	+ 131·7	10·1
South-East and East Anglia	+ 450·4	+ 227·4	+ 174·0	+ 223·0	27·4
South-East and East Anglia (excluding Greater London)	+ 776·4	+ 101·5	+ 49·4	+ 674·9	13·5
Wales	+ 19·4	+ 1·5	+ 2·1	+ 17·9	3·8
West Midlands	+ 152·1	+ 55·3	+ 49·6	+ 96·8	22·8
Yorkshire, Humberside and East Midlands	+ 200·5	+ 41·1	+ 41·3	+ 159·4	11·4
North	+ 11·9	+ 4·7	+ 3·5	+ 7·2	4·1
Scotland	− 11·1	+ 4·5	+ 4·7	− 15·6	4·4
North-West	+ 47·9	+ 30·0	+ 24·0	+ 17·9	8·2
All Regions	+ 1019·8	+ 381·5	+ 309·5	+ 638·3	16·3
Conurbations:					
Greater London	− 326·0	+ 125·9	+ 124·6	− 451·9	47·9
West Midlands	− 3·9	+ 37·4	+ 37·1	− 41·3	35·6
West Yorkshire	+ 4·6	+ 19·3	+ 18·9	− 14·7	20·8
Tyneside	− 23·1	+ 1·1	+ 1·1	− 24·2	5·4
S. E. Lancashire	− 23·8	+ 18·7	+ 15·2	− 42·5	12·2
Merseyside	− 46·7	+ 0·1	+ 1·7	− 46·8	6·0
All Conurbations	− 418·9	+ 202·6	+ 198·6	− 621·5	32·5

* Population minus total immigrants.

Sources: Census of Population 1961, Birthplace and Nationality Tables; Sample Census 1966, Summary Tables. The 1961 figures relate to regions and conurbations as defined in 1966. I am indebted to the National Institute of Economic and Social Research, London, for kind permission to reproduce this table.

Greater London) 13·5, and in Wales 3·8. The one fast-growing region which showed a high absorptive capacity was the West Midlands with an increase of 49,600 and a proportion of 22·8 per 1,000 in 1966. The North and Scotland, like Wales, were hardly in the picture.

The newcomers were a significant input in the labour market, contributing more than a fifth to the increase in the British labour force between 1961 and 1966;[1] but most of this addition took place in areas which were losing indigenous population. Table 6.11 shows that the six conurbations as a whole between 1961 and 1966 absorbed 199,000 immigrants from New Commonwealth countries while losing 622,000 of their indigenous population. In Greater London there was a decline of 5 per cent in manufacturing employment, a decrease of 452,000 in indigenous population, and an absorption of 125,000 New Commonwealth immigrants: in the rest of the South-east and East Anglia employment in manufacturing grew by 11 per cent, the indigenous population increased by 675,000, and the number of New Commonwealth immigrants rose by only 49,000.[2]

The census classification by country of birth cannot tell us the exact number of non-white residents; white persons born abroad must be excluded. There is also reason to believe that there was under-enumeration of some groups, particularly Pakistanis. Careful estimates made by the Institute of Race Relations indicate that in 1966 the total of Commonwealth non-white residents in England and Wales who were born abroad was 711,000, and the number born in the United Kingdom 213,000, giving a non-white total of 924,000, or just under 2 per cent of the population. This total comprised 240,000 from India and Ceylon, 120,000 from Pakistan, 274,000 from Jamaica, 180,000 from the rest of the Caribbean, 51,000 from British West Africa, and 60,000 from the Far East.[3]

The evidence for the conurbations suggests that most of these

[1] See Jones and Smith, op. cit., pp. 36–7.
[2] The figures for manufacturing employment are for 1960 and 1964, years which were at comparable position in the trade cycle. See Ministry of Housing and Local Government, *A Strategy for the South East*, pp. 89 and 92.
[3] For details of these estimates see Rose and associates, op. cit., pp. 96–103 and Appendix III.4.

immigrants tend to establish themselves in areas which are losing population. Are the newcomers replacing local people in areas where economic growth is weak? This can only be tested by an analysis covering a large number of small neighbourhoods. Ceri Peach, in his study of the distribution of West Indians between 1951 and 1961, found that '. . . they have settled most in the large towns, least in the small towns; most in the decreasing towns; most of all in the large decreasing towns and least in the small increasing towns'.[1] He reached the following conclusion.

> In spite of the shortcomings of the available statistics, it seems clear that West Indians have acted as a replacement population in this country. Geographically, they have been drawn to those regions which, in spite of demand for labour, have not been able to attract much net population from other parts of the country. In towns they are proportionately twice as numerous in those that lost population between 1951 and 1961 as in those which increased. They have gone to the decreasing urban cores of expanding industrial regions.[2]

The process is in an early phase but it has in it the seeds of the ghetto; there is an ominous similarity with the experience of the American Negro. In Chapter 5 we found a clear inverse relation between the Negroes' success in establishing themselves in the North and the volume of immigration from Europe.[3] The black people did best in areas where white people were not coming in or were moving out, and they were concentrated in the lower paid jobs. Segregation in Britain is by no means as marked as in the United States but the symptoms are the same. However, since the scale of the problem is so much smaller, it should be feasible to conduct active policies to achieve the highest possible degree of equality of opportunity and geographical dispersal.

[1] Peach, op. cit., p. 81. In 1961 in Birmingham 86 per cent and in London 87 per cent of the West Indians were in local authority areas which had a net decline in white population. Ibid., p. 89.
[2] Ibid., p. 82.
[3] pp. 141–8.

7 The Dynamics of Brain Drain

A striking feature of the international scene since World War II is the high proportion of migrants who can be regarded as human capital, i.e. the 'professional, technical and kindred grades'. Advanced countries are keen to attract qualified manpower and they erect barriers against the entry of the unskilled; the actions of governments suggest that immigration policy has come to resemble tariff policy as an instrument for the pursuit of national gain, as the following statements show.

At the hearings on the 1965 United States immigration bill, the American Secretary of State said:

> The significance of immigration for the United States now depends less on the number than on the quality of the immigrants. The explanation for the high professional and technical quality of present immigration lies in part in the non-quota and preference provisions . . . that favor the admission of the highly qualified migrants. But still more it depends on world conditions of post-war economic and social dislocations . . . Under present circumstances, the United States has a rare opportunity to draw migrants of high intelligence and ability from abroad; and immigration, if well administered, can be one of our greatest national resources. . . . We are in the international market of brains.[1]

In the *White Paper on Immigration*, October 1966, the Canadian Minister of Immigration made the following statement:

[1] House of Representatives (debate), *Hearings of the Sub-committee on the Judiciary*, pp. 389–90 and 401.

Canada has become a highly complex industrialized and urbanized society. And such a society is increasingly demanding of the quality of its work force. If those entering the work force, whether native-born or immigrants, do not have the ability and training to do the jobs available, they will be burdens rather than assets. Today, Canada's expanding industrial economy offers most of its employment opportunities to those with education, training, skill. . . . The high cost of training professional and skilled people – engineers, doctors, skilled technicians, etc. – is a measure of the benefit derived upon their arrival in Canada. . . . Other countries are in competition with us for immigrants.[1]

In the Atlantic economy, 1860–1913, as well as within the United States, 1880–1950, migration helped to bring about the convergence of regional (national or state) growth rates.[2] The question arises whether, in the conditions prevailing in 1950–70, the international flows of human capital tended to widen the gap between developed and less developed countries.

THE STATISTICAL GROUNDWORK

Research on international movements of highly trained manpower has been based largely on the statistics of the main receiving countries, particularly the United States, Canada and Australia. Such countries have always had good reason to keep reasonably accurate records of the number, quality and origins

[1] Department of Manpower and Immigration, Government of Canada (the Hon. Jean Marchand), *White Paper on Immigration*, pp. 8 and 11.
[2] The classic source on the United States is the work of Borts and Stein, *Economic Growth in a Free Market*. Their detailed theoretical and empirical analysis has established beyond doubt the crucial part played by shifts in labour supply functions (via intrastate and interstate migration) in explaining the convergence of state growth rates in the United States, 1880–1950. See also their article, 'Regional Growth and Maturity in the United States: a Study of Regional Structural Change', *Schweizerische Zeitschrift für Volkswirtschaft und Statistik*, pp. 290–321. For further evidence on the Atlantic economy see Thomas, 'International Factor Movements and Unequal Rates of Growth', pp. 7–9.

of immigrants, but they do not have the same interest in measuring outward flows. A word of caution is therefore necessary. When we use statistics showing gross inflows of professional manpower into these countries, we are hampered by a partial eclipse since there are no reliable data on the outward movement of immigrants to their homelands or to other destinations and we cannot satisfactorily measure the emigration of highly trained nationals from these countries. Our knowledge of *net* international flows is incomplete.

In the absence of the required flow data, it is sometimes possible to remedy some of these gaps by using population census statistics. For example, according to the United States census for 1960, only about 50,000 Americans in the professional, technical and kindred grades were living abroad in that year and over 50 per cent of those aged 25 and over had been abroad for only three years or under. Moreover, more than 70 per cent of the American citizens abroad were employees of the Government or dependants of Federal employees. From these figures there can be little doubt that the emigration of highly trained American manpower is an insignificant proportion of the immigration of highly trained foreigners. In fact the *inflow* of foreign immigrants in the professional, technical and kindred grades in the year 1967 alone was 41,652, which was not far short of the total *stock* of Americans in these grades abroad in 1960.

The lack of accurate information on return movements is a serious handicap and not easy to rectify. In the United Kingdom the International Passenger Sample Survey introduced in 1964 cannot yield accurate figures of the inward and outward migration of professionals, since the number of migrants among the sampled passengers is so small as to entail a wide margin of error. Fortunately, the estimates for qualified scientists and engineers have been greatly improved, and we shall be using the new series on the British net balance later in this chapter.

A comprehensive international flow chart should distinguish between the private and public circuits. On the one hand, we have the market-oriented international flow of professional manpower, most of it from poor to rich countries, and on the other, there is a reverse publicly-financed flow of technical and scientific personnel, national and international, from rich to poor countries. If adequate statistics were available, we could estimate for the private and public circuits the annual inward and outward flows for each country. Given accurate benchmark figures of stocks derived from census enumerations at, say, five-year intervals, we could relate net external flows of each category of professional manpower to the corresponding stocks and annual outputs in each country. We may eventually be able to carry out such an exercise for some countries.

THE PATTERN OF INTERNATIONAL FLOWS

A summary view of the pattern of international flows may be obtained by dividing countries into four groups:

(i) advanced countries with a large net inflow;
(ii) intermediate advanced countries with a large two-way traffic;
(iii) advanced countries with a large net outflow;
(iv) developing countries with a large net outflow.

In the first group, advanced countries with a large net inflow, we have the United States and Australia. The United States is by far the largest and the preferred ultimate destination of professional migrants. In the second group are Canada and the United Kingdom. Many migrants of varying degrees of skill move by stages out of low-income countries via intermediate to more advanced ones, forming currents of migration determined by the magnetic influence of the richest destinations. The third group, advanced countries with a large net outflow, consists mainly of European countries such as Norway, the Netherlands and Switzerland. Finally, there is a heterogeneous fourth group of underdeveloped countries with a relatively large net outflow, such as Greece, Iran and Turkey.

The immigration of workers (excluding dependants and persons with no occupation) into the United States, Canada and Australia in the period 1947–67, was as follows: 2,490,000 into the United States, of whom 18 per cent were professional; 1,534,000 into Canada, of whom 13 per cent were professional;

and 1,099,000 into Australia, of whom 8 per cent were professional.[1] In 1967 well over a quarter of the inflow into the United States and Canada was in the professional and technical grades, whereas Australia, where the proportion is about one-tenth, has been relatively more interested in skilled craftsmen.

An analysis of immigration of persons with occupation into the United States in 1967 by skill group gives the following results:

	Percentage of Immigrants with occupation 1967
Professional and entrepreneurial	35
Craftsmen, operatives and clerical	35
Private household and other service workers	19
Labourers	11
All occupations	100

An approximate breakdown for the period, 1907–23, is as follows:[2]

	Percentage of Immigrants with occupation 1907–23
Professional and entrepreneurial	3
Skilled	22
Service and other occupations	24
Labourers	51
All occupations	100

[1] *Annual Reports* of the Immigration and Naturalization Service, Department of Justice, Washington D.C.; *Annual Reports* of the Department of Citizenship and Immigration, Ottawa; Department of Immigration, *Australian Immigration: Consolidated Statistics* (Canberra, 1966). For Australia the period is 1949–66.

[2] Jerome, *Migration and Business Cycles*, p. 48.

The professional and entrepreneurial element in the flow to the United States in 1967 was 35 per cent as against 3 per cent in 1907–23, while the proportion of labourers went down from 51 per cent to 11 per cent.

CANADA: AN INTERMEDIATE COUNTRY

Between 1950 and 1963 Canada received an annual average of 7,790 professional immigrants of whom 1,230 came from the United States; but 4,681 left for the United States and 795 for the United Kingdom. In order to keep 2,314 professional immigrants, Canada had to import 7,790 per annum. The situation in regard to skilled craftsmen is more favourable to Canada, the inflow being 18,284 a year and the outflow 6,210, leaving an annual net gain of 12,074.[1]

The statistics reveal that many scientists and engineers migrated from their country of birth to at least one other foreign country before eventually arriving as immigrants to the United States. For example, in 1962 and 1963 the United States received 2,316 scientists and engineers from Canada as their country of last permanent residence, whereas the number who were Canadian-born was only 1,159. Thus, 50 per cent of the scientists and engineers who crossed the border into the United States as immigrants were non-Canadians who had resided temporarily in Canada. In the decade 1953–63, the number of architects entering Canada was equal to 141 per cent of the number graduating in Canadian universities; the corresponding ratio for engineers

[1] Parai, *Immigration and Emigration of Professional and Skilled Manpower during the Post-War Period*, p. 2.

As far as Canadian-born professionals are concerned, the migration balance as between Canada and the United States became favourable in 1967 and 1968. In 1961–5 the United States had a surplus of about 2,000 a year: in 1967 and 1968 Canada had a surplus of 500 and 1,000 respectively. See Samuel, *The Migration of Canadian-born between Canada and the United States of America, 1955 to 1968*, p. 42. The main reason for this change must be the arrangements operating under the United States Immigration law of 1965 which limits immigration from all Western Hemisphere countries to 120,000 yearly, as from 1 July 1968. Mr Samuel's monograph makes no attempt to determine whether Canada's newly gained surplus is just a temporary phenomenon.

was 73 per cent and for physicians and surgeons 53 per cent. The census of 1961 showed that 25 per cent of the persons qualified as engineers and physical scientists in Canada were post-war immigrants. For other professions the proportions are as follows: architects, 35 per cent; computer programmers, 21 per cent; physicians and surgeons, 19 per cent; professors and college principals, 16 per cent; actuaries and statisticians, 15 per cent; and biological and agricultural professionals, 14 per cent.

The relative gross absorption of human capital by Canada has been phenomenally high. Her intake of professional migrants nearly quadrupled between 1962 and 1967 (from 8,218 to 30,853). With a population one-tenth of that of the United States, Canada's gross absorption in 1967 as a percentage of the gross inflow into the United States was as follows: total professional migrants, 74 per cent; engineers, 42 per cent; natural scientists, 60 per cent; physicians and surgeons, 36 per cent; professional nurses, 88 per cent.

Canada's imports of highly qualified personnel from developing countries have been rising rapidly, with no less than 37 per cent of her intake of professionals in 1967 coming from countries outside Europe and the United States. In proportion to her population, Canada is easily the largest importer of human capital in the world. Her situation next door to the massive American market explains the big difference between the relative magnitude of professional immigration to Canada and to Australia (26 per cent as against 10 per cent). Since the United States is the favourite destination of professional immigrants and the whole of North America is one large market, Canada, as a separate sovereign state, has had to work trebly hard in the immigration business in order to keep her end up. It is not a coincidence that the proportion of professional migrants in the total inflow is almost exactly the same in the United States and Canada, 27 per cent and 26 per cent respectively in 1967. Australia, at the other end of the world, loses relatively few immigrants and has no need to over-import in order to ensure an adequate input of human capital, since she is far away from the special influences operating in the United States.

If we examine the flows of skilled craftsmen as distinct from professional personnel, we find there is less difference between Canada and Australia. Between 1950 and 1963 Canada absorbed on the average 18,284 a year, 1,068 of whom came from the United States, while the outward movement was 6,210, with 5,135 going to the United States. Thus, of the gross import of 18,284, Canada kept 12,074 on the average each year. Australia between 1949 and 1960 absorbed 185,544 skilled craftsmen, or about 16,860 a year, most of whom stayed as permanent immigrants.[1]

IMMIGRANTS TO AMERICA FROM DEVELOPING COUNTRIES

The number of immigrants to the United States in the professional, technical and kindred grades rose from 18,995 in 1956 to 41,652 in 1967, or by 119 per cent; and among them the rate of increase was 215 per cent for engineers (2,804 to 8,822), 189 per cent for scientists (1,002 to 2,893), and 115 per cent for doctors (1,547 to 3,326). The proportion originating in developing countries, which was 25 per cent in 1956, reached no less than 57 per cent in 1967; and in this period immigrant scientists from these countries rose tenfold, engineers sixfold and doctors threefold. The contribution of Asian countries (excluding Japan) to this movement of professional migrants jumped from about 2,000 in 1965 to 13,000 in 1967.

This sudden change in 1966–7 was the result of the Act of 3 October 1965,[2] which abolished the quotas based on national origins and substituted a new system whose philosophy is, within limits, justification by skill instead of by skin. The Act provided for a transition period of three years, 1 July 1965 to 1 July 1968, during which the national origins system was to be phased out by enabling qualified applicants in the 'third preference' category from countries with over-subscribed quotas to be given quota

[1] Department of Immigration, *Australian Immigration, Consolidated Statistics*, No. 1, pp. 54–5.
[2] Immigration and Nationality Act of 1952 (P.L.414, 82nd Congress, 66 Stat. 163) as amended by the Act of 3 October 1965 (P.L.89–236, 89th Congress, 79 Stat.). For a detailed account of these revisions of the basic immigration law and their effect on immigration see U.S. Department of State, *1967 Report of the Visa Office*.

numbers unused by countries with large quotas, until the limit of 17,000 a year was reached. This led to the sharp increase in the number immigrating from developing countries in 1967 and 1968.[1] Because of the limitations, there was a backlog of many thousands of applicants from developing countries who could not be admitted during the transition period and whose entry was delayed until after 1 July 1968.

As from this date, former quota countries were given an overall limit of 170,000 immigrants a year with a maximum of 20,000 for any one country. Members of the professions and people with outstanding ability in the sciences and arts comprise the 'third preference' group which must not exceed 10 per cent of the total of 170,000 in any year. Another 10 per cent is allocated to the 'sixth preference' group covering skilled and unskilled workers, including scientists and engineers, whose immigration has the effect of relieving shortages of labour in the United States. Moreover, as in the past, professional, technical and kindred workers eligible on the basis of, for example, family relationship may enter either within or outside the numerical limitations. The Western Hemisphere, where previously no restrictions applied, is now subject to a limit of 120,000 a year.

The non-return of students plays a significant part in causing the inflow of professional immigrants to be as large as it is. In 1968 as many as 70 per cent of the 4,100 scientists and engineers recorded as immigrants to the United States were students who had entered the country with the declared intention of obtaining education or training and then returning home. They could do this by turning in their 'F' student visa for an immigration visa when they had obtained their degree, provided an immigration quota number was available. The ratio of student to total professional immigration in 1967 was 89 per cent for Taiwan, 80 per cent for Korea, 78 per cent for India, and 71 per cent for Iran. Nearly all the students from developing countries who did not go home were either scientists or engineers.

A valuable source of information on the stock of professional manpower in the United States is the National Register of

[1] Many of them were already in the United States as non-immigrants and changed to immigrant status.

Scientific and Technical Personnel, giving particulars of birth, high school, highest degree and citizenship. The data for foreign-born scientists in 1966 have been analysed by Herbert G. Grubel.[1] The foreign born represent 9·5 per cent of all scientists in the United States and 14·0 per cent of scientists with a Ph.D., the largest contributors being Canada (3,097), China (2,195), United Kingdom (2,041), India (1,382) and Austria (1,099). If we take scientists fully educated in their native country the ranking becomes United Kingdom (1,049), Germany (995), Canada (872), India (378), Austria (296), Japan (282) and Switzerland (264).

In order to gauge the incidence on the countries of origin, Grubel uses the number of scientists in higher education in these countries as a proxy for their stock of scientists, and he finds that the top five are Cyprus, Austria, Canada, Rhodesia and Switzerland. Another set of calculations puts the 1966 stock of foreign-born scientists in relation to general immigration to the United States in the period 1958–67. Viewed in this light India is outstanding, in that the 1966 stock of U.S. scientists fully educated in India equals 32 per 1,000 Indian immigrants to the United States in that period. The next in order are Austria (17·3 per cent), New Zealand (15·4 per cent) and Switzerland (14·7 per cent); the figure for the United Kingdom is 4·3 per cent. The Indian figure brings out clearly the influence of the immigration quotas based on national origins which severely restricted immigration from Asian countries and which could be circumvented most easily by highly educated persons. These are samples of the instructive data, hitherto unavailable, which the records of the National Science Foundation make possible.

Details of the country of last permanent residence of the 12,973 engineers and scientists and the 3,060 physicians and surgeons immigrating into the United States in 1968 are shown in Table 7.1. Western Europe contributed 4,772 engineers and scientists (nearly half of them from the United Kingdom), Canada 1,940, Asia 4,021 (of whom 1,232 were from India, 752 from the Philippines and 626 from Taiwan), and South America 595.

[1] *Characteristics of Foreign Born and Educated Scientists in the United States, 1966.*

TABLE 7.1

Scientists, engineers, and physicians and surgeons admitted to the United States as immigrants, by country or region of last permanent residence. Fiscal year 1968

Country or region of last permanent residence	1968				
	Scientists and engineers				Physicians and surgeons
	Total	Engineers	Natural scientists	Social scientists	
All countries	12,973	9,313	3,110	550	3,060
Europe	4,974	3,648	1,120	206	673
Western Europe	4,772	3,516	1,074	182	572
Austria	101	59	37	5	27
Belgium	64	50	9	5	6
Denmark	105	93	9	3	4
France	207	153	39	15	13
Germany	769	496	241	32	93
Greece	143	109	27	7	34
Ireland	57	39	15	3	21
Italy	145	80	48	17	47
Netherlands	152	101	45	6	18
Norway	148	132	13	3	7
Spain	95	61	28	6	74
Sweden	205	180	20	5	13
Switzerland	251	172	62	17	43
Turkey	61	47	8	6	49
United Kingdom	2,212	1,705	462	45	121
Other	57	39	11	7	2
Eastern Europe	202	132	46	24	101
Czechoslovakia	27	22	5	–	15
Hungary	11	5	6	–	4
Poland	88	57	18	13	36
Rumania	5	3	1	1	5
Yugoslavia	61	39	13	9	41
Other	10	6	3	1	–
North and Central America	2,867	2,041	689	137	743

TABLE 7.1 (*cont.*)

Country or region of last permanent residence	1968				
	Scientists and engineers				Physicians and surgeons
	Total	Engineers	Natural scientists	Social scientists	
Canada	1,940	1,447	417	76	325
Cuba	525	338	156	31	214
Mexico	81	53	20	8	55
Other	321	203	96	22	149
South America	595	406	152	37	341
Argentina	152	93	49	10	95
Bolivia	16	10	5	1	15
Brazil	73	45	21	7	18
Chile	42	32	7	3	16
Colombia	143	110	26	7	116
Ecuador	50	33	16	1	42
Peru	45	33	9	3	15
Venezuela	47	35	8	4	14
Other	27	15	11	1	10
Asia	4,021	2,877	993	151	1,195
Near and Middle East	522	380	116	26	238
Far East	3,499	2,497	877	125	957
China (mainland)	190	134	54	2	6
Hong Kong	200	130	66	4	42
India	1,232	944	241	47	96
Japan	109	57	43	9	23
Philippines	752	591	151	7	639
Taiwan	626	390	209	27	21
Other	390	248	113	29	130
Africa	358	249	94	15	87
All other areas	158	92	62	4	21

Note: Data include professors and instructors.
Source: National Science Foundation, *Reviews of Data on Science Resources*, No. 18, p. 7.

Of the 3,060 physicians and surgeons, nearly 40 per cent were from Asia (as many as 639 from the Philippines), 572 from Western Europe, 325 from Canada and 341 from South America.[1]

IMMIGRATION IN RELATION TO U.S. OUTPUT OF EDUCATED MANPOWER

It is of interest to assess the significance of America's imports in relation to her own output of human capital. The information set out in Table 7.2 leads to the following conclusions for the period 1956–67.

(a) U.S. output of scientists more than doubled, while imports nearly trebled until in 1967 they were 2·6 per cent of U.S. output. In 1967 50 per cent of the immigrants were from developing countries.

(b) U.S. output of engineers rose by 72 per cent, while imports increased more than threefold until in 1967 they were 16 per cent of U.S. output. In 1967 48 per cent of the immigrants were from developing countries.

(c) U.S. output of physicians remained virtually unchanged, while imports more than doubled until in 1967 they were nearly one-third of U.S. output. In 1967 two-thirds of the immigrants were from developing countries.

An official American report summed up the position as follows:

In 1967 U.S. domestic output of 173,210 graduates was an increase of 14,334 over the number graduated in 1966 of 158,876. Thus, the 7,913 scientific immigrants from the developing countries represent a supply equal to more than half of an entire year's growth in the production of U.S. scientific manpower. . . . These facts do not support a common

---

[1] For a guide to the vast literature on the brain drain see Dedijer and Svenningson, *Brain Drain and Brain Gain. A Bibliography on the Migration of Scientists, Engineers, Doctors and Students.* The most comprehensive assessment of the world situation is the report on an international research project initiated by Education and World Affairs, The Committee on the International Migration of Talent, *The International Migration of High-Level Manpower. Its Impact on the Development Process.*

TABLE 7.2

Annual additions to professional manpower by U.S. educational institutions and by immigration, 1956 and 1962–7

Fiscal Year	Scientists			Engineers			Physicians		
	Graduates of U.S. Institutions	Immigrants Number	% of U.S. Graduates	Graduates of U.S. Institutions	Immigrants Number	% of U.S. Graduates	Graduates of U.S. Institutions	Immigrants Number	% of U.S. Graduates
1956	45,948	1,022	2·2	31,646	2,804	8·9	9,862	1,547	15·7
1962	71,307	1,104	1·5	44,851	2,940	6·6	10,392	1,912	18·4
1963	77,149	1,612	2·1	44,471	4,014	9·0	10,469	2,270	21·7
1964	86,574	1,676	1·9	47,746	3,725	7·8	10,538	2,409	22·9
1965	93,368	1,549	1·6	50,975	3,455	6·8	10,482	2,194	20·9
1966	99,145	1,852	1·9	51,785	4,921	9·5	10,580	2,761	26·1
1967	107,510	2,893	2·6	55,090	8,822	16·0	10,610	3,326	31·4

Source: Committee on Government Operations, *The Brain Drain into the United States of Scientists, Engineers and Physicians. A Staff Study for the Research and Technical Programs Subcommittee of the Committee on Government Operations*, p. 3; and *Scientific Brain Drain from the Developing Countries, Twenty-Third Report by the Committee on Government Operations*, pp. 3–4.

impression that scientific immigration into the United States is largely a phenomenon affecting a few advanced countries nor the view that the brain drain from the developing countries is insignificant in size.[1]

Finally, it must be noted that the above figures are an under-estimate of the true gross inflows of human capital from poor countries, since they omit professional immigrants from developing countries who enter the United States via intermediate developed countries such as Canada, the United Kingdom and Japan. It is estimated that in 1962–4 only 1,844 out of 3,460 scientists immigrating into the United States from Canada were Canadian born, and there is evidence that a number of students from South-east Asia stay in Japan until they can qualify for permanent residence in the United States.

BRITAIN'S NET BALANCE

The picture given for the United States, although it rests on figures of gross immigration, is a reasonably good approximation since the outward movement is known to be relatively small. For Britain it is important to be able to measure the two-way traffic.

In the light of new statistics based on the censuses of 1961 and 1966, it is possible to present firm estimates of the annual outward and inward movements of qualified scientists and engineers. What happened between 1961 and 1966 can be summarized as in Table 7.3.

In the five years under review the 'natural increase' of engineers was 42,315; a net emigration of 5,555 born in Great Britain was half offset by a net immigration of 2,680 Commonwealth, Irish and foreign born, giving an overall net loss of 2,875. In the case of scientists there was a net inflow of 455 born in Great Britain in addition to the 2,860 inward balance of persons born outside Britain, so that the 'natural increase' of 39,635 British scientists was augmented by 3,315.

In interpreting these figures allowance must be made for the

[1] Committee on Government Operations, *Scientific Brain Drain from the Developing Countries. Twenty-third Report by the Committee on Government Operations*, p. 4.

differences between the quality of the outward and inward flows. According to an official report, '. . . the indications are that the immigrants contain a higher proportion of people from the newly-independent Commonwealth countries than the emigrants, and that they will generally lack the training and experience which is taken out of the country by the emigrants.'[1]

The year-to-year changes from 1958 to 1969 (see Table 7.4 and fig. 7.1) show a substantial rise in the net outflow of engineers

TABLE 7.3

Net changes in numbers of qualified scientists and engineers (1961–6)

	Engineering and technology	Science
Overall change	+39,440	+42,950
Natural increase		
(New graduates minus deaths)	+42,315	+39,635
Gain or loss by migration	− 2,875	+ 3,315
Foreign born	+ 2,460	+ 2,030
Commonwealth or Irish born	+ 220	+ 830
Great Britain born	− 5,555	+ 455

Source: Department of Trade and Industry, *Persons with Qualifications in Engineering, Technology and Science, Studies in Technological Manpower, No. 3,* p. 33.

to a peak of 3,740 in 1967, a sharp reduction to 1,755 in 1969. The peak net loss of engineers was no less than a third of the output three years earlier. There was a fluctuating net gain of scientists for most of the period until 1967 when the net loss was relatively large, and in 1969 there was again a net gain.

In a book published in 1964 B. Abel-Smith and Kathleen Gales estimated that between 1955 and 1962 doctors born and trained in Britain had been leaving the country at the average rate of 392 per year, or about a quarter of the annual output of British medical schools.[2] About 30 per cent of British doctors

[1] Committee on Manpower Resources for Science and Technology, *The Brain Drain. Report of the Working Group on Migration,* p. 13.
[2] Abel-Smith and Gales, *British Doctors at Home and Abroad.*

TABLE 7.4

United Kingdom: balance of migration of qualified scientists and engineers 1958–69

| | Persons with qualifications in engineering and technology | | | Persons with qualifications in science | | |
	Emigration	Immigration	Net balance	Emigration	Immigration	Net balance
1958	2,725	1,785	− 940	2,885	3,405	+ 520
1959	2,525	2,025	− 500	2,855	3,935	+1,080
1960	2,530	2,110	− 420	2,695	4,100	+1,405
1961	2,430	3,215	+ 785	3,135	4,035	+ 900
1962	2,735	3,025	+ 290	3,100	4,285	+1,185
1963	3,065	2,240	− 825	3,490	4,220	+ 730
1964	3,750	2,355	−1,395	3,880	3,910	+ 30
1965	4,050	3,125	− 925	4,240	4,880	+ 640
1966	5,255	2,760	−2,495	4,470	4,720	+ 250
1967	6,180	2,440	−3,740	4,895	4,160	− 735
1968	4,945	2,865	−2,080	4,995	4,970	− 25
1969*	4,685	2,930	−1,755	4,830	5,020	+ 190

* Provisional figures.

Source: Department of Trade and Industry, Persons with Qualifications in Engineering, Technology and Science, Studies in Technological Manpower, No. 3, 1971, p. 31.

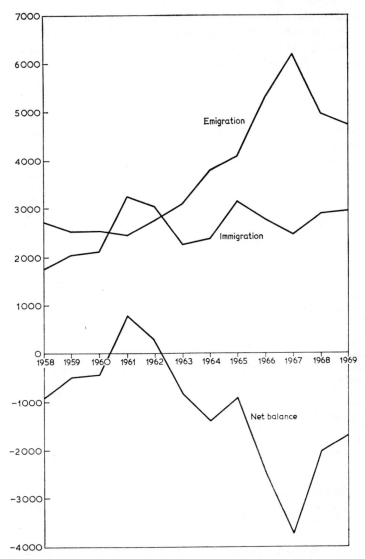

Figure 7.1 United Kingdom: inward and outward migrants with qualifications in engineering and technology, 1958–69.
Source: Table 7.4.

resident abroad were in low-income countries, and the majority of the rest were in the United States, Australia and Canada.

Subsequent analysis has thrown light on the scale and characteristics of inward as well as outward movements,[1] as shown in Table 7.5. The results for 1962–4 can be summed up as follows.

TABLE 7.5

Migration of doctors to and from Great Britain, by country of origin and destination, 1962–4

Country to or from which migration occurred	Emigrants		Immigrants or returned emigrants		Net gain or loss	
	Born U.K. or Irish Republic	*Born elsewhere*	*Born U.K. or Irish Republic*	*Born elsewhere*	*Born U.K. or Irish Republic*	*Born elsewhere*
Total	1,648	1,919	1,075	2,377	−573	+458
N. Ireland or Irish Republic	171*	51	255*	188	+ 84	+137
India	44	473	48	709	+ 4	+236
Pakistan	11	82	9	346	− 2	+264
Ceylon	–	40	3	84	+ 3	+ 44
Canada	283	97	66	44	−217	− 53
Australia	233	304	76	365	−157	+ 61
New Zealand	65	83	21	103	− 44	+ 20
Other Commonwealth	369	428	315	284	− 54	−144
U.S.A.	229	114	102	24	−127	− 90
South Africa	32	125	23	117	− 9	− 8
Other foreign	125	98	93	92	− 32	− 6
Unknown	86	24	64	21	− 22	− 3

* Represents movements between Great Britain and Northern Ireland or the Irish Republic of doctors born in the United Kingdom or the Irish Republic.
Source: Ash and Mitchell, 'Doctor Migration, 1962–1964', p. 571.

Of British or Irish born doctors 1,648 emigrated from Britain and 1,075 entered or re-entered the country, the net loss being 603 or 300 a year. Of doctors born outside the United Kingdom or

[1] Ash and Mitchell, 'Doctor Migration, 1962–1964', pp. 569–72.

the Irish Republic, 2,377 took up residence in Great Britain and 2,034 emigrated, the net gain being 343 overseas doctors or 170 a year. This latter figure, however, is an underestimate since it does not include foreign born doctors who decided to stay in Britain after graduating in British medical schools or those who obtain registrable qualified status after coming to Britain. If allowance is made for this omission, the true net gain of overseas doctors was about 300 a year. After extending the analysis to September 1965, the authors reached the following conclusion. 'The current estimate of the movement in the three years ended September 1965 of fully or provisionally registered doctors born overseas indicates that the true total net gain to medical manpower in Great Britain of such doctors seems to counterbalance the net loss of doctors born in the United Kingdom and Irish Republic.'[1]

In 1965 Great Britain had a stock of 62,700 'economically active' doctors, or 1,181 per million of the population.[2] Of these over 10,000 working in the National Health Service were born outside the British Isles (8,000 in the hospital service and 2,600 in general practice in England and Wales),[3] and two out of every three of these non-British doctors had come from developing countries, mainly India and Pakistan. In 1967 the graduates of non-British medical schools who established practice in Britain (2,053) outnumbered those who had qualified at home (1,933).[4]

One effect of the American immigration law of 1965 has been to deflect overseas doctors from Britain. To obtain a licence to practise in America doctors must pass the examination of the Educational Council for Foreign Medical Graduates, and the number of candidates each year is a good index of the propensity to emigrate. The number rose from 254 in 1964 to 620 in 1965 and 802 in 1966; in 1968 the American Embassy in London revealed that over half the doctors sitting the examination for entry

[1] Ibid., p. 572.
[2] Royal Commission on Medical Education, 1965–8, *Report*, p. 133.
[3] Gish, 'The Royal Commission and the Immigrant Doctor'.
[4] The Committee on the International Migration of Talent, *The International Migration of High-Level Manpower. Its Impact on the Development Process*, p. 602.

to America were non-British. This new factor has added to the difficulties facing the British National Health Service.

Both Britain and the United States are drawing medical personnel from the developing countries, but there is an important difference. The United States has very little leakage outward; her stocks gain by almost the amount of her imports. The supply of graduates from American medical schools hardly increased at all in the 1960s. Britain, on the other hand, is very much part of the international circular flow; it is the high rate of emigration to the United States, Canada, Australia and similar countries which makes it necessary to import so much medical personnel from developing countries.

DYNAMIC SHORTAGE AND BRAIN DRAIN

The trends brought out by our statistical survey, and the contrast with the nineteenth-century pattern which emerges from the survey, can be summed up in a generalization. The combination of mass unskilled migration, population-sensitive capital formation and portfolio foreign investment has been replaced by professional elite migration, science-based capital formation and direct foreign investment. The question raised by 'brain drain' is whether, in this new setting, there is a tendency for the growth potential of countries of emigration (particularly the less developed) to be reduced in favour of that of countries receiving a large net immigration.

Some economists, using the techniques of welfare economics, have tried to show that there is no significant possibility of 'world loss' from the international migration of educated people.[1] Such reasoning implies a 'world social welfare function', and it is hard to see what possible meaning could be attached to such a notion. It must be recognized that, since there are strong barriers to the international movement of unskilled labour, we are confronted with a 'second-best' situation. The issue turns on the presence of externalities. Given the maximization of world output as the value criterion, there can be no dispute as to the existence of several

[1] E.g. Grubel and Scott, 'The International Flow of Human Capital', pp. 268–74.

theoretical possibilities of world loss through the loss of externalities to sending countries, which are not offset by gains of externalities to receiving countries, and which also more than counterbalance the increase in private income received by the migrants.[1]

The formidable difficulties of operating a 'world social welfare
function' have been pointed out by Don Patinkin, in his paper 'A
"Nationalist" Model'.[2] He made a highly relevant point in the
following passage:

> Countries which are concerned with their losses from the 'brain
> drain' have been criticized by some economists as acting in
> accordance with 'anachronistic' concepts of 'economic and
> military power' and national prestige. (Grubel and Scott, op.
> cit., p. 274.) An implicit assumption of this criticism is that
> such 'nationalistic' actions are interfering with the free flow
> of manpower resources in an international market which would
> otherwise reflect the welfare-maximizing behaviour of in-
> dividuals. But this is simply not the case for the 'brain drain'
> as it exists today. For this market already reflects to a highly
> significant degree a demand for manpower generated by the
> nationalistic considerations of the U.S. government defense and
> space programs. Correspondingly, the nationalistic influences
> which the 'brain-losing' countries attempt to exert on the *supply*
> side of the international manpower market can to a large extent
> be seen as an offset of the nationalist forces on the *demand* side.[3]

This comment is fully borne out by the evidence on the causes of
dynamic shortage presented in this chapter.

The diagnosis to be put forward here receives support from
developments in growth theory. Of particular interest are models
based on the notion of a gap between the discovery of new techniques and the application of them in industry, for example, the

[1] See Thomas, 'The International Circulation of Human Capital',
pp. 489–94; Johnson, 'Some Economic Aspects of Brain Drain', pp.
388–9; Thomas, 'The International Circulation of Human Capital: a
Reply to Harry G. Johnson', pp. 423–7.
The main contributions to this controversy have been reprinted in
Blaug, ed., *Economics of Education*, Vol. 2, pp. 241–301.
[2] In Adams, ed., *The Brain Drain*, pp. 99–108.
[3] Ibid., pp. 105–6.

one by R. R. Nelson and E. S. Phelps which states that the rate at which the most advanced known technology is applied in industrial practice depends on the degree of human capital intensity and the level of technology in practice. The rate of increase of technology in practice is an increasing function of human capital intensity and proportional to the gap. These authors have indicated the bearing of these ideas on human capital and growth.

> According to these models, the rate of return to education is greater the more technologically progressive is the economy. This suggests that the progressiveness of the technology has implications for the optimal capital structure in the broad sense. In particular, it may be that society should build more human capital relatively to tangible capital the more dynamic is the technology. . . . If innovations produce externalities, because they show the way to imitators, then education – by its stimulation of innovation – also yields externalities. Hence, the way of viewing the role of education in economic growth set forth here seems to indicate another possible source of a divergence between the private and social rate of return to education.[1]

The importance of science-based capital formation has added greatly to the role of Research and Development. That this is highly relevant to an analysis of the international circulation of professional manpower is borne out by the fact that more than half the foreign born scientists in the United States are in R. and D. compared with 35 per cent of all U.S. scientists, and 41 per cent of foreign born engineers are in R. and D. compared with 27 per cent of all U.S. engineers. Promising work has been done on the R. and D. factor as an explanatory variable in international trade and international investment and in inter-State productivity differentials in industry and agriculture.[2] The results suggest

[1] Nelson and Phelps, 'Investment in Humans, Technological Diffusion, and Economic Growth', pp. 72–5.
[2] For example, Gruber, Mehta and Vernon, 'The R. and D. Factor in International Trade and International Investment of United States Industries', and Keesing, 'The Impact of Research and Development

interesting hypotheses concerning human capital flows and differentials between growth rates of countries at different levels of development.

The highest grades of professional manpower are expensive to produce and they take a long time to train; they play a far more crucial role in the process of growth than they did in the nineteenth century, as the pace is now set by science-based industries. Human capital is highly mobile internationally and is attracted to areas where real private productivity is highest. Because of the increasing demand for educated manpower in the technologically progressive economies and the externalities yielded by education-intensive investment through the stimulation of innovations, there is keen competition between advanced countries for supplies of top skills.

An important reason for the upward shifts in the demand for scientists and engineers in the United States after 1950 was the prominent part played by the Federal Government in financing Research and Development. Expenditure on R. and D. in industry rose from $7,731 million in 1957 to $14,197 million in 1965, and 55 per cent of it came from Federal funds. In 1965 the number of Federally-financed R. and D. scientists and engineers totalled 162,900, or nearly half of all such personnel (346,000) in industry. The Department of Defence supported 59 per cent, and the National Aeronautics and Space Administration 30 per cent, of all R. and D. scientists and engineers engaged in Federal projects. Total expenditure on R. and D. (public and private sectors) rose from $5,210 million in 1953 to $25,000 million in 1968, and $15,500 million of the latter, or over 60 per cent, came from the Federal Government.

The number of R. and D. scientists and engineers in industry rose from 243,800 in January 1958 to 358,900 in January 1966, i.e. by 47 per cent; in the same period industrial R. and D.

---

on United States Trade', pp. 20–48. Griliches, 'Production Functions in Manufacturing: Some Preliminary Results' in Brown, ed., *The Theory and Empirical Analysis of Production*; 'Research Expenditure, Education, and the Aggregate Agricultural Production Function', pp. 961–74. Besen, 'Education and Productivity: Some Cross-Section Evidence', pp. 494–7.

funds increased by 84 per cent. The expansion of employment of R. and D. scientists and engineers in two industries in this period was outstanding, 43,300, or 90 per cent, in electrical equipment and communications, and 42,100, or 72 per cent, in aircraft and missiles; and it is in these industries that Federal financing is paramount, 63 per cent and 88 per cent respectively. It is a

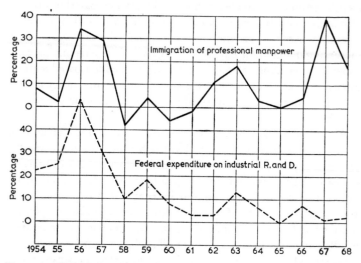

Figure 7.2 United States: immigration of professional manpower and Federal expenditure on industrial R. and D., 1954–68 (annual percentage rate of change).
Sources: National Science Foundation, *Science Manpower Bulletin*, p. 2; id., *Reviews of Data on Science Resources*, No. 12, p. 4; id., *Science Resources Studies Highlights*, 25 May 1970, pp. 1–2; Department of Justice, Immigration and Naturalization Service, *Annual Reports of the Commissioner of Immigration and Naturalization*; id., *Annual Indicator of the In-migration into the United States of Aliens in Professional and Related Occupations*.

striking fact that no less than 74 per cent of the all-industry growth in the employment of R. and D. scientists and engineers between 1957 and 1965 occurred in these two industries, largely governed by the defence and space programmes of the Federal Government. In January 1966 the aircraft and missiles industry alone employed 28 per cent of all R. and D. scientists and engineers.

Fig. 7.2 shows a close relationship between the annual percentage rates of change in Federal expenditure on Research and Development and in immigration of professional manpower over the period 1953–68. There can be little doubt that Federal expenditure on R. and D. was a major determinant, and the statistics show that immigrant scientists and engineers were on the average of superior quality and more heavily engaged in R. and D. than their U.S. counterparts.

Let us draw a distinction between skills which are 'general' and those which are 'specific'.[1] General training equips the trainee with a skill which is as useful elsewhere as in the firm providing the training. Consequently the marginal productivity of the trainee is raised equally both outside and inside the firm, and under competitive conditions the costs of training will be borne by the trainee. In the case of purely specific training the marginal productivity is raised only within the firm and not outside, so that the training costs are borne by the firm. The United Kingdom has a large capacity for producing educated manpower whose skills are general rather than specific. Scientists and technologists are a good example of human capital which is universally usable, and this is particularly true of British personnel going to other English-speaking countries.

The production of educated manpower in the United Kingdom is heavily subsidized out of public funds. It would not be doing undue violence to the facts to conceive of the United Kingdom as a gigantic public firm with a large annual output of general skills, the cost of whose production is borne mainly by the firm itself. In a situation where public investment in general skills is financed in a manner appropriate to specific skills, i.e. the firm paying the costs and not the trainee, it is easy to attract a plentiful supply of trainees but not so easy to keep them when they are qualified.

Following Arrow and Capron[2] we can say that, if there is a steady upward shift in the demand for scientists and engineers

---

[1] Becker, *Human Capital: A Theoretical and Empirical Analysis, with Special Reference to Education.*
[2] Arrow and Capron, 'Dynamic Shortages and Price Rises: the Engineer-Scientist Case'.

over a period of time, and if there continue to be unfilled vacancies in positions where salaries are the same as those being currently paid in others of the same type and quality, there is a dynamic shortage. With every shift in the demand curve the market price tends to rise towards the equilibrium price but the equilibrium price moves and the market price does not catch up with it. The magnitude of this dynamic shortage depends on the rate of increase of demand, the reaction speed in the market (i.e. the ratio of the rate of price rise to the excess demand), and the elasticity of supply and demand.

The reaction speed in the market for engineers and scientists in America has been low, because of long-term contracts, the diversity and special requirements within each profession causing an imperfect spread of information, and the dominance of oligopolistic firms in research and development. The elasticity of supply of scientists and engineers in the short run is necessarily low because of the time it takes to train new ones, but even over the long period the evidence suggests that the engineering profession in the United States has been becoming relatively less attractive. Engineering students as a proportion of all freshmen declined from 22 per cent in 1957 to 13·5 per cent in 1965. A more significant symptom is the change in the preferences of the most gifted students reported on by the National Merit Scholarship Corporation. The proportion of the Merit Scholars opting for engineering fell from 33·6 per cent in 1957 to 20·2 per cent in 1965, whereas the proportions going in for teaching and law rose from 8 per cent to 15·5 per cent and 6·5 per cent to 11 per cent respectively. Furthermore, whereas 23 per cent of Merit Scholars going to college in 1956 planned to enter engineering, a follow-up study revealed that only 4 per cent of these same students had the same goal in 1964.[1]

To sum up, there were two powerful forces pushing the American demand curve for human capital to the right during the 1950s and most of the 1960s: first, autonomous public investment – the large-scale expansion in the education-intensive space and defence programmes of the Federal Government, and secondly,

[1] See Engineering Manpower Commission of the Engineers' Joint Council, *Engineering Manpower, Bulletin 6.*

the endogenous factor in the economy – the tendency of private investment to require increasing doses of human capital to sustain its rate of growth. The dynamic shortage thus generated coexisted with heavily subsidized production of general skills together with administered salary levels in a large sector of the economy in the United Kingdom and other countries, and this played a crucial part in causing brain drain.

When I put forward this interpretation in a lecture in March 1967, I added the qualification that

> . . . we must be careful about prophesying a permanent dynamic shortage in the market for professional manpower in the United States. One recalls how preoccupied people were with the 'dollar shortage' in the 1950s and how that shortage soon gave way to a dollar glut. . . . It is conceivable that changes in the elements governing dynamic shortage in the United States could bring a relaxation in the world market for skills at the very time when the current flow of output of professional manpower in Europe is sharply rising as a result of an increase in investment undertaken a few years earlier in circumstances of extreme scarcity.[1]

As it turned out, this prognosis proved to be justified. By the end of the 1960s the motive force governing dynamic shortage had weakened, but the reality was temporarily blurred by the effects of the change in the American immigration law. Although the data do not allow us to measure with any precision some of the operative elements, e.g. the ratio of the rate of increase in the salaries of engineers and scientists to the excess demand (the reaction speed) and the elasticities of supply and demand, we do know fairly accurately what was happening to our main explanatory variable, Federal expenditure on R. and D.

We have already noted the clear correlation between annual rates of change in Federal expenditure on industrial R. and D. and in immigration of professional, technical and kindred grades, 1953–68 (fig. 7.2). The only exception was the year 1967, and

[1] 'The International Circulation of Human Capital', a lecture delivered under the auspices of the University of London at the London School of Economics on 2 March 1967. Published in *Minerva*, quotation on p. 502.

this will need to be looked at in the light of the change in the immigration law.

To get a closer picture we shall examine the market for engineers, the available information for which is given in fig. 7.3 and Table 7.6. First, we can see how steep was the rise in Federal

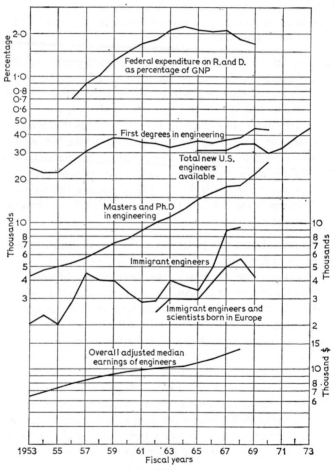

Figure 7.3 United States: internal supply, immigration, and earnings of engineers, 1953–73.
Sources: Table 7.6.

TABLE 7.6 United States: internal supply, immigration, and earnings of engineers, 1953–73

Year	Federal expenditure on R. and D. as % of GNP	Total new U.S. engineers available	Masters and Ph.D. in engineering	Immigrant engineers	Immigrant engineers and scientists born in Europe	Overall adjusted median earnings of engineers($)
1953	–	–	4,227	2,066	–	6,450
1954	–	–	4,668	2,304	–	–
1955	–	–	4,978	2,021	–	–
1956	0·7	–	5,199	2,804	–	7,975
1957	0·9	–	5,689	4,547	–	–
1958	1·02	–	6,316	4,032	–	8,300
1959	1·3	–	7,329	3,950	–	–
1960	1·5	–	7,775	3,354	–	9,650
1961	1·7	–	8,920	2,890	–	–
1962	1·8	–	10,116	2,940	2,431	10,025
1963	2·1	–	10,838	4,014	3,002	–
1964	2·25	–	12,520	3,725	2,982	10,475
1965	2·10	31,700	14,370	3,446	2,978	–
1966	2·04	31,800	15,980	4,915	3,412	11,850
1967	2·1	31,800	17,780	8,821	5,023	–
1968	1·8	35,300	18,085	9,313	5,660	13,900
1969	1·7	35,600	21,400	7,150	2,850	–
1970	–	29,800*	25,670	–	–	–
1971	–	33,100*	–	–	–	–
1972	–	38,600*	–	–	–	–
1973	–	45,500*	–	–	–	–

* Projections.

Sources: National Science Foundation, Science Resources Studies Highlights, 14 August 1970, p. 2; id., Scientists, Engineers, and Physicians from Abroad, 1966 and 1967, pp. 2–5; id., Science Resources Surveys Release, 24 February 1970, p. 4; Engineering Manpower Commission of the Engineers' Joint Council, Prospects of Engineering and Technology; Graduates 1968, p. 29; id., Professional Income of Engineers 1968–1969, p. 20; id., Engineering Manpower Bulletin, No. 17, p. 3.

expenditure on R. and D. as a proportion of GNP – from o·7 per cent in 1956 to a peak of 2·25 per cent in 1964 and an average of 2·12 per cent in the years 1963–7. In the late 1950s the number of students taking first degrees in engineering rose sharply from 22,000 to 38,000 but this was followed by a decade of stagnation, the number graduating in 1968 being no higher than it had been in 1959. Meanwhile, the number of M.Sc. and Ph.D. degrees awarded in engineering soared from just over 5,000 in 1956 to nearly 18,000 in 1967. The recruitment of immigrants, with year-to-year variations in line with Federal expenditures, had a strong upward trend, and one can infer from the course of the earnings of engineers that the reaction speed was low.

The interesting question is whether the sharp fall in immigration in 1969 indicates a temporary relaxation or a more lasting phase in which dynamic shortage will have lost much of its force. One cannot be certain. The market for professional manpower in the inflationary boom of the late 1960s was complicated by the effects of selective service and changes in the immigration law. In the transition, when the national origins system was being phased out, qualified applicants from countries with small quotas were given quota numbers unused by countries with large quotas, and the dramatic consequence of this is quantified in fig. 7.4. In the three years, 1966–8, no less than 25 per cent of the 32,701 engineers and scientists who 'immigrated' were former students resident in the United States who obtained immigrant visas, and 90 per cent of these former students were Asian-born. Admission on a 'first-come, first-served' basis according to skill categories began to operate in the fiscal year 1969, and there was a backlog from the transition period. In that year Asian-born immigrants were the largest group of engineers and scientists admitted – 5,300 as compared with 4,400 in 1968. The introduction of a quota for the Western Hemisphere was an additional factor. Persons born in Asia were able to compete more effectively for available immigrant visas.

We can now return to the main question. The major determinant – Federal expenditure on R. and D. as a proportion of GNP – fell from 2·1 per cent in 1967 to 1·7 per cent in 1969, and total R. and D. outlay (private as well as public), which had levelled at

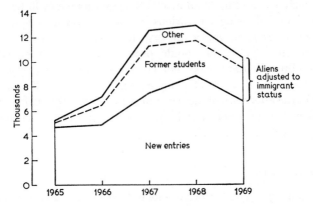

Figure 7.4 United States: immigrant scientists and engineers as new entries and alien residents changing status, fiscal years 1965–9.
Sources: National Science Foundation, *Reviews of Data on Science Resources*, Nos. 13 and 18; id., *Scientists, Engineers and Physicians from Abroad, 1966 and 1967;* id., *Science Resources Surveys Release*, No. 2.

3 per cent of GNP in the mid-1960s, was also sagging. It was estimated that defence spending planned for the year ended 30 June 1971 would be $17,000 million less (in constant dollars) than at the peak of the Vietnam war, and the number of people employed in industries connected with defence declined by 400,000 in 1969–70. There was also a cutback in the space programme. A new and sombre phenomenon darkened the scene; there was widespread professional unemployment in the industries and areas which had profited so handsomely from the spectacular rise of the Federally-supported 'military-industrial complex'.[1]

The number of European-born engineers and scientists immigrating in 1969 was 50 per cent less than in the previous year (fig. 7.3). The Engineering Manpower Council's projection for

[1] Under the heading, 'Brain Drain from California back to Europe', the Los Angeles correspondent of *The Guardian* reported as follows on 5 August 1971. 'California's population used to grow by 1000 immigrants a day. Now for the first time, the State is exporting people and expects a net loss this year. By saving the Lockheed TriStar, the American Government has only prevented bad unemployment in the Pacific Coast aircraft industry from assuming disastrous proportions. A quarter of America's aerospace workers live on the West Coast where jobs have gone down

the early 1970s of the total new U.S. engineers who will be available (after allowing for various leakages) gives a decline from 35,600 in 1969 to 29,800 in 1970 followed by a steady rise to 45,500 in 1973. If this should prove correct, and the Federal expenditure variable does not change its course (fig. 7.3), the relaxation in the market for engineers and scientists will continue; but in the aftermath of the new immigration law this can be quite consistent with a not insignificant absorption of educated people from developing countries.

CONCLUSION

Our main purpose has been to identify the determinants of brain drain by concentrating on demand conditions in the United States, the largest market for human capital, and supply conditions in the leading countries of emigration. The quantitative evidence suggests that the model of dynamic shortage helps to explain the course of events in the period 1950–70. The main cause of the excess demand in the international market for skills was an autonomous factor – the huge public investment programme of the United States Government. It is not possible to measure the extent, if any, to which the absorption of human capital by the main net importers restricted the growth of the countries supplying the migrants. The annual real growth rate *per capita* in developing countries as a whole was 2·5 per cent in 1960–7 compared with 2·3 per cent in 1950–60; the corresponding rates for industrialized countries were 3·6 per cent and 2·8 per cent respectively. This indicates a substantial divergence, due largely to the differential rate of growth of population. Any estimate of the role of brain drain as a factor contributing to this

---

from 615,000 in 1967 to 435,000, a drop of nearly 30 per cent. . . . In Seattle, where Boeing has its plant, 105,700 workers in July 1968 dwindled to 39,400 in May this year, and unemployment is 12 per cent. In Los Angeles local unemployment is 7½ per cent. . . . Those who came to California as part of the brain drain from Europe are going back. Germany has vacancies for its own nationals, and for Americans too.' The chairman of the American Civil Aeronautics Board was quoted as saying: 'Other Governments are buying our brains and therefore our technology.'

divergence would have to be done by examining each developing country separately, as conditions vary so much.

At the beginning of this chapter attention was drawn to the two international circuits – the movement of professional manpower from poor to rich countries and the reverse flow of publicly-financed technical personnel into the poor countries; and we have seen how large a part is played in the brain drain by the non-return of students. The Pearson Commission on International Development concluded that

> . . . indiscriminate scholarship awards for study in advanced countries, as well as some training programs, have contributed to acceleration of the 'brain drain' out of poor countries. This problem is of disturbing dimensions. The present flow of skilled and qualified personnel from poor to rich countries actually outnumbers the number of advisory personnel going from rich to poor. In 1967, the developing countries obtained the temporary services of 16,000 foreign advisers (out of a total of over 100,000 technical assistance personnel), but the U.N. estimates that close to 40,000 of their own national professionals emigrated to the industrialized countries.[1]

Whether this emigration is to be regarded as brain drain in the technical sense, i.e. a brake on growth, depends on conditions in the country concerned. There is abundant evidence that a number of underdeveloped countries have been producing far more graduates than could possibly be gainfully employed at home;[2] stocks of university graduates have been going up at the rate of about 10 per cent a year, whereas GNP has been rising at about 5 per cent a year.[3] The situation in India has been described as follows.

> Expansion acquires a momentum which cannot be easily resisted when altered circumstances require a change of policy. The ultimate limitation of resources dictates a decline in

[1] Pearson and associates, *Partners in Development, Report of the Commission on International Development*, pp. 201–2.
[2] See The Committee on the International Migration of Talent, op. cit., pp. 685–9.　　　　　　　　　　　　　[3] Ibid., p. 685.

standards, which accelerates the scramble for higher education by further postponing the saturation of labour markets, only to recreate a still more intractable problem later on. The process has probably gone further in India than anywhere else, but India is the mirror in which the developing countries of Africa and Asia can see the problem they will be facing in the decade of the 1970s.[1]

Clearly, the overflow of talent from these countries will continue as long as they maintain an educational system which '. . . only too easily becomes an instigator of maladjustment and structural unemployment rather than an essential source of growth and development'.[2] Unfortunately, this overflow contains men of exceptional ability, such as leaders of teams, and their departure is a real economic loss, particularly where the infant industry argument applies.

In the case of some of the middle group of countries, including the United Kingdom as well as some developing countries in the Middle East and East and Central Africa, the incidence of brain drain can be more clearly established since the growth of the economies presupposed adequate inputs of particular skills and there is less unemployed human capital. Here, for reasons previously referred to, the leakage of talent means an economic loss. When the United States, in pursuit of her national goals, absorbed human capital which other countries have paid for by taxation to promote the achievement of their own goals, there is brain drain in the true sense. It behoves the United States, Canada and Australia to spend more of their own resources in expanding their capacity to produce expensive skills, particularly medical graduates, so as to reduce their reliance on other countries' public investment. Our model showed that in the country of emigration, public subsidizing of the production of general skills together with administered salary levels in the public sector tended to increase the outflow; if appropriate policies were applied to change these supply conditions, the incidence of brain drain would be reduced.

[1] Blaug, Layard and Woodhall, *The Causes of Graduate Unemployment in India.*   [2] Pearson and associates, op. cit., p. 68.

As to the future, any projection is bound to be hazardous. The propensity of American professionals to emigrate may increase and the attractiveness of America for Europeans may diminish, thereby enlarging the scope for qualified immigrants from the poorer countries. The method of financing higher education in the United Kingdom and other countries may be changed, e.g. by the substitution of loans for grants, so that the costs of training in general skills are borne in greater measure by the beneficiaries. A continuing pronounced shift in the interest of American students away from science and technology could have a profound effect on future supplies of engineers and scientists, whereas a combination of a static output of graduates from American medical schools and a high income elasticity of demand for medical service would mean an increasing levy on the supplies of graduates from other countries' medical schools. The revival of public and private demand for human capital in a buoyant American economy could entail another phase of serious dynamic shortage.

Finally, we must remember that the 1950s and 1960s were unique in that the emergence of the American science giant involved an immense accelerator effect; the steep rate of growth of R. and D. expenditure as a proportion of GNP was bound to level off. The demand for human capital cannot go on growing faster than the economy, and there has to be a limit to the number of Ph.D.'s who can be absorbed by the science establishment.[1] There must be some natural rate at which the growth of demand for human capital will ultimately tend to settle, and the movement towards this equilibrium will bring problems with international repercussions very different from those of dynamic shortage.

[1] For a formal presentation of this line of thought see Martino's valuable paper, 'Science and Society in Equilibrium'.

Epilogue on the Kuznets Cycle

The Atlantic economy of the period 1840–1924 was succeeded after World War II by a different balance of forces which gave the phenomenon of brain drain a special but passing significance. We now come to the solemn question of whether we should say farewell to the Kuznets cycle. Abramovitz, as chief mourner, has written a moving epitaph. 'The Kuznets cycle in America lived, it flourished, it had its day, but its day is past. Departed, it leaves to us who survive to study its works many insights into the kinds of connections and responses which go together to make for spurts and retardations in development. We are the wiser for its life, but it is gone. *Requiescat in pace.* Gone but not forgotten.'[1] For my own part, I am inclined to repeat Mark Twain's remark when he read an obituary of himself in the papers; he said that the news was somewhat exaggerated.

It is not possible here to do justice to the powerful arguments presented by Abramovitz. What he is saying is that the old Kuznets cycle was '. . . a form of growth which belonged to a particular period in history and that the economic structure and institutions which imposed that form on the growth process have evolved, or been changed, into something different'.[2] He is anxious '. . . to guard the integrity and usefulness of the Kuznets-cycle hypothesis for interpreting development in the United States, Canada and Western Europe from about the 1840s to 1914 by shielding it from an inappropriate confrontation with the different form which the growth process is taking, and is likely to take, in the contemporary world'.[3] He is not saying that

[1] Abramovitz, 'The Passing of the Kuznets Cycle', p. 367.
[2] Ibid., p. 349.   [3] Ibid.

long swings have had their day. This he makes clear in the following sentence. 'What I do wish to argue is that the specific set
of relations and response mechanisms which were characteristic
of pre-1914 "long swings" in growth are unlikely to be characteristic of future long swings. These will be of a different sort and
may, indeed, not have much in common with one another in,
say, their durations, amplitudes or internal structure.'[1] It would
appear, then, that the deceased mourned by Abramovitz was that
well-known member of the family, the American Kuznets Cycle,
Born 1840: Departed this Life 1914.

One feature of the modern world which is weighing heavily in
the argument is the ending of mass immigration; it is held to be a
matter of chance whether long swings produced merely by the
echo effects of past fluctuations in births will generate the pre-
1914 type of Kuznets cycle. Then there is the point that governments now know how to prevent serious depressions. Another
factor is the greatly increased volume of Federal, State and local
government expenditures in the United States and the promin-
ence of government grants and loans in the outflow of capital.
However, Abramovitz admits that '. . . the adaptive variation in
the flows of capital funds which, before 1914, made possible regular divergent fluctuations in the growth rates of Europe and the
United States, may well continue to operate in the future. But it
will probably be called on to operate only sporadically; not regu-
larly. For with the disappearance of the migration link, the chief
cause of regular divergent fluctuations between the two halves
of the Atlantic Community has been removed.'[2] This emphasis
on the migration link as the basic cause of the inverse rates of
growth in the pre-1914 period is in line with the main thesis of
this book; but as to the future, one should keep an open mind
despite the disappearance of trans-Atlantic mass migration. Much
more research needs to be done on long swings in the post-1945
period.[3]

Changes in population structure and their echo effects on both

---

[1] Ibid., pp. 349–50.   [2] Ibid., p. 366.
[3] For an instructive pioneering study see Bernstein, 'The Post-War
Trend Cycle in the United States', pp. 1–10. See also Hickman, 'The
Post-war Retardation: Another Long Swing in the Rate of Growth?'

sides of the Atlantic must continue to be reckoned with, and the demographic determinants of construction cycles will not disappear, particularly in an age in which problems of population and urbanization are going to be crucial. Waves of internal or intra-continental migration can be a potent generator of long swings and in the United States even the demographic force of immigration is by no means a thing of the past. As we saw in Chapter 5, the North and West between 1950 and 1970 received a massive influx of 3 million young blacks, the echo effects of which are bound to entail demographic cycles with a powerful social and economic impact. If we add the 5 million immigrants from abroad, we get a decennial rate of over 4 million for 1950–70 which is half the record inflow into the United States in 1901–10. Since the future demographic and economic consequences in America are likely to conform to well-established patterns, the old American Kuznets cycle may yet show that it is not half as dead as it looks. Finally, the ending of the Bretton Woods international monetary regime in 1971 may be the beginning of a new process of interaction which could entail systematic long swing divergencies between growth rates in the United States and an enlarged European Economic Community of comparable magnitude.

Bibliography

FURTHER READING

A bibliography of 397 items is contained in Brinley Thomas, *International Migration and Economic Development: A Trend Report and Bibliography*, Paris, Unesco, 1961.

For literature on urban history reference should be made to H. J. Dyos, ed., *The Study of Urban History*, London, Edward Arnold, 1968; *Research in Economic and Social Research: A Social Science Research Council Review*, London, Heinemann, 1971, pp. 47–54; Asa Briggs, *Victorian Cities*, London, Penguin, new edition 1968.

REFERENCES

ABEL-SMITH, B. and GALES, K. *British Doctors at Home and Abroad*, London, Bell, 1964.

ABRAMOVITZ, M. 'The Nature and Significance of Kuznets Cycles', *Economic Development and Cultural Change*, Chicago, IX (3), April 1961, pp. 225–48.

—, *Evidences of Long Swings in Aggregate Construction since the Civil War*, National Bureau of Economic Research, New York, Columbia University Press, 1964.

—, 'The Passing of the Kuznets Cycle', *Economica*, XXXV (140), November 1968, pp. 349–67.

ADELMAN, IRMA. 'Long Cycles – Fact or Artifact?', *American Economic Review*, June 1965, pp. 444–63.

ADLER, J. H. (ed.) *Capital Movements and Economic Development*, London, Macmillan, 1967.

Bibliography

AMERICAN PHILOSOPHICAL SOCIETY, *Population Redistribution and Economic Growth, United States, 1870–1950* (Philadelphia): Vol. I (1957) by Everett S. Lee, Ann Ratner Miller, Carol P. Brainerd and Richard A. Easterlin; Vol. II (1960) by Simon Kuznets, Ann Ratner Miller and Richard A. Easterlin; Vol. III (1964) by Hope T. Eldridge and Dorothy S. Thomas.

ARROW, KENNETH J. and CAPRON, WILLIAM N. 'Dynamic Shortages and Price Rises: the Engineer-Scientist Case', *Quarterly Journal of Economics*, LXXIII (2), May 1959, pp. 302–8.

ASH, R. and MITCHELL, H. D. 'Doctor Migration, 1962–1964', *British Medical Journal*, 2 March 1968, pp. 569–72.

BALFOUR, RT. HON. A. J. *Economic Notes on Insular Free Trade*, London, Longmans, 1903.

BARNÉNAS, J. 'International Movement of Public Long-term Capital and Grants, 1951–2', *International Monetary Fund, Staff Papers*, V, 1 February 1956.

BARRACLOUGH, GEOFFREY, *An Introduction to Contemporary History*, London, Penguin, 1967.

BEACH, W. E. *British International Gold Movements and Banking Policy, 1881–1913*, Cambridge, Mass., Harvard University Press, 1935.

BECKER, G. S. *Human Capital: A Theoretical and Empirical Analysis, with Special Reference to Education*, New York, National Bureau of Economic Research, Columbia University Press, 1964.

BERNSTEIN, EDWARD M. *International Effects of U.S. Economic Policy*, Study Paper No. 16, prepared for the Joint Economic Committee, Congress of the United States, 25 January 1960, Washington D.C. 1960.

—, 'The Post-war Trend Cycle in the United States', New York, Model Roland and Co., *Quarterly Review*, First Quarter 1963, pp. 1–10.

BESEN, STANLEY M. 'Education and Productivity: Some Cross-Section Evidence', *Journal of Political Economy*, 76 (3), May–June 1968, pp. 494–7.

BIRD, R. C., DESAI, M. J., ENZLER, J. J. and TAUBMAN, P. J. 'Kuznets Cycles in Growth Rates: the Meaning', *International Economic Review*, VI, May 1965, pp. 229–39.

BLACKER, C. P. 'Stages in Population Growth', *The Eugenics Review*, 39 (3), October 1947, pp. 89–94.

BLAUG, M. (ed.) *Economics of Education*, Vol. 2, Harmondsworth, Penguin Modern Economics Readings, Penguin, 1969.

BLAUG, M., LAYARD, P. R. G. and WOODHALL, M. H. *The Causes of Graduate Unemployment in India*, London, Allen Lane, The Penguin Press, 1969.

BLOOMFIELD, ARTHUR I. *Monetary Policy under the International Gold Standard, 1880–1914*, New York, Federal Reserve Bank of New York, October 1959.

—, *Patterns of Fluctuation in International Investment before 1914*, Princeton, N.J., Princeton Studies in International Finance No. 21, International Finance Section, Department of Economics, Princeton University, 1968.

BORTS, GEORGE H. and STEIN, JEROME L. 'Regional Growth and Maturity in the United States: A Study of Regional Structural Change', *Schweizerische Zeitschrift für Volkswirtschaft und Statistik*, 98 (3), 1962, pp. 290–321.

—, *Economic Growth in a Free Market*, New York and London, Columbia University Press, 1964.

BOWLEY, A. L. 'Area and Population' in *The New Survey of London Life and Labour*, Vol. I: *Forty Years of Change*, London, P. S. King, 1930, pp. 58–83.

BROWN, THOMAS N. *Social Discrimination against the Irish in the United States*, New York, The American Jewish Committee, November 1958.

BUCKLEY, K. A. H. 'Urban Building and Real Estate Fluctuations in Canada', *Canadian Journal of Economic and Political Science*, February 1952, pp. 51–62.

—, *Capital Formation in Canada 1896–1930*, Toronto, Toronto University Press, 1955.

—, *Population, Labour Force and Economic Growth, 1867–1962*, Banff, Alberta, Banff School of Advanced Management, 1964.

BUTLIN, NOEL G. *Investment in Australian Economic Development, 1861–1900*, Cambridge, Cambridge University Press, 1964.

CAGAN, PHILLIP, *Determinants and Effects of Changes in the Stock of Money 1875–1960*, New York, National Bureau of Economic Research, New York, Columbia University Press, 1965.

Bibliography

CAIRNCROSS, A. K. 'Internal Migration in Victorian England', *The Manchester School of Economic and Social Studies*, XVII (1), January 1949, pp. 67–87.

—, *Home and Foreign Investment 1870–1913*, Cambridge, Cambridge University Press, 1953.

—, 'The English Capital Market before 1913', *Economica*, XXV (98), May 1958, pp. 142–6.

CAIRNES, J. E. 'Fragments on Ireland' (1866), in *Political Essays*, London, Macmillan, 1873.

CAMPBELL, BURNHAM O. *Population Change and Building Cycles*, Urbana, Ill., Bureau of Economic and Business Research, University of Illinois, 1966.

CARPENTER, NILES. *Immigrants and their Children*, U.S. Population Census, 1920, Monograph VII, Washington D.C. 1927.

CARRIER, N. H. and JEFFERY, J. R. *External Migration: a Study of the Available Statistics, 1815–1950*, London, General Register Office, HMSO, 1953.

COALE, ANSLEY J. 'The Population of the United States in 1950 Classified by Age, Sex and Color – a Revision of Census Figures', *Journal of the American Statistical Association*, L, March 1955, pp. 16–54.

COMMITTEE ON GOVERNMENT OPERATIONS. *The Brain Drain into the United States of Scientists, Engineers and Physicians. A Staff Study for the Research and Technical Programs Sub-committees of the Committee on Government Operations*, House of Representatives, 90th Congress, 1st Session, U.S. Government Printing Office, Washington D.C. 1967.

—, *Scientific Brain Drain from the Developing Countries, Twenty-third Report by the Committee on Government Operations*, 90th Congress, 2nd Session, House Report No. 1215, U.S. Government Printing Office, Washington D.C. 1968.

COMMITTEE ON THE INTERNATIONAL MIGRATION OF TALENT. *The International Migration of High-Level Manpower. Its Impact on the Development Process*, New York, Praeger, 1970.

COMMITTEE ON MANPOWER RESOURCES FOR SCIENCE AND TECHNOLOGY. *The Brain Drain. Report of the Working Group on Migration*, Cmnd. 3417, London, HMSO, October 1967.

DALY, D. J. 'Long Cycles and Recent Canadian Experience', *Report of the Royal Commission on Banking and Finance*, Ottawa, Government Printing Office, 1964. Appendix volume, pp. 283–301.

DEDIJER, S. and SVENNINGSON, I. *Brain Drain and Brain Gain. A Bibliography on the Migration of Scientists, Engineers, Doctors and Students*, Lund, Research Policy Program, 1967.

DEPARTMENT OF ECONOMIC AFFAIRS. *A Strategy for the South East. A First Report by the South East Economic Planning Council*, London, HMSO, 1967.

DEPARTMENT OF IMMIGRATION. *Australian Immigration: Consolidated Statistics, No. 1*, Canberra, 1966.

DEPARTMENT OF MANPOWER AND IMMIGRATION. *White Paper on Immigration*, Ottawa, October 1966.

DEPARTMENT OF TRADE AND INDUSTRY. *Persons with Qualifications in Engineering, Technology and Science, Studies in Technological Manpower, No. 3*, London, HMSO, 1971.

DU BOIS, W. E. B. *The Philadelphia Negro*, New York, Benjamin Blom, 1899, reissued 1967.

DUNNING, JOHN H. *American Investment in British Manufacturing Industry*, London, Allen & Unwin, 1958.

DYOS, H. J. *Victorian Suburb: A Study of the Growth of Camberwell*, Leicester, Leicester University Press, 1961.

EASTERLIN, RICHARD A. 'Influences in European Overseas Emigration before World War I', *Economic Development and Cultural Change*, Chicago, IX (3), April 1961, pp. 331–51.

—, *Population, Labor Force, and Long Swings in Economic Growth: the American Experience*, National Bureau of Economic Research, New York, Columbia University Press, 1968.

ELDRIDGE, HOPE, T. and THOMAS, DOROTHY S. *Population Redistribution and Economic Growth, United States, 1870–1950*, Vol. III: *Demographic Analyses and Interrelations*, Philadelphia, American Philosophical Society, 1964.

ENGINEERING MANPOWER COMMISSION OF THE ENGINEERS JOINT COUNCIL. *Engineering Manpower Bulletin*, No. 6, April 1967; No. 17, September 1970. New York.

—, *Professional Income of Engineers, 1968–1969*, April 1969. New York.

ENGINEERING MANPOWER COMMISSION . . . *Prospects of Engineering and Technology Graduates 1968,* September 1968. New York.

EZEKIEL, MORDECAI. 'The Cobweb Theorem', *Readings in Business Cycle Theory,* selected by a Committee of the American Economic Association, Philadelphia, The Blackiston Co., 1944, pp. 422–42.

FABRICANT, S. *Basic Facts on Productivity Change,* New York, National Bureau of Economic Research, Occasional Paper 63, 1959.

FARLEY, REYNOLDS, *Growth of the Black Population: a Study of Demographic Trends,* Chicago, Markham Publishing Co., 1970.

FEINSTEIN, C. H. *Home and Foreign Investment, 1870–1913,* unpub. Ph.D. thesis, University of Cambridge, 1959.

—, 'Income and Investment in the United Kingdom, 1856–1914', *Economic Journal,* LXXI (282), June 1961, pp. 367–85.

FEIS, HERBERT. *Europe: the World's Banker, 1870–1914,* New Haven, Conn., Yale University Press, 1930.

FERENCZI, I. and WILLCOX, WALTER F. *International Migrations,* National Bureau of Economic Research, New York, Columbia University Press, 1929, Vol. I.

FISHLOW, ALBERT. *American Railroads and the Transformation of the Ante-Bellum Economy,* Cambridge, Mass., Harvard University Press, 1965.

FOGEL, ROBERT W. *Railroads and American Economic Growth,* Baltimore, Johns Hopkins University Press, 1964.

—, and ENGERMAN, STANLEY L. *The Reinterpretation of American Economic History,* New York, Harper & Row, 1971.

FORD, A. G. *The Gold Standard 1880–1914: Britain and Argentina,* London, Oxford University Press, 1962.

FRANKS, CHARLES M. and MCCORMICK, WILLIAM W. 'A Self-Generating Model of Long Swings for the American Economy, 1860–1940', *The Journal of Economic History,* XXXI (2), June 1971, pp. 295–343.

FRIEDMAN, MILTON and SCHWARTZ, ANNA J. *A Monetary History of the United States, 1867–1960,* National Bureau of Economic Research. Princeton, N.J., Princeton University Press, 1963.

GALLMAN, ROBERT E. 'Gross National Product in the United

States, 1834–1909', in *Output, Employment and Productivity in the United States after 1800*, Studies in Income and Wealth, Vol. 30, by the Conference on Research in Income and Wealth, New York, National Bureau of Economic Research, Columbia University Press, 1966.

GENERAL REGISTER OFFICE. *Sample Census 1966, Great Britain*, Summary Tables, London, HMSO, 1967.

—, *Registrar General's Quarterly Return for England and Wales*, 4th Quarter, 1968, No. 480, London, HMSO, 1968.

GISH, O. 'The Royal Commission and the Immigrant Doctor', *The Lancet*, 29 June 1968, pp. 1423–4.

GLAZER, NATHAN and MOYNIHAN, DANIEL P. *Beyond the Melting Pot: The Negroes, Puerto Ricans, Jews, Italians and Irish of New York City*, second edition, Cambridge, Mass., The M.I.T. Press, 1970.

GRILICHES, Z. 'Research Expenditure, Education, and the Aggregate Agricultural Production Function', *American Economic Review*, LIV, December 1964, pp. 961–74.

—, 'Production Functions in Manufacturing: Some Preliminary Results', in BROWN, M., ed., *The Theory and Empirical Analysis of Production*, New York, National Bureau of Economic Research, Columbia University Press, 1967.

GRUBEL, HERBERT G. *Characteristics of Foreign Born and Educated Scientists in the United States, 1966* (mimeographed). Prepared by Herbert G. Grubel, University of Pennsylvania, under National Science Foundation Grant 1678, 1968.

—, and SCOTT, ANTHONY D. 'The International Flow of Human Capital', *American Economic Review, Papers and Proceedings*, LVI (2), May 1966, pp. 268–74.

GRUBER, W., MEHTA, D. and VERNON, R. 'The R. and D. Factor in International Trade and International Investment of United States Industries', *Journal of Political Economy*, February 1967, pp. 20–48.

HABAKKUK, H. J. 'Fluctuations in House-building in Britain and the United States in the Nineteenth Century', *The Journal of Economic History*, XXII (2), 1962. Reprinted in HALL, A. R. (ed.), *The Export of Capital from Britain 1870–1914*, London, Methuen, 1968, pp. 103–42.

HALL, A. R. 'Some Long-period Effects of the Kinked Age Distribution of the Population of Australia, 1861–1961', *The Economic Record*, 39 (85), March 1963, pp. 43–52.

HALL, A. R. (ed.) *The Export of Capital from Britain 1870–1914*, London, Methuen, 1968.

HAMILTON, HORACE C. 'The Negro leaves the South', *Demography*, 1, 1964, pp. 273–95.

HARKNESS, JON P. 'A Spectral-Analytic Test of the Long-Swing Hypothesis in Canada', *Review of Economics and Statistics*, 1(4) November 1968, pp. 429–36.

HARRIS, S. E. (ed.) *The New Economics: Keynes' Influence on Theory and Public Policy*, London, Dennis Dobson, 1947.

HAUSER, P. (ed.) *Population and World Politics*, Glencoe, Ill., Free Press, 1958.

HAWTREY, R. G. *A Century of Bank Rate*, London, Longmans, 1938.

HEGELAND, H. (ed.) *Money, Growth and Methodology and other Essays in Economics in Honour of John Åkerman*, Lund, C. W. K. Gleerup, 1961.

HICKMAN, BERT G. 'The Post-war Retardation: Another Long Swing in the Rate of Growth?', *American Economic Review*, LIII (2), May 1963, pp. 490–507.

HICKS, J. R. *A Contribution to the Theory of the Trade Cycle*, London, Oxford University Press, 1950.

—, *A Theory of Economic History*, London, Oxford University Press, 1969.

HIGONNET, RENÉ T. 'Bank Deposits in the United Kingdom 1870–1912', *Quarterly Journal of Economics*, LXXI (3), August 1957, pp. 329–67.

HOUSE OF REPRESENTATIVES, *Hearings of the Sub-Committee on the Judiciary*, House of Representatives, Part II, Serial No. 13, July–August 1961.

HOWARD, R. S. *The Movement of Manufacturing Industry in the United Kingdom, 1945–1965*, London, HMSO, Board of Trade, 1968.

IMLAH, ALBERT H. 'The Balance of Payments and the Export of Capital of the United Kingdom, 1816–1913', *Economic History Review*, Second Series, V (2), 1952, pp. 208–39.

IMLAH, ALBERT H. *Economic Elements in the Pax Britannica*, Cambridge, Mass., Harvard University Press, 1958.

Immigration from the Commonwealth, Government White Paper, Cmnd. 2739, London, HMSO, August 1965.

JEROME, HARRY. *Migration and Business Cycles*, New York, National Bureau of Economic Research, 1926.

JOHNSON, HARRY G. 'The Transfer Problem and Exchange Stability', in JOHNSON, HARRY G., *International Trade and Economic Growth*, London, Allen & Unwin, 1958, pp. 169–90.

—, 'Some Economic Aspects of Brain Drain', *Pakistan Development Review*, 7 (3), Autumn 1967, pp. 379–411.

JONES, K. and SMITH, A. D. *The Economic Impact of Commonwealth Immigration*, National Institute of Economic and Social Research, Occasional Paper No. XXIV, Cambridge, Cambridge University Press, 1970.

KALDOR, N. *The Causes of the Slow Rate of Growth of the United Kingdom*, Cambridge, Cambridge University Press, 1966.

—, 'Productivity and Growth in Manufacturing Industry: a Reply', *Economica*, XXXV (140), November 1968, pp. 385–391.

— (ed.) *Conflicts in Policy Objectives*, London, Basil Blackwell, 1971.

KEESING, DONALD B. 'The Impact of Research and Development on United States Trade', *Journal of Political Economy*, February 1967, pp. 20–48.

KELLEY, ALLEN C. 'Demographic Change and Economic Growth: Australia, 1861–1911', *Explorations in Entrepreneurial History*, Series 2, 5, Spring/Summer 1967/68, pp. 207–77.

KENDRICK, JOHN W. *Productivity Trends in the United States*, National Bureau of Economic Research, Princeton, N.J., Princeton University Press, 1961.

KEYNES, J. M. *The Economic Consequences of the Peace*, London, Macmillan, 1920.

KUZNETS, S. *Secular Movements in Production and Prices*, Boston and New York, Houghton Mifflin, 1930.

—, 'Long Swings in the Growth of Population and in Related Economic Variables', *Proceedings of the American Philosophical Society*, 102 (1), February 1958, pp. 25–52.

Bibliography

KUZNETS, S. *Capital in the American Economy: Its Formation and Financing*, National Bureau of Economic Research, Princeton, N.J., Princeton University Press, 1961.

—, and RUBIN, E. *Immigration and the Foreign Born*, New York, National Bureau of Economic Research, Occasional Paper 46, 1954.

LAYTON, WALTER T. and CROWTHER, GEOFFREY. *An Introduction to the Study of Prices*, London, Macmillan, 1938.

LEAGUE OF NATIONS. *Industrialisation and Foreign Trade*, Geneva, 1945.

LEBERGOTT, STANLEY. *Manpower in Economic Growth: the American Record Since 1800*, New York, McGraw-Hill, 1964.

—, 'Labor Force and Employment 1800–1960', in *Output, Employment and Productivity in the United States After 1800*, Studies in Income and Wealth, Vol. 30, National Bureau of Economic Research, New York, Columbia University Press, 1966, pp. 117–210.

LEE, C. H. 'A Stock-Adjustment Analysis of Capital Movements: the United States-Canadian Case', *Journal of Political Economy*, July/August 1969, pp. 512–23.

LEONTIEF, W. 'Factor Proportions and the Structure of American Trade', *Review of Economics and Statistics*, November 1956, pp. 386–407.

LEWIS, CLEONA. *America's Stake in International Investments*, Washington, Brookings, 1938.

LEWIS, J. PARRY. 'Growth and Inverse Cycles: a Two-country Model', *Economic Journal*, LXXIV (293), March 1964, pp. 109–18.

—, *Building Cycles and Britain's Growth*, London, Macmillan, 1965.

LIPSEY, ROBERT E. *Price and Quantity Trends in the Foreign Trade of the United States*, National Bureau of Economic Research, Princeton, N.J., Princeton University Press, 1963.

MARSHALL, ALFRED. *Principles of Economics*, eighth edition, London, Macmillan, 1922.

MARTINO, JOSEPH P. 'Science and Society in Equilibrium', *Science*, 165, 22 August 1969, pp. 769–72.

MATTHEWS, R. C. O. *The Trade Cycle*, Cambridge, Cambridge University Press, 1959.

246

MATTILA, JOHN M. and THOMPSON, WILBUR R. 'Residential-Service Construction: a Study of Induced Investment', *Review of Economics and Statistics*, 38, 1956, pp. 465–73.

MEIER, AUGUST. *Negro Thought in America, 1880–1915*, Ann Arbor, University of Michigan Press, 1963.

MITCHELL, B.R. and DEANE, PHYLLIS. *Abstract of British Historical Statistics*, Cambridge, Cambridge University Press, 1962.

MOYNIHAN, DANIEL P. *The Negro Family: the Case for National Action*, Department of Labor, Office of Policy Planning and Research, Washington D.C., 1965.

—, 'On Ethnicity', *The New York Times*, 2 May 1971

MYRDAL, GUNNAR. *An American Dilemma: the Negro Problem and Modern Democracy*, New York, Harper, 1944; Twentieth Anniversary edition, 1962.

NATIONAL SCIENCE FOUNDATION. *Science Manpower Bulletin*, NSF 58-4, No. 8, February 1958, Washington D.C.

—, *Scientists, Engineers, and Physicians from Abroad, 1966 and 1967*, NSF 69-10, January 1969. Washington D.C.

—, *Reviews of Data on Science Resources*, NSF 68-5, No. 12, January 1968; NSF 68-14, No. 13, March 1968; NSF 69-36, No. 18, November 1969. Washington D.C.

—, *Science Resources Studies Highlights*, NSF 70-12, 25 May 1970; NSF 70-28, 14 August 1970. Washington D.C.

—, *Science Resources Surveys Release*, NSF 70-123, No. 2, 24 February 1970. Washington D.C.

NELSON, R. R. and PHELPS, E. S. 'Investment in Humans, Technical Diffusion and Economic Growth', *American Economic Review, Papers and Proceedings*, LVI (2), May 1966, pp. 72–5.

NEW YORK TIMES COMPANY. *Report of the National Advisory Commission on Civil Disorders*, New York, Bantam Books, 1968.

—, *New York Times Encyclopedia Almanac 1971*, New York, 1971.

O'LEARY, P. J. and LEWIS, W. ARTHUR. 'Secular Swings in Production and Trade, 1870–1913', *The Manchester School of Economic and Social Studies*, XXIII (2), May 1955, pp. 113–252.

PARAI, LOUIS. *Immigration and Emigration of Professional and Skilled Manpower during the Post-War Period*, Special Study

No. 1, prepared for the Economic Council of Canada, Ottawa, Queen's Printer and Controller of Stationery, 1965.

PARKER, WILLIAM N. and KLEIN, JUDITH L. V. 'Productivity Growth in Grain Production in the United States, 1840–60 and 1900–10', in *Output, Employment and Productivity in the United States after 1800*, Studies in Income and Wealth No. 30, National Bureau of Economic Research, New York, Columbia University Press, 1966, pp. 523–80.

PATINKIN, DON. 'A "Nationalist" Model', in ADAMS, W. (ed.), *The Brain Drain*, New York, Macmillan, 1968, pp. 92–108.

PEACH, CERI. *West Indian Migration to Britain*, London, Institute of Race Relations, Oxford University Press, 1968.

PEARSON, RT. HON. L. B. and ASSOCIATES, *Partners in Development, Report of the Commission on International Development*, London, Pall Mall Press, 1969.

PHELPS BROWN, E. H. and HOPKINS, SHEILA V. 'The Course of Wage-Rates in Five Countries 1860–1939', *Oxford Economic Papers* (New Series) 2 (2), June 1950, pp. 226–296.

PHINNEY, J. T. 'Gold Production and the Price Level: the Cassel Three Per Cent Estimate', *Quarterly Journal of Economics*, XLVII, 1933, pp. 647–79.

PIGOU, A. C. *Industrial Fluctuations*, London, Macmillan, 1927.

PONSONBY, G. and RUCK, S. K. 'Travel and Mobility' in *The New Survey of London Life and Labour*, Vol. I: *Forty Years of Change*, London, P. S. King, 1930, pp. 171–99.

RIESSER, J. *The German Great Banks and their Concentration*, Washington D.C., National Monetary Commission, 1911.

ROBERTSON, D. H. 'New Light on an Old Story', *Economica*, New Series, XV (60), November 1948, pp. 294–300.

RODERICK, A. J. (ed.) *Wales through the Ages*, Vol. II, Llandybie, Carmarthenshire, Christopher Davies, 1960.

ROSE, E. J. B. and ASSOCIATES. *Colour and Citizenship: A Report on British Race Relations*, London, Institute of Race Relations, Oxford University Press, 1969.

ROSTOW, W. W. *British Economy of the Nineteenth Century*, London, Oxford University Press, 1948.

ROYAL COMMISSION ON MEDICAL EDUCATION, 1965–8. *Report*, Cmnd. 3569, London, HMSO, April 1968.

SAMUEL, T. J. *The Migration of Canadian-born between Canada and the United States of America, 1955 to 1968*, Research Branch, Program Development Service, Department of Manpower and Immigration, Ottawa, 1969.

SAUL, S. B. 'House Building in England 1890–1914', *The Economic History Review*, Second Series, XV (1), August 1962, pp. 119–37.

SAVILLE, JOHN (ed.) 'Studies in the British Economy, 1870–1914', Special Number, *Yorkshire Bulletin of Economic and Social Research*, 17 (1), May 1965.

SCHUMPETER, J. A. *Business Cycles: A Theoretical, Historical and Statistical Account of the Capitalist Process*, New York and London, McGraw-Hill, 1939, 2 volumes.

SHEPPARD, DAVID K. *The Growth and Role of U.K. Financial Institutions 1880–1962*, London, Methuen, 1971.

STAMP, JOSIAH C. *British Incomes and Property*, London, P.S. King, 1916.

STOVEL, JOHN A. *Canada in the World Economy*, Cambridge, Mass., Harvard University Press, 1959.

SUNDBÄRG, G. *Emigrationsutredningen*, Bilaga IV, *Utvandringsstatistik*, Stockholm, Kungl. Boktryckeriet, 1910.

SWEEZY, ALAN. 'The Economic Explanation of Fertility Changes in the United States', *Population Studies*, 25 (2), July 1971, pp. 255–67.

TAEUBER, KARL E. and ALMA, F. 'White Migration and Socio-economic Differences between Cities and Suburbs', *American Sociological Review*, XXIX, October 1964, pp. 718–29.

—, 'The Changing Character of Negro Migration', *American Journal of Sociology*, LXX, January 1965, pp. 429–41.

THOMAS, BRINLEY. *Migration and Economic Growth: a Study of Great Britain and the Atlantic Economy*, Cambridge, Cambridge University Press, 1954.

—, 'Migration and International Investment' in THOMAS, BRINLEY (ed.), *The Economics of International Migration*, London, Macmillan, 1958, pp. 3–16.

THOMAS, BRINLEY (ed.) *The Economics of International Migration*, London, Macmillan, 1958.

—, 'Wales and the Atlantic Economy', *Scottish Journal of Political Economy*, November 1959, pp. 169–92.

—, 'Recent Trends in American Investment in Western Europe', *The Three Banks Review*, No. 47, September 1960.

—, 'International Factor Movements and Unequal Rates of Growth', *The Manchester School of Economic and Social Studies*, XXIX (1), January 1961, pp. 1–21.

— (ed.) *The Welsh Economy: Studies in Expansion*, Cardiff, University of Wales Press, 1962.

—, 'Long Swings in Internal Migration and Capital Formation', *Bulletin of the International Statistical Institute, Proceedings of the 34th Session*, XL, Book 1, Toronto, 1964, pp. 398–412.

—, 'The International Circulation of Human Capital', *Minerva*, V (4), Summer 1967, pp. 479–506.

—, 'The International Circulation of Human Capital: A Reply to Harry G. Johnson', *Minerva*, VI (3), Spring 1968, pp. 423–7.

UNITED NATIONS. *International Capital Movements in the Inter-War Period*, Lake Success, 1949.

URQUHART, M. C. and BUCKLEY, K. A. H. *Historical Statistics of Canada*, Cambridge, Cambridge University Press, 1965.

U.S. DEPARTMENT OF COMMERCE. *Negroes in the United States, 1926–1932*, Bureau of the Census, U.S. Government Printing Office, Washington D.C. 1935.

—, *Historical Statistics of the United States, 1789–1945*, Bureau of the Census, U.S. Government Printing Office, Washington D.C. 1949.

—, Bureau of the Census, *Historical Statistics of the United States: Colonial Times to 1957*, Series A, U.S. Government Printing Office, Washington D.C. 1960.

—, *U.S. Census of Population 1960. Special Reports. Characteristics of Professional Workers*, Final Report, PC (2)-7E, Bureau of the Census, U.S. Government Printing Office, Washington D.C. 1964.

—, *U.S. Census of Population 1960. Special Reports. Socio-economic Status*, Final Report, PC (2)-5C, Bureau of the Census, U.S. Government Printing Office, Washington D.C. 1967.

U.S. DEPARTMENT OF COMMERCE. Bureau of the Census, *Census of Population 1960, U.S. Summary,* PC (1)-1B, Government Printing Office, Washington D.C., 19.

—, Bureau of the Census, *Census of Population 1970,* PC (V2)-1, U.S. Government Printing Office, Washington D.C., 1970.

U.S. DEPARTMENT OF JUSTICE. *Annual Reports of the Commissioner of Immigration and Naturalization,* Immigration and Naturalization Service, U.S. Government Printing Office, Washington D.C.

—, *Annual Indicator of the In-migration into the United States of Aliens in Professional and Related Occupations, Fiscal Years 1967 and 1968,* Immigration and Naturalization Service, U.S. Government Printing Office, Washington D.C. 1968 and 1969.

U.S. DEPARTMENT OF STATE. *1967 Report of the Visa Office,* Bureau of Security Consular Affairs, U.S. Government Printing Office, Washington D.C. 1967.

VINER, JACOB. *Canada's Balance of International Indebtedness, 1900–1913,* Cambridge, Cambridge University Press, 1924.

—, 'Clapham on the Bank of England', *Economica,* New Series, XII (46), May 1945, pp. 61–8.

WEBER, B. 'A New Index of Residential Construction 1838–1950', *Scottish Journal of Political Economy,* II (2), June 1955, pp. 104–32.

WEINER, M. L. and DALLA-CHIESA, R. 'International Movements of Public Long-term Capital and Grants, 1946–50', *International Monetary Fund, Staff Papers,* IV, 1 September 1954.

WELTON, THOMAS A. *England's Recent Progress,* London, Chapman and Hall, 1911.

WILKINSON, MAURICE. 'European Migration to the United States: An Econometric Analysis of Aggregate Labor Supply and Demand' (mimeographed). Presented to the European meeting of the Econometric Society, Brussels, September 1969.

WILLIAMS, DAVID. *A History of Modern Wales,* London, John Murray, 1950.

WILLIAMSON, JEFFREY G. *American Growth and the Balance of Payments 1820–1913,* Chapel Hill, University of North Carolina Press, 1964.

Index

Abel-Smith, B., 213
Abramovitz, M., 5, 10–11, 18, 234–6
absorption, ethnic and in-migrants to
 U.S., 160–1, 169
accelerator-multiplier process, 99–109
Adelman, Irma, 17, 19
Africa, British investment in, 107
agriculture: and exports from U.S.,
 74–5; U.S. investment in, 74; in
 U.S. in Great Depression, 152;
 Welsh, 181; *see also* rural sector
Argentina, 113, 124; British investment in, 111, 113; and investment
 swings, 75, 83
armed forces, 156, 158, 183
Arrow, K. J. and Capron, W. N., 223
Ash, R. and Mitchell, H. D., 216–17
Atlantic community, 3; and migration link, 235
Atlantic economy, 127–8, 170, 234;
 and migration, 199; model of, 90;
 and Wales, 170–8
Australia: British investment in, 65;
 building cycles in, 93; capital inflow in relation to exports, 83; and
 demographic determinants of long
 swing, 92; demographic variables
 in economic [growth, 86; and domestic determination of economic
 growth, 6–7; exports, 114; and
 flow of professional migrants, 201–
 202, 204–5; immigration waves,
 87; and infrastructure investment,
 86, 91; and investment swings,
 75; long swings pattern in, 91–3;
 population cycles in, 87–8; railway
 investment, 91
automobile(s), 72, 132

balance of payments, 129
Balfour, Rt. Hon. A. J., 72

bank(s): central, 3; deposits in
 Britain, 77–8
Bank of England, 76, 114; gold stock,
 112; policy, 16; reserve, 103, 105,
 109, 114–15, 118, 124–5
Bank rate, 103, 109, 111–12, 115–16,
 118–19
banking: 1893 panic, 112; system in
 U.S., unit, 105n.
Baring crisis of 1890, 111, 113
Barraclough, Geoffrey, xiii
Beach, W. E., 118
Belgium, 60–1
Bernstein, E. M., 133
birth rate in England and Wales
 (1870–1913), 37; *see also* population
Blacker, C. P., 151
Blaug, M., Layard, P. R. G. and
 Woodhall, M. H., 232
Bloomfield, Arthur I., 20n., 89, 91
Borts, G. H. and Stein, J. L., 127, 199n.
brain drain, 198–236; Britain and,
 212–18, 232; determinants of, 230;
 from developing countries, 212;
 literature on, 210n.
British Empire: and British foreign
 investment to 1913, 60; and European emigrants, 60
building/construction: alternation of
 American and British cycles, 39–
 43; and cobweb theorem, 41;
 demographic/population factors
 relevant to, 24, 41, 236; and Export
 Sector, 32, 71; and Home-Construction Sector, 32; and immigration, 39–40, 43; and internal migration, 41, 43; methods of assessment of population change, 51–2;
 and migration, 51–4; and population change, 114; — regional cycles,
 see under regional building cycles

Index

building in Australia, 93; and population change/demographic variables 88

building in Britain, 7, 20–44; and 1890s boom, 111–12, 114; and Canada, 90; and emigration, 22, 37; evidence of cycles in, 21; and foreign investment, 72; and investment, 20, 22; and migration, 24–6, 33–4, 37, 41, 43, 51–4, 178, 183; and population change/demographic variables, 22, 24–6, 33, 37, 45–58; *see also* building/construction, regional building cycles

building in U.S.A.: and migration, 43; and population change/demographic variables, 24; and required additions by age group, 40; swings in, 81, 83

business cycles, 19

Butlin, Noel, 6–7, 91, 93

Cagan, Phillip, 77, 105, 126

Cairncross, A. K., 37, 39, 67, 73, 174, 183

Cairnes, J. E., 161

California, and Negro migration, 143–4

Camberwell (London), demographic history of, 36

Campbell, Burnham O., 25n., 39–40

Canada, 124; British investment in, 65, 117, 119; and European emigrants, 131; export of public capital, 130–1; exports, 114; and flow of professional migrants, 201–205; immigration and net capital imports, correspondence between, 89–90; imports/exports, 90–1; and infrastructure investment, 86, 90–1; and investment swings, 75, 83; long swings pattern in, 88–91; railway construction in, 90; spectral analysis of long cycles in, 17–18

capital construction, 4

capital exports in Britain: primacy of, 109n.; swings in, and terms of trade, 67, 69, 71; *ex post*, 105, 107

capital exports in U.S., 116–17, 129–131; *see also* capital outflow

capital flows, 97, 220–1

capital formation: in countries of new settlement, and long swings, 101; domestic, and foreign lending/exports, 69, 71, 118, 129; export-sensitive, 105; migration-sensitive, 139; 'other', 8–10, 66–7, 85–6, 120; population-sensitive, *see under* population-sensitive capital formation; science-based, 218, 220; two components of, 8–10; in U.S., 12–13, 118

capital inflow, 12, 102

capital movement: and terms of trade, relationship between, 67–71; in U.S., and monetary changes, 79

capital outflow: from Britain, and terms of trade (1862–1913), 69; — (1907–13), and gross domestic capital formation, 72; — to Australia (1861–1900), 6–7; from Europe (1845–1913), 59–61; — to America (1845–1913), 4, 59; *see also* investment, foreign

Cheshire, building in, 32–3

coal exports, Welsh, 170, 173–5, 178, 181

coalfields of England, 175

cobweb: monetary, 81, 98; theorem, 98n.; — and Argentina, 113; — and building cycle, 41

Colean, Miles L., 39

Commonwealth Immigrants Act (1962), 191–2

construction/house building, *see* building

'consumption-led' growth, 129

cycle(s): inverse, *see* inverse; Kuznets, *see under* Kuznets; self-generating, and migration, 87

Daly, D. J., 18

Death Registration Area, 149n.

demographic: factors, *see* birth rate; marriage rate; population; revolution (1890–1940), xiii

Depression, Great, in Britain, 182

Depression, Great, in U.S., 151, 152

Development Areas, 189

doctors: and brain drain in Britain, 213, 216–18; U.S. training for, 232–3

dollar: convertibility suspended (1971), 130, 135–6; glut, 129, 134, 225; scarcity, 129, 134, 225; stability, 113; standard, xii, 129

Du Bois, W. E. B., 163

dynamic shortage and brain drain, 218, 224–5, 228, 230, 233

Dyos, H. J., 36

early expanding phase and demographic cycles, 151

58,450

JV
6118
•T5
1972

Thomas, Brinley,
1906-

Migration and ur-
ban development

DATE DUE

DEC 14 1992			
APR 0 3 1996			
MAR 2 8 1996			
APR 1 8 1996			
APR 1 0 1996			
OCT 2 0 1998			
SEP 3 0 1998			